TAXATION AND
SOCIAL POLICY

TAXATION AND SOCIAL POLICY

Edited by
Cedric Sandford, Chris Pond
and Robert Walker

 Heinemann Educational Books · London

Heinemann Educational Books Ltd
22 Bedford Square, London WC1B 3HH

LONDON EDINBURGH MELBOURNE AUCKLAND HONG KONG
SINGAPORE KUALA LUMPUR NEW DELHI IBADAN NAIROBI
JOHANNESBURG EXETER (NH) KINGSTON PORT OF SPAIN

© Cedric Sandford, Chris Pond and Robert Walker
First published 1980

British Library Cataloguing in Publication Data

Sandford, Cedric Thomas
    Taxation and social policy. – (Studies in social policy and welfare).
    1. Great Britain – Social policy
    2. Great Britain – Social conditions – 1945 –
    3. Taxation – Great Britain
    4. Fiscal policy – Great Britain
    I. Title   II. Pond, Chris
    III. Walker, Robert   IV. Series
    300′.941   HN385.5

ISBN 0–435–82789–8
ISBN 0–435–82790–1 Pbk

Published by Heinemann Educational Books Ltd
Filmset by Northumberland Press Ltd
Gateshead, Tyne and Wear
Printed in Great Britain by Richard Clay (The Chaucer Press) Ltd
Bungay, Suffolk

Contents

Preface

The post-war period has witnessed a dramatic extension in the scope and coverage of both taxation and social policy. Each system has developed in an independent and largely *ad hoc* manner. This process of separate development has created an overlap and interaction between the two systems which makes it impossible to consider satisfactorily either system in isolation from the other.

It was for this reason that the Civil Service College organised a three-day seminar held at Sunningdale, 9–11 July 1979, which considered the interaction of social and fiscal policies and critically examined proposals for reform. The seminar brought together officials working particularly in taxation on the one hand and in aspects of the social services on the other; the majority of participants were therefore drawn from the Treasury, Inland Revenue, Department of Health and Social Security and Department of the Environment.

This book arose from the seminar. Just as the interaction between taxation and the welfare services creates a need to bring together the policymakers from both fields, so that same interaction creates the need for these two subject areas to be brought together to meet the needs of students of each. Students of taxation rarely examine, in other than the most cursory way, the social policies on which taxation impinges; whilst many students of the social services, of social administration or of social policy are innocent of the facts and theory of taxation. This book seeks to remedy the deficiency; to fill the gap. Whilst each chapter is founded on a paper presented by the author at the Sunningdale seminar,* the chapters often differ significantly from the conference papers. They have been substantially re-written with three objectives in view. First, to present them more suitably, for papers prepared for oral delivery can rarely be satisfactorily transmuted unchanged into publishable form. Second, to impose on the book a somewhat tighter structure, more

* The exception is Chapter 12 which was written especially for publication and was not presented at the Sunningdale seminar.

unity than was possible in the seminar where each contributor was not acquainted in advance with the exact coverage of his fellow contributors. Third, to enable valuable points from the discussion to be incorporated in the chapter. Nonetheless it must be stressed that the opinions expressed remain those of the individual authors and do not necessarily reflect the views of other participants in the seminar, or the policy of any government department or other organisation with which they are associated.

The book covers only some of the areas of social policy and also has little to say about indirect taxes. It concentrates on those social policies with the most pronounced and significant interface with taxation – the social security system, housing, pensions and the general treatment within the tax and social security systems of women and the family. The book thus has little or nothing to say, for example, on education, the National Health Service, or the personal social services, where the inter-relationships with taxation, whilst they exist, are less obtrusive and important. On the tax side, for parallel reasons, the emphasis is on direct taxation, reference to VAT or local rates cropping up only in the chapter on housing.

The pattern of the book is as follows. Chapter 1 presents an overview of the subject. It offers some signposts to the rest of the book and indicates common themes and linkages. It includes some aspects of the theme of the book, such as public *perception* of the link between taxation and government spending on social services which, whilst important, hardly justify a separate chapter. It also touches on some issues, like the relationship between economic growth and spending on social policies, which are related peripherally to the theme of this book, but if explored in depth would require a book to themselves.

In Part I a macro-look is taken of the overall effect of taxation and public expenditure on the distribution of income – or rather, this topic is examined as far as existing data permits, for one of the crucial conclusions from this part of the study is how little we can say with confidence about overall redistribution. Chapter 4, which deals with what the Americans have called 'tax expenditures', reinforces this conclusion. Tax expenditures are the value of the reliefs and concessions within the tax system, which amount to an implicit welfare system alongside the explicit system of positive public spending. For the first time, in the Public Expenditure White Paper of January 1979 (Cmnd 7439), the government published estimates of the cost in terms of revenue sacrificed, of the direct tax allowances and reliefs; but the data are incomplete and there are no official estimates of the distributional effects of the tax expenditures nor is it possible to make unofficial estimates which are comprehensive and wholly reliable.

Part II of the book explores in depth the inter-relations between taxation and four aspects of social policy. Chapters 5, 6 and 7 examine, respectively, social security, housing and pensions. Chapter 8 reviews the treatment of women and the family under income taxation and the child benefit scheme, revealing inequities in the current treatment of women and children and at the same time demonstrating the difficulties inherent in seeking to apply one of the objectives of a tax system – horizontal equality – the equal treatment of equals.

In Part III the failures of the present system and the possibilities of reform are reviewed. The first chapter in this section examines the deficiencies of our present direct tax system and briefly suggests possible directions of reform. Chapter 10, which follows, contains a corresponding review of the social security system, taking us back to Beveridge, indicating what went wrong and possibilities for reform drawing on some, if not all, of the principles of the Beveridge Report. From there we move to more radical proposals for reforming both the social security and income tax systems and conclude this section with a review of the arguments and main practical conclusions of a debate on policy held at the Sunningdale seminar. The debate was introduced by three eminent speakers, each associated with one of the main reform proposals previously outlined – Frank Field, MP, with 'Back to Beveridge', Sir Brandon Rhys Williams, MP, son of the originator of the social dividend and campaigner for social reforms, and Tony Crocker, a former Under Secretary in the Department of Health and Social Security with special knowledge of the tax credit scheme.

The final chapter attempts to sum up the general conclusions, with particular policy recommendations, which emerge from the study.

Biographical Notes on Contributors

David Collard: Professor of Economics at the University of Bath. He has written widely on welfare economics and the history of economic thought and his publications include *The New Right: A Critique* (1968), *Prices Markets and Welfare* (1972) and *Altruism and Economy* (1978).

Ken Judge: Senior Research Fellow, and Assistant Director of the Personal Social Services Research Unit, at the University of Kent. He was previously a lecturer in social policy at the Civil Service College and the University of Bristol. He has recently been appointed editor of the *Journal of Social Policy*, is the general editor of *Studies in Social Policy* published by Macmillan, and a former scientific adviser to the Department of Health and Social Security. His publications include articles in a wide range of journals and three books: *Rationing Social Services* (1978), *Charging for Social Care* (1980), and *Pricing the Social Services* (1980).

Ruth Lister: Director of the Child Poverty Action Group. She has worked with the Group since 1971 as legal research officer, Assistant and Deputy Director. Her publications include *Supplementary Benefit Rights* (arrow 1974); *As Man and Wife* (1973), *Justice for the Claimant* (1974), *Social Security: The Case for Reform* (1975), *Patching up the Safety Net* (1977), *Wasted Labour* (with Frank Field 1978), *Social Assistance: The Real Challenge* (1978), *The No Cost No Benefit Review* (1979), *A Budget for the Year of the Child* (1979), all published by CPAG. She has also contributed to Fabian Society publications and written extensively in journals such as New Society, Community Care, Social Work Today and Poverty. She is currently writing a book on welfare benefits for the Sweet & Maxwell Social Work and the Law series.

Michael O'Higgins: Lecturer in Social Policy and member of the Centre for Fiscal Studies at the University of Bath. He was previously employed at the Policy Studies Institute. His research interests are mainly in the area of income distribution and public policy, and recent publications include a contribution to *The Yearbook of Social Policy in Britain* (1979).

David Piachaud: Lecturer in Social Administration at LSE. He has previously worked in the Department of Health and Social Security and the Prime Minister's Policy Unit. He has published numerous papers on poverty, social security and other aspects of social policy.

Chris Pond: Director of the Low Pay Unit. Previously he was a Lecturer in Economics at the Civil Service College and Research Officer at the Low Pay Unit. He is joint author of *Inflation and Low Incomes* (Fabian Society 1975), *Trade Unions and Taxation* (WEA 1976), *To Him Who Hath* (Penguin 1977) *Taxing Wealth Inequalities* (Fabian Society 1980) and author of *The Poverty Trap* (Open University 1978). He has contributed to *Are Low Wages Inevitable?* (Russell Press 1977), *The Conscript Army* (Routledge and Kegan Paul 1978), *The Wealth Report* (RKP 1979), *Why the Poor Pay More* (Macmillan 1978), *Labour and Equality* (Heinemann 1979) and the *Yearbook of Social Policy* (RKP 1980). He is a regular contributor to New Society.

Mike Reddin: Lecturer in Social Administration at the London School of Economics. He is currently trying to make sense of the partnership between the State and company pension sectors and has previously undertaken research on social policy in the United States and Denmark. Among his publications are *Social Services for All* and *Universality and Selectivity: Strategies in Social Policy*, and contributions to *Social Services for All* and *The Yearbook of Social Policy 1976*.

Cedric Sandford: Professor of Political Economy and Director of the Centre for Fiscal Studies at the University of Bath. He was a member of the Meade Committee. He has written and broadcast widely on economic and fiscal affairs. His publications include *Taxing Personal Wealth* (1971); *Hidden Costs of Taxation* (1973); (With J. R. M. Willis and D. J. Ironside) *An Accessions Tax* (1973) and *An Annual Wealth Tax* (1975); *Economics of the Public Finance* (2nd edition 1978); *Social Economics* (1977).

Geoffrey Stephenson: Consultant with the Statistical Office of the European Community in Luxembourg. He was until recently head of the Redistribution of Income Section within the Social Statistics

Division of the Central Statistical Office, which is responsible for producing statistics on the effects of taxes and benefits on household income, and the annual article on this subject in *Economic Trends*.

Robert Walker: Lecturer in Social Policy at the Civil Service College. He previously worked at the Department of Environment undertaking research into various aspects of housing management. He has written numerous articles and papers on means-tested benefits, housing management and research methodology.

Christine Whitehead: Lecturer at the London School of Economics and Senior Research Associate in the Department of Land Economy, University of Cambridge. In the past she has acted as economic adviser to the House Policy Review and is now a Special Adviser to the House of Commons Select Committee in Environment. Publications include *The UK Housing Market: An Econometric Model* (1974) and many articles on housing especially in the CES Review.

Geoffrey Whittington: Professor of Accounting and Finance in the University of Bristol, having previously held a similar post at the University of Edinburgh. After graduating from the London School of Economics, he qualified as a chartered accountant and spent ten years in research at the Department of Applied Economics, Cambridge. From 1975 to 1977 he was a member of the Meade Committee on the Structure and Reform of Direct Taxation. he is currently engaged in research on inflation accounting, sponsored by the Social Science Research Council.

1   Taxation and Social Policy: An Overview
Cedric Sandford

Introduction

This chapter takes a very broad look at the main inter-relationships between taxation and social policy; it seeks to present an overview – to trace out the territory as seen from a high-flying aircraft.

Some ideas and material are included in this chapter which do not recur in the book – for there are some points which, whilst important enough to our theme to deserve mention, do not justify a separate chapter. But, in the main, the purpose of the chapter is to provide signposts to topics pursued at more depth later in the book, to raise questions which will be examined, if not wholly answered, in subsequent chapters, to stress the relevance of the various chapters to the theme and to identify links between chapters.

In this chapter we first identify and examine a number of ways in which taxation and social policy are linked. We then briefly consider some of the policy failings and policy constraints which have been made apparent by the previous analysis.

Links between Taxation and Social Policy

Taxation finances social policy
It is a truism that almost all social policy requires expenditure and that the main means of financing that expenditure (at any rate in the long term and if taxation is suitably defined) is taxation. Truism or not, this statement raises a series of related questions of which the first is, how widely recognised is the link between taxation and social policy? Studies of how people perceive the relationship between taxation and public expenditure are still in their infancy, but there are a few on which we can draw.

Eva Mueller (1963) records a study conducted by the Survey

Research Centre of the University of Michigan where respondents were asked whether they favoured more or less spending on a list of specific federal programmes; the majority of respondents tended to favour increased federal spending. When, however, respondents were asked if they favoured more spending even if taxes had to be raised, support fell away dramatically, leaving no single programme so popular that a majority were prepared to pay higher taxes for it.

A more specific study was undertaken by David Piachaud (1974) on English data on attitudes to pensions. He first asked a group of some six hundred male respondents drawn from the electoral register whether they wished to see an increase in pensions and by how much. He then questioned them on whether they would be prepared to be worse off in order to pay for it, by presenting them with the relationship that 'pensions could go up by £y for single pensioners if each working person were prepared to be £x per week worse off'. The results were that people were only prepared to contribute extra taxes for *half* the increase in the level of pensions which they themselves thought desirable.

A similar kind of difference in people's views is to be found in a survey by Harris and Seldon (1979) of a sample of some 1900 electors in Great Britain. Fifty-seven per cent of the sample thought it 'a good idea' to impose a limit on taxation, but this figure fell to 33 per cent (with a big increase in abstentions) when the rider was added, 'even if, as a result, government might cut some services'.

A small study by Lewis (1980) revealed again the incongruence of electors' opinions – considerably more of the respondents favouring reductions in taxation than favoured cuts in public expenditure. His study also showed considerable differences in the political popularity of various public expenditure programmes.

If, as this limited empirical work seems to indicate, people do not link public spending and taxation in a specific way, ought measures to be taken to encourage that awareness? In particular, should budgetary procedures be reformed so that expenditure changes and tax changes are brought into closer relationship with each other and considered side by side both by government and by Parliament?

A Committee of the Institute for Fiscal Studies, under Lord Armstrong's Chairmanship, is examining this issue and will be publishing a report. In the meantime the Committee's secretary, Melvyn Westlake, has outlined the need for budgetary reform in a recent article (1979). Perhaps more significant, Lord Cockfield, when adviser to the Conservative Party in Opposition, expressed his approval of such a change (1979) and his translation to the Treasury as Minister of State may mean that some action can be expected, though the issue is more complex than may appear at first sight.

Several of the surveys to which we have referred indicated different degrees of popularity for different expenditure programmes and perhaps the most significant issue for our time is not whether aggregate tax receipts and expenditure outlays should be brought into closer relationship but whether we should go in for hypothecated taxes – taxes pledged for use on specific kinds of expenditure such as a special tax for the NHS. This raises various questions. Would such a tax meet less taxpayer resistance? If an increase in spending on a particular service necessarily meant an increase in the hypothecated tax, would it mean more responsibility in expenditure? How important are the disadvantages – such as more complex overall budgeting?

In essence the national insurance contribution (NIC) is an hypothecated tax, except that not all the cost of NI benefits is met from it – some comes from a general Exchequer contribution. This raises the questions: are people as employees or self-employed persons more willing to pay NIC than they would be to pay additional income tax because they see NIC as related to a particular set of benefits? Is there a psychological influence both on willingness to pay and on willingness to claim benefits? Has the notion of 'insurance' a value? This notion was fundamental to the original Beveridge proposals which envisaged equal benefit for equal contributions; and there is no doubt that the take-up of NI benefits is high and that they are free of stigma. If the way to rationalise the tax and social security systems is to return to Beveridge principles in whole or in part (see Chapters 10 and 13), is this a part of Beveridge which we wish to retain or reinstate?

There are strong contrary arguments. The general contribution from the Exchequer always made the 'insurance' principle a little phoney. With income-related contributions and benefits we have moved a long way from Beveridge. The existence of a large and probably growing number of people on supplementary benefit, especially the long-term unemployed who have exhausted their right to NI benefit, raises serious doubts about the validity of the present system; it gives practical force to the philosophical appeal of rights derived from citizenship (see Chapter 13) rather than contributions. Moreover to scrap NIC and replace it by a payroll tax on employers and extra income tax on employees would simplify the tax structure, get rid of the regressiveness of NI contributions with the particular regressive 'kink' at the upper limit and abolish the myth that 'contributors' have covered the full cost of NI benefits by their NI contributions. Herein lies one of the fundamental issues of the relationship between tax and social security.

Taxation is itself an instrument of social policy

Some tax measures are deliberately introduced as instruments of social policy; in other cases there may be no clear social policy objective, but a tax or group of taxes may nevertheless affect social policy by way of their impact, for example, on the distribution of income and wealth.

Let us start with an example of a tax specifically introduced with a social purpose. To judge by ministerial statements, such a tax was the capital transfer tax (CTT) (see Chapter 9). In his Budget speech, March 1974, The Chancellor of the Exchequer, Mr Healey, presented CTT as part of a 'Determined attack on the maldistribution of wealth in Britain'. Mr Healey's proposal to introduce a wealth tax, announced in the same Budget, had the same objective.

The overall structure of the tax system may have implications for social policy, in particular the balance between direct and indirect taxes. Direct taxes can be more closely adjusted to prevailing concepts of ability to pay than indirect taxes. Nonetheless we must be careful in our judgement. The conventional equation of direct = progressive and indirect = regressive is not necessarily or invariably true. Thus the employee's NIC is a direct but regressive levy, whilst, because of the wide zero-rating, VAT is in fact slightly progressive, measured in relation to disposal income.

The *rate* structure of the main taxes is obviously of prime importance in affecting the distribution of income and wealth. Income tax in the United Kingdom is progressive, but because of the unique feature of a very wide band of income (£9250 in 1979/80) taxed at a constant marginal rate, the element of progression over certain income ranges is not very pronounced (see Chapter 9).

Exemptions or reliefs in the tax structure are used for purposes of social policy and influence the progression of the tax system. They constitute a kind of implicit welfare system, the distribution of the benefits from which is not precisely known nor necessarily rational in relation to overall objectives of social policy. These so-called 'tax expenditures' are the subject of Chapter 4, but also figure very prominently in Chapter 6 on Housing and Chapter 7 on Pensions. In subtle ways tax concessions affect the distribution of income and wealth and may indeed frustrate the purpose for which they were intended. Concessions become 'capitalised' within the structure of market prices. Thus, as Christine Whitehead explains in Chapter 6, tax concessions to house owners raise the value of houses, providing a capital gain to present owners but reducing the capacity of would-be purchasers to buy their first house.

How the tax unit is defined is particularly related to the concept of horizontal equity – the equal treatment of those of the same taxable capacity. Should individuals be taxed as such whether they are single or married or should there be a special married 'unit'? These considerations significantly affect the distribution of income as between families. They enter into the discussion of women and the family in Chapter 8 and that on the tax credit scheme, Chapter 12.

Taxation may negate social policy

A negative feature of the tax system may have very marked effects on the distribution of income or wealth – if the system fails to provide for the neutralisation of external distortions. An outstanding instance was the failure to index the UK income tax system against inflation. In the decade of the late 1960s to late 1970s income tax allowances were not increased in line with either the price level or average earnings and tax bands were not widened in proportion to the rate of inflation. Consequently particular categories of taxpayers were hit with exceptional severity; there was a largely unplanned and haphazard effect on the distribution of income. Three groups suffered most. Those with most allowances were hit heavily, for example, people with a large family and therefore with a number of child allowances. Then people at particular junctures of the income tax scale were hit; thus those who before the inflation were just below the threshold were brought into taxpaying at the relatively high rate of 30–5 per cent plus the NIC; from paying no income tax these people found themselves paying a significant proportion of their income in tax. Also those who were previously at or near the top of the basic-rate band, or in the lower reaches of higher-rate band, were heavily hit; as the bands were not widened in proportion to inflation, these people shot up the higher-rate scale and found themselves paying at a marginal tax rate perhaps 20–30 per cent above that which they were previously paying on the same real income. Conversely those already in the middle to upper range of basic rate, who remained on basic rate, fared relatively well. (See Field, Meacher and Pond 1977.)

Further we need to mention the extent of evasion and avoidance of taxes, which affects the distribution of income and wealth. Evasion is illegal tax dodging. Avoidance is less easy to define in a satisfactory way, but for our purposes we can simply say that it is the adoption of methods to reduce tax bills which are within the law but contrary to the intention of the government. Both activities have the effect of bringing about a redistribution of income in a way never intended by governments; evasion is likely to mean a transfer from the honest to the dishonest and avoidance a transfer from the unsophisticated to the sophisticated. (Sandford 1980.)

One attraction of an expenditure tax is that, by partially eliminating the distinction between income and capital for tax purposes, it might reduce the scope for avoidance (see Chapter 9). A fully comprehensive income tax which included gifts, legacies and capital gains as income would have similar effects.

Data from the Family Expenditure Surveys suggests that, when you take the tax system as a whole, the extent of progression within it is not very marked (Chapter 2). However, this may be of no importance if the distributional effects of government expenditure result in a 'satisfactory' overall progression. One difficulty here is our limited knowledge of these distributional effects (Chapters 2 and 3).

Overlap between taxation and social policy provisions
The outstanding case of overlap between taxation and social policy provisions is the so-called poverty trap – the situation in which someone in receipt of various means-tested benefits, such as family income supplement (FIS), rent rebate or allowance, rate rebate and free school meals, may obtain little benefit, and sometimes even suffer loss, by obtaining an increase of gross income; the higher income leads to a reduction of benefits and is also subject to income tax and NIC. The relationship between benefits and tax is made abundantly clear by the terms sometimes used to describe the situation. On the one hand, there are the explicit tax rates (income tax and NIC); on the other, the 'implicit tax rates' – the reduction in benefits as income rises (Prest 1970.) Although conditions for dif-

ferent benefits and the time periods for eligibility vary, so that the effect of the poverty trap is muted somewhat and less apparent to the victim, it is possible, as we have already implied, for the combined marginal explicit and implicit tax rates to exceed 100 per cent of an increase of income. This situation is intolerable for a number of reasons. It becomes almost impossible for the poor to pull themselves out of poverty. There is in theory at least a very obvious disincentive effect on willingness to work. Poverty itself is not adequately alleviated. Further, the effectiveness of incomes policies designed to help the low paid is undermined by the existence of the trap. The elimination of the poverty trap is central to any fundamental reform of the tax and social security systems.

A somewhat similar if less serious salary trap applies, mainly to the middle class, in respect of means-tested grants for students in higher education. The effect is to add to the explicit income tax rate an implicit tax rate of between 10 and 20 per cent, depending on the position of the parent on the scale of 'residual income' used to assess means.

Another area of overlap of taxation and social security, or at least of logical inconsistency, arises from the taxation of some social benefits but not others. Thus state-retirement pensions are subject to income taxation while sickness and unemployment benefits are tax-free. These short-term benefits remain untaxed for practical administrative reasons; but there is no good social policy reason for the different treatments (see Chapters 5 and 13). The Conservative government is seeking to find ways of taxing them.

A further overlap exists with indirect taxes. The prices paid for goods which include indirect taxes affect the cost of living so that the index of retail prices reflects changes in indirect taxation. Where benefits are linked to the retail price index they have to be increased to offset the increase in indirect taxes. Again the government is concerned about this overlap, especially when the rise in indirect taxes is associated with a reduction in direct taxes – hence the government's experiments with a standard of living index.

There are two other relationships between taxation and social benefits, of a more problematical nature, but too important to be ignored and we shall deal with them briefly.

Taxation, economic growth and welfare provision
The rate of economic growth is very relevant to the capacity of the

economy to afford improvements in social benefits. Thus any effects that taxation may have on economic growth indirectly affect the prospects of improvements in welfare provision. The most common argument advanced under this head would be that high income tax rates, especially high marginal rates of tax, are a disincentive to work. On the whole, the studies which have been done on this subject do not bear out that contention (Godfrey 1975). Income tax has a twofold effect on people's willingness to work, one acting as an incentive and the other as a disincentive. Thus, an increase in income tax makes people worse off in terms of the goods and services they can enjoy and they may react by trying to increase income, i.e. do *more* work (the 'income effect' resulting from changes in aggregate income). On the other hand, higher tax rates make leisure relatively more attractive because an extra hour of work brings in a lower return and people may therefore substitute leisure for income, i.e. do *less* work ('the substitution effect' resulting from changes in marginal tax rates). Perhaps more significant is the effect of high taxation in providing an incentive to evade and avoid tax, with income distributional effects which we have already described. Finally, probably the most important influence of taxation on economic growth is the way that it may generate investment distortion. Thus in the United Kingdom the concessions given under the tax system to housing, to insurance policies and to pension funds may well have the effect of diverting savings into relatively safe and rentier-type investments rather than promoting innovation and risk-taking. This theme is pursued in Chapter 9; one of the strongest arguments for a progressive expenditure tax, outlined in that chapter, is that it would eliminate such investment distortions, as would a fully comprehensive income tax.

The effect of social policy on economic growth

How far does social policy itself promote economic growth? In other words, how far are the social services self-financing? The argument that they may be so applies particularly to education and health, which can be thought of as investment in human capital. There can be no doubt that investment in education does something to promote economic growth. But whether it does more than would be achieved by applying some of the resources in other directions may be doubted, and over the past ten or twenty years in the United Kingdom there would appear no obvious positive correlation between the increase in education expenditures and rate of economic growth. In health, the Guillebaud Committee (1955) produced the slogan that health expenditures were 'wealth producing as well as health producing'. Undoubtedly there is some scope for expenditure on medical care to improve output by reducing the amount of time lost through sickness, and conceivably by increasing the fitness of workers whilst at work; but the nineteenth-century situation no longer holds, when expenditure on medical care, along with expenditure on public health, reduced mortality rates largely amongst the working population and thereby brought about an increase in output. In the twentieth century the effect of further reduction in mortality rates is primarily to extend retirement and to increase a section of the population which makes heavy demands on medical care. There is little prospect today of justifiying health care expenditure in terms of investment benefit (Lees 1960).

Whilst some level of health and education expenditure makes a substantial contribution to economic growth, in the sense that to stop all education and health spending would seriously reduce GNP, additional spending on education and health have little self-financing element about them and this must be even more true of other social policy measures. The call which such measures make on scarce resources must be justified in terms of a consumption benefit rather than any investment benefit. There are, indeed, some social policy provisions which, perhaps in conjunction with taxation and other features of the economy such as low wages in some occupations, may have positively detrimental effects on output. Thus an earnings rule on pensions acts as a disincentive to work; a few people, for example those with very large families, may be discouraged from taking a job because they are better off on social security; and the poverty trap situation discourages workers from making extra effort.

Policy Failings and Policy Constraints

Arising from this survey of the link between taxation and social policy it is possible to identify a series of policy failings and policy constraints. One constraint, to which we have already referred, is the imperfect data about the distributional effects of the whole system of taxation and welfare benefits (Chapters 2 and 3). In so far as the distributional effects of social policies are not fully known or appreciated, the scope for rational and consistent policy is reduced.

However, even perfect data does not guarantee rationality or consistency. Politicians are particularly prone to embark on policies with insufficiently clear objectives, and this is true of social policies as of other policies. Thus, for example, we have mentioned that both capital transfer tax (CTT) and the wealth tax were proposed (though the latter was never introduced) for a specific purpose: to reduce inequality in the distribution of wealth. Yet it is clear that their purpose and their structure were insufficiently thought out.

There is no evidence that the Labour Party or Government developed, or even sought to develop, any consistent philosophy about the distribution of wealth; yet the philosophy affects the tax instruments. Thus the characteristic of a wealth tax is that, in principle, it taxes wealth irrespective of its source or use. Yet it might be thought appropriate to distinguish between, say, wealth derived from inheritance, from gambling earnings or from hard work and enterprise; or between wealth immobilised in agriculture and that spent by the West End playboy. (Sandford 1979.)

Even if such subtleties are ignored, the structure of CTT and the proposals for a wealth tax seem ill-designed to achieve their declared purpose. The deficiencies of CTT are spelt out in Chapter 9. As to the wealth tax, the latest Labour Party proposals, as set out in the Manifesto of 1979 (p. 14), envisage a threshold of £150 000, which would only affect a fraction of the top 1 per cent wealth holders. But this is just the category of wealth holders whose share of wealth has halved in the past fifty years and continues to decline quite rapidly (Cmnd 1979). The tax would leave unaffected wealth holders below that level, such as the top 2–10 per cent, where no such notable reduction has taken place. In short, the wrong target has been chosen to achieve the declared objective.

Another failure has been the apparent lack of co-ordination both between central government departments and between central government and local government. The supreme example of this is of course the poverty trap which shows the lack of co-ordination both between the Inland Revenue and the DHSS and between central and local government pursuing their own series of means-tested benefits. This raises the question: is government too big? Is this lack of co-ordination an inevitable outcome of too large an organisation? If we do not take that point of view – or even if we do, but cannot immediately remedy the situation – we must seek ways of improving co-ordination. More openness in government might help.

It is possible that the unique concern with budget secrecy in the United Kingdom may have created problems of co-ordination because of the restriction on the number of people who are made privy to major tax changes before Budget day. Wider pre-Budget discussions might reveal overlaps before governments become committed to particular lines of policy so that problems were avoided or, at least, realised and solved at an earlier stage.

The imperfectly progressive rate structure of the United Kingdom income tax and the inability to tax short-term benefits both stem from administrative constraints (see Chapters 5 and 9) – the legacy of a cumulative Pay-As-You-Earn system. PAYE was a remarkable wartime innovation to adapt the income tax to a situation in which millions of wage earners who had never been income tax payers before would be brought into the net. It has the great merit that, by and large, the right amount of tax is extracted from the large majority of taxpayers without any end-of-year adjustments. But it may be time to ask if the costs do not outweigh the benefits.

Some other constraints spring from the predilections, not to say human failings, of Chancellors and the inevitable features of a democratic system. Chancellors like the maximum of discretion. This is why the relationship between the allowances under the income tax, e.g. the ratio of married man's to single person's allowance, have never been standardised; and also why, if not the only reason, Chancellors have resisted the indexation of tax allowances and tax bands. As we have seen such predilections result in anomalies in income distribution. Again, politicians may be tempted to adopt policies which they think will catch votes even though they know the measures to be detrimental to the economic health of the nation; once adopted they become almost impossible to remove. Who is likely to attempt to remove the tax privileges which the owner-occupier has come to possess when owner-occupiers constitute such a large part of the electorate? In the same vein politicians are subject to the influence of pressure groups. Before a Budget, Chancellors receive hundreds of representations and these representations continue during the passage of the Finance Bill and beyond. Some of the tax expenditures (Chapter 4) have resulted from the influence of pressure groups seeking to espouse particular causes, often worthy ones; but their success frequently introduces anomalies into the tax system.

Conclusion

Most of the issues touched on this introduction are considered at more depth in later chapters; in the light of this treatment they are further discussed and brought into closer relationship with each other in the final chapter.

References
Cockfield, Lord 1978, *Too Much of a Good Thing*, London, Institute for Fiscal Studies, para 7–10.
Field, F., Meacher, M. and Pond, C. 1977, *To Him Who Hath: a study of poverty and taxation*, Harmondsworth, Penguin Books, pp. 34–8.
Godfrey, L. 1975, *Theoretical and Empirical Aspects of the Effects of Taxation on the Supply of Labour*, Paris, OECD.
Harris, R. and Seldon, A. 1979, *Over-ruled on Welfare*, London, Institute for Economic Affairs, pp. 26–39.
Lees, D. S. 1960, 'The economics of health services', *Lloyds Bank Review*, no. 56.
Lewis, A. 1980, 'Attitudes to public expenditure and their relationship to voting preferences', *Political Studies*, forthcoming.
Mueller, E. 1963, 'Public attitudes toward fiscal programmes', *Quarterly Journal of Economics*, vol. LXXVII, pp. 210–35.
Piachaud, D. 1974, 'Attitudes to Pensions', *Journal of Social Policy*, vol. 3, no. 2, pp. 137–46.
Prest, A. R. 1970, *Social Benefits and Tax Rates*, London, Institute for Economic Affairs.
Report of the Committee of Inquiry into the Cost of the National Health Service (Guillebaud Committee) 1955, Cmnd 9663, London, HMSO.
Royal Commission on the Distribution of Income and Wealth (Diamond Commission) 1979, Report no. 7, Cmnd 7595, London, HMSO, tables 4.4 and 4.5.
Sandford, C. T. 1979 'The wealth tax debate' in F. Field, (ed), *The Wealth Report*, London, Routledge and Kegan Paul.
Sandford, C. T. 1980, 'Tax compliance costs, evasion and avoidance' in D. A. Collard, R. C. Lecomber and M. D. Slater, (eds) *Income Distribution: the Limits of Redistribution*, Bristol, John Wright for Colston Research Society.
Westlake, M. 1979, 'The need for budgetary reform', *Fiscal Studies*, vol. 1, no. 1, pp. 51–9.

Part I
Taxation as an Instrument of Social Policy

While much of this book is concerned with the contradictions between taxation and social policy, the first group of essays explores the complementary nature of the two systems. In particular, we are interested in the way in which the tax system is, or could be, used to pursue certain 'social policy' objectives.

One important aspect of this relationship is the extent to which taxes and benefits can be used to redistribute resources between households of different type and at different levels of income. Virtually any government activity, from raising a tax to installing a bus lane, has some impact on the distribution of resources. The purpose of many such activities has nothing to do with the distribution of incomes, and it is a mistake to assume that all necessarily redistributed income in a 'positive vertical' (e.g. from rich to poor) or 'positive horizontal' (e.g. from employed to unemployed, towards families with children) direction. Nor would it be sensible for governments to determine their policies *solely* on the basis of redistributive effects. But policymakers do at least benefit from knowing what the distributive effects of their activities are likely to be.

The first two chapters in this section explore the evidence which is currently available on the impact of taxes and public expenditure on the distribution of incomes. Geoffrey Stephenson first describes in Chapter 2 the results of recent analyses for which he has been responsible at the Central Statistical Office (CSO). The analysis suggests that the tax system as a whole has little impact on the level of economic inequality. Many indirect taxes, especially local rates and taxes on beer and tobacco are regressive; VAT appears broadly neutral (when measured against disposable income); and even the direct tax system is only mildly progressive. While, on average, households paid about 20 per cent of their original income in direct taxes, the richest ten per cent of households still paid only

23 per cent in such taxes. However, the CSO argues that, when the benefits of the public spending which these taxes finance are taken into account the net effect of government activity is generally equalising – resources are distributed from working households with relatively high incomes to low income families mainly dependent on state transfers. Families with children also gain at the expense of those without.

A more sceptical view is taken in Chapter 3 by Michael O'Higgins who suggests that the CSO conclusions may be based on too partial an analysis. Almost a third of all government receipts and a half of government spending is missing from the analysis. If taxes other than those on incomes and household spending were included together with public spending other than social security, social services and subsidies, the picture might, he argues, be different. Chapter 3 also discusses some of the methodological issues involved in the official analysis. An important defect, in his view, is that public expenditure on particular services only takes account of cash expenditures ignoring 'tax expenditures', that is the effects of tax allowances and reliefs. It is this aspect of the relationship between taxation and social policy to which we turn in Chapter 4. Here the concept of tax allowances both as forms of public expenditure and as a vehicle of 'fiscal welfare' are explored. Chris Pond argues that the independent system of welfare administered through the tax system, and represented by tax allowances and reliefs, has received too little attention from those concerned with social policy. The chapter explores some of the implications of the existence of such 'tax expenditures' for social policy.

2 Taxes, Benefits and the Redistribution of Income
Geoffrey Stephenson

Introduction

Since the early 1960s the Central Statistical Office has produced reports on the impact of taxes and social security benefits, published each year in Economic Trends (CSO 1980). Their general purpose has been to show how taxation and public expenditure on social services, cash benefits and consumer subsidies affect the observed distribution of income between households of different types and at different levels of income.

Government Expenditure and Financing

Government spending and taxes vary in their aims and in their impact on households. Whatever the aim of a particular measure, whether it be to provide an income during periods of unemployment or sickness or to raise tax revenue, the measure has redistributional consequences.

General government expenditure is taken to be the combined expenditure of central government and local authorities and includes expenditure on goods, services and transfer payments, i.e. payments for which no goods and services are received in return (see CSO 1968). Thus defined, general government expenditure in 1978 amounted to £71 thousand million. It was financed by receipts of £23 thousand million from direct taxes on persons, by £23 thousand million from indirect taxes falling on expenditure and by £25 thousand millions from other sources such as corporation tax and borrowing. Households both contribute to and benefit from this expenditure. They pay taxes directly in the form of income tax and national insurance contributions, and indirectly through local rates and the taxes levied on the goods and services they buy. They benefit from government spending on social services including state education, the National Health Service and housing and rail travel subsidies, as well as payments in cash.

There are considerable difficulties in moving from these aggregates to apportioning taxes and benefits to individual households. We can obtain information about the types of households that receive cash benefits and pay direct taxes through surveys such as the Family Expenditure Survey (FES). From the replies respondents give to questions on their expenditure, we can estimate their payments of indirect taxes. From information they supply about such factors as their age and the number of children in the household, we can estimate the average costs of providing them with social services, such as health and education. But there are other kinds of financing, such as corporation tax and government receipts from public corporations, which are not covered in the FES and which are difficult to apportion to individual households. Indeed, most people would probably not think of these as leading to a reduction in their personal incomes. Similarly, there are other items of government expenditure, such as capital expenditure, expenditure on defence and on the maintenance of law and order, for which there is no clear conceptual basis for allocation, or for which we do not in any event have sufficient information to make an allocation.

Consequently, in the estimates given here, only some 47 per cent of total government expenditure and 59 per cent of total government receipts in 1978 are in the categories which are directly allocated to individual households. Details of the allocated and unallocated taxes and benefits are shown in Table 2.1. Allocated expenditure comprises all cash benefits, including retirement pensions and supplementary benefits; subsidies on housing, food and rail travel, and current expenditure on the health and education services. Allocated revenue comprises income tax, employees' national insurance contributions and indirect taxes such as VAT and local authority rates. Complete methodological details are given in the articles published in Economic Trends (e.g. CSO, 1980). This partial and unbalanced coverage limits the significance to be attached to precise figures of gains or losses from redistribution, particularly for households in the middle ranges of the income distribution; for them even the direction of the true net effect is somewhat uncertain.

Table 2.1   Government expenditure and financing 1978

	£ ooom.	%
Allocated financing		
Direct taxes		
Income tax	19	26
Employees' and self-employed		
NI contributions	4	6
Indirect taxes		
On final goods and services	14	20
On intermediate goods and services	6	8
	42	59
Unallocated financing		
Unallocated taxes	14	20
Other receipts	6	8
Government borrowing requirement	9	13
Total financing	71	100
Allocated expenditure		
Cash benefits	15	21
Subsidies		
Housing		
(including rent rebates and allowances)	2	3
Food and rail	*a*	*a*
Benefits in kind		
Health Service	7	10
Education	8	11
School meals, milk, welfare foods	*a*	*a*
	33	47
Unallocated expenditure		
Other current expenditure on social,		
environmental and protective services	7	9
Capital expenditure protective services	5	7
Other expenditure	27	37
Total expenditure	71	100

a Positive but less than 1.0.
Source: CSO 1979.

Distributional Impact

The starting point for the measurement of the distributional impact is household *original* income, that is income before the addition of any cash benefits or the deduction of any taxes. Table 2.2 shows how this income is made up for successive fifths (quintile groups) of the household population ranked by their original income. In this table, and indeed throughout the chapter, the averages shown are those of all households in a particular group, not just those households in the group in receipt of a particular type of income or benefit. Thus, the low average wages and salaries of households in the lowest fifth of the distribution reflect the very few workers in the group rather than a low level of wages of individual workers: the sum of their wages is divided by the total number of households in the group.

Table 2.2   Distribution of original income by source 1978
(£ per household per annum)

	Lowest 20%	2nd 20%	3rd 20%	4th 20%	Top 20%	All households
Wages and salaries	33	1509	3792	5570	8763	3934
Self-employment	3	119	248	263	743	275
Other	206	634	479	626	1134	616
Original income	242	2262	4519	6459	10640	4825
Number of workers per household	0.15	0.90	1.50	1.85	2.40	1.40

Source: Family Expenditure Survey.

Table 2.2 shows that households with greater incomes contain on average more workers than those with lower incomes. Between 40 and 50 per cent of the variation in household incomes is due to the differing numbers of workers per household. Thus, if everyone received the same wage and had no other income, there would still be considerable spread in household income, as some households are composed entirely of retired persons without any workers, whilst other households contain three or more workers.

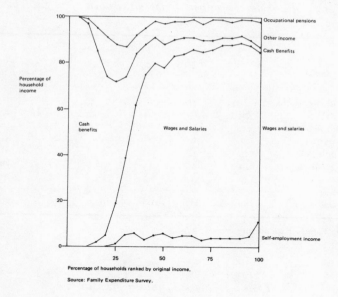

Figure 2.1 shows this step, and indicates

Figure 2.1   Sources of household income, 1978

The first step in the analysis of distributional effects is to add cash benefits to original income. Figure 2.1 shows this step, and indicates the importance of cash benefits in relation to other sources of income. In the lowest 5 per cent of the distribution, households are very dependent on government benefits in the form of cash receipts: this group consists predominantly of retired people with no other source of income. In Table 2.3 we can see that 76 per cent of households in the lowest quintile group of the original income distribution are composed of one and two adult retired households. Over 30 per cent of cash benefits go to this group of retired households. Unemployment benefit and sickness benefit help to make good interruptions in original income. Thus they tend to be inversely related to original income: this goes some way in explaining the slow tapering of cash benefits as income rises. Both the presence of retired people in households with working members (and thus high incomes) and the universal coverage of child benefit mean that cash benefits add to the income of households at all levels in the original income distribution. This is shown at the top of Table 2.4.

Table 2.3   Household composition of the distribution of original income 1978

	Lowest 20%	2nd 20%	3rd 20%	4th 20%	top 20%	All households
	Percentages					
One and two adults retired	76	26	4	1	1	22
One and two adults non-retired	11	42	38	36	28	31
Two adults, one to four children	4	19	43	38	24	26
Others	9	13	15	25	47	22
Total	100	100	100	100	100	100

Source: Family Expenditure Survey.

Table 2.4   Stages of redistribution 1978

	Lowest 20%	2nd 20%	3rd 20%	4th 20%	Top 20%	All households
	£ per household per annum					
Original income	240	2260	4520	6460	10640	4830
+ cash benefits	1470	890	430	300	260	670
− direct taxes	10	280	810	1250	2380	950
Disposable income	1710	2870	4140	5510	8520	4550
+ subsidies	210	120	110	80	80	120
− indirect taxes	340	640	900	1140	1580	920
+ direct benefits in kind	480	550	690	750	820	660
Final income	2050	2900	4040	5200	7840	4410
No. of persons per household	1.7	2.2	3.0	3.2	3.5	2.7
No. of children per household	0.3	0.5	1.0	1.0	0.8	0.7

Source: Family Expenditure Survey.

The second step is the deduction of direct taxes, and employees' national insurance contributions (see Table 2.4). Together the adjustments for cash benefits and taxes give *disposable* income, which is a measure of income available to households for spending. As Table 2.4 shows, direct taxes and cash benefits have the major impact in redistributing income. Not surprisingly, better-off households pay a higher proportion of their income in direct taxes (income tax and national insurance contributions). These take about 22 per cent of the original income of the top quintile, compared with an average for all households of just under 20 per cent and for the lowest quintile of 4 per cent.

However, tax payments are determined not only by size of original incomes but also by tax reliefs such as those on mortgage interest and life insurance premiums. The tax figures are shown net of these reliefs because of the nature of the available data. The alternative of treating the reliefs as tax subsidies or tax expenditures, showing a notional tax liability before reliefs and a corresponding cash benefit might be of some interest (see Chapter 4). However, it would not alter the overall redistributive effect of taxes.

Disposable income reflects the net 'gains' and 'losses' of direct taxes and cash benefits and is much more evenly distributed than original income. The lowest fifth of households received 8 per cent of disposable income compared with 1 per cent of original income, and the top fifth received 37 per cent of disposable income and 44 per cent of original income.

The final step in the redistribution analysis is to add subsidies, deduct indirect taxes, including local-authority rates and add direct benefits in kind, so far as they can sensibly be allocated. This gives *final* income. The largest subsidy to households is through housing provided by local authorities. Indirect taxes, for example, VAT, are closely related to the level of expenditure of households and are thus roughly proportional to disposable income and have little redistributive impact. Subsidies and indirect taxes are considered at the same stage, as they both act through prices paid by consumers.

Direct benefits in kind that can be allocated to households are the health and education services. The approximate benefit is estimated from the cost of providing the service to differential households. Using estimates of the education cost per pupil at different types of schools and colleges, education benefit to individual households is estimated from the number of members in each form of full-time education. Thus, generally, households with two or three children are shown to benefit more from government spending on education than on households with none or one child, and a household with a member at university is shown to receive greater benefit than a household with a member at a nursery school.

The estimated cost of health services to individuals varies according to age and sex. It is, generally speaking, greater for the elderly and children than for persons of other ages. The redistributive effect of health expenditure, like education expenditure, varies with the size and composition of households. Table 2.4 shows that average direct benefits in kind rise with income, households are larger on average and contain greater numbers of children in the higher-income ranges; average benefits in the lower ranges are substantial too because of the presence of elderly persons.

Table 2.4 also shows with some certainty that for the top two-fifths of households final income is substantially less than original income while the reverse is true for the lowest fifth. As noted above, the different extent to which taxes and benefits have been allocated to households in this study limits the usefulness of the net results for the intervening groups. The average gains by the poorest fifth of households, which contains 13 per cent of individuals, are comparatively large. Their average original income in 1978 increased from £240, a 1 per cent share of original income, to £2050, or 9 per cent of final income. On the other hand, the average original income of the top fifth of households, which contains 26 per cent of individuals, was reduced from £10 640 to £7840; that is a reduction from a 44 per cent share of original income to a 36 per cent share of final income.

The explanation of this pattern and scale of redistribution lies in the differences between cash benefits and tax payments at different levels of income. For example, in 1978 the average cash benefits received by the lowest fifth of households was £1470, compared with £260 received by the top fifth. Direct tax payments were on average £10 and £2380 for these two groups respectively. Indirect taxes, which are correlated with disposable income, were on average £340 and £1580. Direct benefits in kind and subsidies taken together were £690 and £900. Although the value was higher for the higher-income groups in cash terms this represented a considerably higher proportion of income for the lower than the higher group.

Effect on Different Household Types

Figures 2.2, 2.3 and 2.4 summarise the overall effect on incomes of allocated taxes and benefits for three household types. The types are two-adult retired households, households with two adults and one to four children and those with two adults who are non-retired. There is no chart for one-adult households because it would be broadly similar to that for two adults. Also there is none for the 'others' category which is not very homogeneous, including both families with and those without children. The charts distinguish original income, disposable income and final income for 1978.

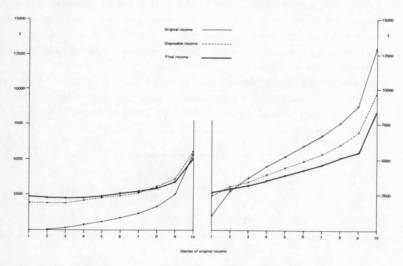

Figure 2.2   *The impact of taxes and benefits on households* (a) *two adults retired,* (b) *two adults non-retired*

For two-adult retired households – Figure 2.2(a) – cash benefits form the bulk of their disposable income. Those in the lower half of the distribution pay on average little or no direct taxes and their original income and disposable income rise together. For those in the upper half, direct taxes reduce the value of their income until for the top tenth of households direct taxes are almost equal to the cash benefits they receive (mainly state retirement pensions). Over the range as a whole, final income and disposable income are roughly equal for retired households. The lower-income groups tend to have a

higher final income than disposable income and the reverse is true
for the higher-income groups. This is due mainly to the decline in
the proportion of local-authority tenants, and thus housing subsidy,
as we consider groups of households with higher incomes.

Two-adult non-retired households – Figure 2.2(b) – have final
income less than original income, and thus taxes exceeding benefits,
for all but the lowest 20 per cent of these households. The lowest
decile is a rather heterogeneous group with a low number of
workers per household and more unemployed persons than other
deciles. It also includes relatively large numbers of semi-retired
households, households with invalids and some student households.
As a result, high benefit levels in the lowest deciles quickly taper off
to a state where the majority of benefit arises from the health
service. Final income is consistently lo~'er than disposable income
with indirect taxes being markedly higher than indirect benefits and
benefits in kind.

Two-adult households with one to four children (Figure 2.3) have,
except at the extremes, an original income profile similar to that of
two-adult non-retired households. The bulk of benefits consist of

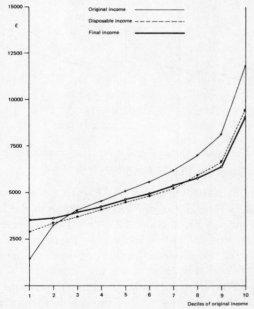

Figure 2.3   Two adults and one to four children

education and health services and they are fairly constant over all income bands. Disposable and final income are very similar except for the lowest-income deciles. This means that indirect taxes and non-cash benefits are approximately equal. For the lowest deciles the deviation from this pattern, with final income appreciably greater than disposable, is due partly to the higher levels of housing subsidy at this end of the distribution (as with retired households) and partly to the higher rates of education benefit due to higher than average numbers of children and the existence of some student households in this group.

Change over Time

Table 2.5 shows how the shares of original, disposable and final income for successive quintile groups in the distribution of original income have changed over the period 1973–8. The chief observation is that, despite significant changes in government expenditure and fiscal policies, the relative distribution of household final income remained broadly the same during this period.

The stable pattern of final income is largely explained by two factors. First, as Table 2.5 shows, the starting-point, i.e. the percentage distribution of original income, was itself remarkably stable throughout the period 1973–8. (Although, since the share of original income in final income is small for the bottom quintile group of households, even large percentage changes in it would not materially affect the share of final income; and vice versa.) Secondly, annual changes in the redistributive components and other factors often offset one another. For example, the share of original income received by the second lowest quintile group of households fell from 11 per cent to 9 per cent, without a corresponding reduction in its share of final income. The share of original income fell because the number of retired households in the population increased and because most of this increase appeared in the second lowest quintile group, rather than being confined to the lowest quintile group, where retired households already predominated. As retired households generally have very small original incomes, their larger numbers in the second lowest quintile group led to a reduction in its share of original income. However, these larger numbers of retired households also led to offsetting changes; the share of subsidies rose, the share of direct taxes fell, and, more important, the share of cash benefits

Table 2.5   Percentage distribution of original, disposable and final income 1973–8 Households are ranked by original income

	Percentages Original income					
	1973	*1974*	*1975*	*1976*	*1977*	*1978*
Quintile group						
Top 20 per cent	44	44	43	44	44	44
21–40 per cent	26	26	26	26	27	27
41–60 per cent	19	19	19	19	19	19
61–80 per cent	11	11	10	10	10	9
81–100 per cent	1	1	1	1	1	1
Total original income	100	100	100	100	100	100
	Disposable Income					
Quintile group						
Top 20 per cent	39	38	37	38	37	37
21–40 per cent	24	24	24	24	24	24
41–60 per cent	18	18	18	18	18	18
61–80 per cent	13	13	13	13	13	13
81–100 per cent	7	7	7	7	8	8
Total disposable income	100	100	100	100	100	100
	Final Income					
Quintile group						
Top 20 per cent	37	36	35	35	35	36
21–40 per cent	24	24	24	23	23	24
41–60 per cent	18	18	19	18	18	18
61–80 per cent	13	13	14	14	14	13
81–100 per cent	8	8	7	9	9	9
Total final income	100	100	100	100	100	100

increased. As cash benefits form a relatively large part of final income of this quintile group, the share in final income did not fall in line with the share of original income.

Conclusion

This analysis of the impact, of those taxes and benefits we can allocate, on the distribution of original income, suggests that the principal redistribution is from working households with high original incomes to retired households with few workers and little original income. There is also some redistribution from households without children to those with children, particularly those with older children, which receive considerable benefit from the education service. The main redistributive impact is from income tax and cash benefits. The analysis suggests that without the tax benefit subsidy system the distribution of income and of welfare would have been much more unequal than it was.

References
CSO 1968, *National Accounts Statistics, Sources and Methods*, London, HMSO.
CSO 1979, *National Income and Expenditure 1968–78*, London, HMSO.
CSO 1980, *Economic Trends*, no. 315, pp. 99–130, London, HMSO.

3 The Distributive Effects of Public Expenditure and Taxation: An Agnostic View of the CSO Analyses*
Michael O'Higgins

Introduction

In the previous chapter, Geoffrey Stephenson reported the results of the latest analysis by the Central Statistical Office (CSO) of the effects of taxes and benefits on household incomes. Since their beginning, almost twenty years ago, these analyses, and the related papers by their initiator, J. L. Nicholson (e.g. 1974, 1977), have dominated this area of study in the United Kingdom, particularly with respect to empirical investigation. The other purely empirical work on redistribution has consisted of a paper by Merrett and Monk (1966) and a series of studies by Brown (1971, 1972, 1973) and his successors, Jackson and McGilvray (1973); these focus on policy issues and essentially ignore methodological questions. The only papers to combine methodological analysis with empirical investigation are those by Webb and Sieve (1971), Barg (1974), Peretz (1975) and Nicholson and Britton (1976), and each of these is rather limited in the extent to which empirical assessment of methodological differences is carried out. This situation in the UK contrasts markedly with that in North America where a number of investigators (Gillespie 1965; Musgrave *et al.* 1974; Pechman and Okner 1974; and Ruggles 1979) have combined methodological and empirical investigation, discussing methodological alternatives and presenting their empirical consequences. The CSO exercises do not do this and the absence, thus far, of the American practice amongst

* I am grateful to Della Nevitt, Julian le Grand and the editors for helpful comments; and am particularly indebted to Pat Ruggles for the stimulus of our joint work on income distribution, in the course of which many of these ideas have developed. Responsibility, however, rests with me.

non-official investigators means that our options appear to be simply to accept or reject the official 'facts'. This chapter does neither – hence the choice of the label 'agnostic' – but rather sets out the main worries raised by the CSO approach (both in commission and in omission) and indicates the alternative ways in which these worries might be met. In short, the chapter spells out the *caveats* to be borne in mind when using the CSO data.

These criticisms lead to the second part of the argument which is that many of the unsatisfactory elements of the methodology betray the absence of a policy context in which the data are to be used. In other contexts, methodological questions which are not immediately susceptible to resolution by theoretical analysis may be dealt with by a pragmatic application of the technique which seems most relevant to the purpose for which the analysis is being undertaken. However, since the CSO analyses have a general information rather than a specific policy objective, this guideline of pragmatism is no help either. Thus, one is left in a situation which led one pair of commentators to suggest that 'it seems that the inclusion of a tax or benefit (in the CSO analyses) depends on the ease with which it is directly allocable to individuals' (Peacock and Shannon 1968, p. 38).

This, then, is the critique, in principle, of the CSO approach: that the absence of an explicit methodological basis for the exercise renders suspect, because partial, the results and incidentally reveals the absence of a policy context for the exercise. This chapter concentrates on discussing in detail the specific methodological criticisms, but concludes with some examples of the policy questions which seem to be missed out on in the CSO exercises.

Questions of Methodology

The problems of tax and expenditure allocation may be examined under the following headings (though some problems could be discussed under more than one of the headings):

1. Coverage – which revenues and expenditures to include?
2. The Balanced Budget Question – should equal amounts of government revenue and expenditure be allocated and, if so, how?
3. Allocation – who benefits?
4. Valuation – by how much?
5. Comparison – with what does one compare the post-tax and expenditure allocation situation? If one is examining allocations by income level, what concept of income is valid?

Coverage

Table 2.1 of the previous chapter set out the details of the allocation of general government revenue and expenditure in 1978.
Government expenditures which were allocated to households consisted of all cash benefits, subsidies on housing, food and rail travel,
and current expenditure on health, education and school meals, milk
and welfare foods. The allocated revenue was made up of income
tax, national insurance contributions, rates, VAT and excise duties
(though not all of each of these items was included). Since the CSO
studies began, the proportion of revenue allocated has hovered at
about the 60 per cent mark (in 1978 it was 59 per cent), whilst
the corresponding figure for expenditure has gradually risen from
about one-third to almost one-half (47 per cent in 1978). Throughout this period, however, methodological refinements have been
directed at improving existing allocations rather than at extending
them to the unallocated balances.

The reason why the majority of public expenditure is not allocated
in the CSO analyses is explained by Boreham and Semple:

> The three classes of public expenditure which are not allocated
> in the current analysis in Economic Trends are (1) those which
> are not generally seen as conferring benefits on individual house-
> holds (e.g. defence); (2) those where it is impossible to assess the
> extent to which households, rather than other sectors of the
> economy, benefit from the expenditure (e.g. roads); and (3) those
> where insufficient information is available about variations in
> accessibility and the individual usage of services (e.g. libraries,
> parks). (1976, p. 281)

Nicholson and Britton state more starkly, 'It is not possible to
devise satisfactory procedures for allocating all the items in the
public authorities current account' (1976, p. 320).

Boreham and Semple illustrate these difficulties when they argue
that to allocate all government expenditure one must

> provide some objective criteria for choosing between a number of
> possible methods of allocation. For example, assuming that current
> expenditure on defence can be treated as a benefit, which, if any,
> of the following is the best method of allocating such expenditure:
> (i) per capita, (ii) per equivalent adult, (iii) in proportion to
> household income, (iv) in proportion to rateable value, or (v)
> in proportion to the number of expected remaining years of life?
> (1976, p. 292)

Prest also notes this problem with respect to defence:

> defence expenditure may be primarily useful for the defence of
> tangible property and the income derived therefrom – but insofar
> as it prevents wage-earners from being killed or disabled, it makes
> for a greater present value of their prospective earnings stream.
> (1968, p. 87)

and Roskamp notes that 'per capita allocation, distribution according to income received, property owned and total taxes paid have
been suggested' as methods of allocation, adding that 'it seems that
income received is in recent studies the preferred allocation index'
(1968, p. 104).

Peacock, however, believes that a failure to allocate some parts
of government expenditure may lead to 'seriously misleading' distributional information, if, for example, the government finances
new (allocated) expenditure by cutting unallocated expenditure (or
vice versa) (1974, p. 155). Rather than being blinded by the range
of alternative methods which might be used to allocate expenditures
such as defence, Peacock and Shannon argue that '*differing* assumptions about the allocation of taxes and benefits *must* be made ... the
official calculations make no attempt to show the effect on the final
results of utilizing different allocations and valuations' (1968, p. 44).

Webb and Sieve similarly argue that 'Indivisible benefits generally may be presumed to accrue to some or all members of society
and to make no allocation of them ... is to invite other users of
the statisitics to make assumptions about the likely beneficiaries'
and they conclude that 'indivisible benefits should be allocated
preferably on two or more sets of assumptions' (1971, pp. 76–7).
More recently, these arguments have been put by Maynard (1976
pp. 308–9) and Harrison (1976, p. 346).

Many of the objections to the allocation of such expenditures as
those on roads, defence, etc., rest upon theoretical uncertainty as to
which of the various possible modes of allocation is most appropriate; but, as has been argued, one can at least indicate how
sensitive the results are to the various allocation options, and discover
to what extent theoretical differences actually affect the empirical
outcome. Preliminary results of some recent research along these
lines suggests that if unallocated expenditures are allocated, whether
on a per capita basis, in proportion to income, or in proportion to
capital, the overall picture of UK redistribution is less equalizing
than is suggested by the current incomplete picture. (For the final

results of this more detailed analysis see Ruggles and O'Higgins (1981).)

On the revenue side, the argument is essentially similar: with respect to capital and corporation taxes and those parts of indirect taxes which are assumed to fall on investment or on general government final consumption, one could test the consequences of the various assumptions which might be made. However, non-tax revenue accounted for almost 20 per cent of total government income in 1977 and it seems inappropriate to treat it as if it were tax revenue. An alternative treatment is suggested below (pp. 34–35).

Apart from these general matters relating to coverage, two specific questions, relating to capital expenditures and to tax expenditures, deserve further discussion.

Peretz follows CSO procedure in not allocating capital expenditure 'on the grounds that the benefits of it accrue to future households in each group', but acknowledges that 'each group of households does of course benefit from capital expenditure in the past, and some allowance might be made for this by allocating imputed rents' (1975, p. 9).

This latter argument is developed by Boreham and Semple who suggest that 'some element of the past capital input to current services' be included in current allocations. 'If a suitable way of compounding to a present value could be found this (present value of past investment) could be added to the current costs of providing services etc. in order to obtain a more adequate picture of the current benefits received' (1976, p. 274).

Boreham and Semple recognise that the logic of this extends to 'excluding the (small) element of current expenditure which contributes to future services' (1976, p. 292), and in areas such as health and education it may be argued that a considerable proportion of current expenditure is effectively investment in human capital, which, if 'capital expenditure' is not to be allocated, should consequently be excluded from the analyses. Essentially then, this viewpoint holds that those parts of public expenditure which effectively constitute investment should not be allocated when they occur but (possibly) as the benefit is realised.

Peacock disagrees, however; having noted that Aaron and McGuire (1970) criticised the inclusion of government capital expenditure as a benefit to individuals in the year in which it occurs 'on the grounds that the only benefits relevant to individuals are the current benefits', he sets out his case. 'Remembering that what we are trying to do is to reallocate a given national income ... there is no reason ... why the money value of government invest-ment expenditure should be treated any differently from the money value of current expenditures on goods and services and not be allocated to the period in which investment occurs, for the value of the investment at the margin is the present consumption foregone' (1974, pp. 157–8).

The argument rests on an assumption about collective choice, that investment takes place now presumably because the community derives a present satisfaction from conferring benefits on future users of government services, a satisfaction which is greater than that derived from alternative current private or public users. If we do not exclude investment expenditures made by private individuals from their incomes, why should social investment be excluded from measures of national income and its distribution? If we are working in the context of the national accounts and trying to take snapshots to see who is getting the value of total government expenditures at different times, then the question about capital expenditure becomes 'how should it be allocated?' rather than 'should it be included?'. Again sensitivity analysis – the use of alternative assumptions – seems the way forward.

The second specific issue of coverage concerns 'tax expenditures' – reliefs or exemptions from taxes – which, it is increasingly accepted, may be treated as equivalent to more 'conventional' expenditures both in their costs to the government and in their public impact (see Chapter 4). As yet, however, relatively little is known about their distributive effect and they are not specifically dealt with in the CSO analyses, although FES data on payments of income tax are net of tax relief. Both Webb and Sieve (1971, pp. 75–6) and Field, Meacher and Pond (1977, p. 193) have argued that tax expenditures should be included as a separate stage in these analyses. This could be done with a minor modification to existing procedures whereby recorded tax payments were increased to their 'notional' level and the value of the tax expenditures entered as a quasi-cash or fiscal benefit. In other words, the existing data on (net) income tax payments should become two sets of figures, gross liability and tax expenditures.

The Balanced Budget Question

A related question, first raised by Peacock and Shannon (1968), is the CSO procedure of allocating unbalanced amounts of government revenue and expenditure, which has a profound effect on the pattern of measured net benefit. They suggested either that all benefits (and by implication all taxes) should be allocated, or that a synthetic social welfare budget be drawn up so as to include only those taxes regarded as paying for the allocated social service benefits. The allocation of these social service taxes and benefits would then allow one to examine the redistributive impact of the social welfare system (so defined). (However, Peacock later changed his views and regarded his earlier advocacy of social welfare budgets as 'no more than a plausible subterfuge', arguing that 'partial results are no substitute for the overall effects of the budget' (1974 p. 156).)

In response to this criticism, Nicholson and Britton (1976) examined how the pattern of net benefits changed if the residual (the aggregate excess of taxes paid over benefits received in the FES sample) is regarded as unallocated expenditure and allocated (i) per capita and (ii) in proportion to household income. Using these alternatives redistribution amongst different household types is little affected. They also measure the effect on inequality of allocating the residual equally to households and find it to be equalising – in general the reduction in inequality is greater the larger the excess of taxes over benefits.

Barg (1974) similarly analyses the sensitivity of the CSO results to a number of assumptions designed to balance the amounts of tax and expenditure allocated, and, as Maynard notes, 'the difference between his redistributive impact results and those of the (CSO) approach exceeds 100% in some cases' (1976, p. 308).

Both of these studies, therefore, basically attempted imputations in order to bring to a balance the average amounts of tax paid and benefit received (as distinct from attempting to allocate all taxes and benefits). Yet in retrospect the balanced budget argument may be seen as more of a support to the argument that all taxes and benefits should be allocated than as a distinct argument in its own right. Government income may include payments from non-residents, trading income and borrowing as well as taxation; it may be that some or all of these non-tax elements should not be allocated as charges on households in the UK, but more properly regarded as beneficial 'leaks' into the household sector. (A similar treatment might be preferred by some for corporation or capital taxes). Some items of government expenditure might also be thought of as 'leaks' out of the household sector – expenditure on non-residents, debt interest and capital expenditure are possibilites; again, payments to and from people in institutions could be treated as separate from household sector transactions (if the data were available), with only a net leak in one or other direction being allocated. Whatever range of items are so treated, it is unlikely that positive and negative leaks will be equal and so some imbalance (albeit a much smaller one than is currently the case) will continue to exist. It is not apparent that this is conceptually objectionable.

Allocation and Valuation of Expenditures

The actual procedures used by the CSO to value and allocate government expenditures have been outlined in the previous chapter and need not be repeated here; but it should be noted that whilst cash benefits are allocated to those sample respondents who report having received them in the previous twelve months, other benefits are dealt with by allocating their running *costs* according to the approximate pattern of service use. Hence, the cost of administering the social security system is not assumed to be a benefit to those receiving social security, but any growth in administration costs in the NHS or in state education will result in a measured increase in benefit. Consequently, a salary rise for people in the middle management of the NHS, for example, would appear in the analysis as a reduction in the inequality of the distribution of 'final' income, even though its effect in reality may be to increase the inequality of the 'original' distribution.

Many commentators have set out theoretical objections to using cost data as a measure of benefit. For example, Prest argues: 'In principle, the valuation of public expenditure by reference to costs of inputs is wrong. What is really needed is some system of valuing outputs' (1968, p. 86). This objection is often a prelude to the somewhat predictable conclusion that 'The use of input cost as an estimate of output benefit is intuitively repugnant but practically inevitable' (Maynard 1976, p. 309). Many of these objections stem from a desire to place a market or exchange value on public service benefits. But in a situation where the state sector is dominant and there is little or no charge at the point of use for public services, this cannot be done with much confidence. In fact if one's concern is to measure the distribution of the current flows of resources from the government to households as valued in the national accounts (i.e. by service costs) there is a robust common-sense case for the CSO procedures.

The more serious objection relates to the policy relevance of the data rather than to methodology, though in principle it is the same as that voiced by Prest and others. The cost-based procedure, if it is to be a guide to public perception of service benefits, requires that people see the costs as benefiting them and that they value these benefits as highly as they would the money value of the costs. If the value placed on a service by taxpayers fails to increase as rapidly as its cost to them as taxpayers, then the gap between the real income position of various family types and income groups as depicted in the CSO analyses, on the one hand, and as perceived by themselves, on the other, will increase. The effects for policy may be hazardous. That such a gap has indeed emerged would provide one explanation of a number of recent tendencies in the UK, in that the benefits of the social wage (the average value to households of government social services expenditure) do not appear to enter on a pound-for-pound basis into the decision-making or preference func-tions of many households, especially in wage-bargaining situations. If this sort of gap does exist then the use of cost data to measure the distribution of benefit is more likely to mislead than to inform the policymakers. (A particular example, suggested by David Piachaud, concerns the proposal in the London Borough of Southwark to build a new town hall at some considerable expense. Most of the evidence on the reactions of the inhabitants of that borough indicates that these costs are not at all seen as a benefit).

Using costs as a benefit measure, therefore, seems acceptable if one wishes to provide data for some professional judgement on where resources go (e.g. if one wishes to make the flow of resources accord with some normatively-defined criteria of need) but not if one is sliding over into a tax-justificatory appraisal of public expenditure. In other words, the CSO data on benefits in kind do not provide a certain indication of the distribution of economic welfare arising from those services, but are only an apportionment of the costs among the service clients.

The question which follows from this is whether, even if the use of cost data as a benefit measure is accepted, the cost-apportionment is accurate. Most of the recent criticism of the CSO on this point arises from the work of Julian Le Grand (1978a, 1978b) on the social class distribution of the benefits of the health and education services. Le Grand's work has generally been interpreted as indicating that the middle classes do better out of these services than the working classses, and the CSO procedures have been criticised by, among others, Field, Meacher and Pond (1977) for ignoring this class differential. However, Le Grand's results (1978a) actually show that whilst working-class households make less use of the NHS relative to their self-reported incidence of sickness, the higher incidence of sickness in working-class households means that actual service use is approximately similar as between the (broadly defined) social classes. This may not be a satisfactory situation in social policy terms, but since the CSO analyses assume no class differential in service use they accord (rather coincidentally) with Le Grand's results.

Similarly on education, Le Grand (1978b) has shown that, as expected, the major class differences in the use of publicly funded education occur after the minimum school-leaving age. As the CSO allocation of benefits distinguishes the costs of attendance at different types of institution, and also makes a division between the cost of educating those over and under sixteen, it deals adequately with these points. The analysis is less satisfactory in its treatment of students living away from home whilst attending a third-level institution. They are not counted as members of the household, hence the public costs which benefit such students (who are disproportionately from the higher social classes) are not reflected in the benefits received by their families. As the students, if sampled, are likely to be members of relatively low-income households, the data which emerge on the distributive impact of the education system portray a picture more egalitarian than is really the case. This inequality is apart from any which may exist if, as Field, Meacher and Pond (1977) have argued, middle-class children benefit more, firstly, because they are better attuned to the norms and values of the system, and, secondly, because they ultimately benefit to a much greater extent from the investment aspect of education.

Another practical objection to the CSO procedures is that they take no account of regional variations in costs. For a number of years it has been part of government policy, as manifested in the Resource Allocation Working Party, to reallocate health service resources more equitably between the various health regions. Yet the CSO analyses assume that a person of a given sex and age group receives the same benefit from the NHS no matter what part of the country he or she lives in. Similarly, education spending varies throughout the country, without such differences being reflected in the CSO analyses. The policy significance of the CSO data would be substantially improved if they allowed for examination of the extent to which inter-regional inequalities contributed to inequality in the nation as a whole. The absence of any regional element in the health and education data both reduces the validity of the CSO analyses and illustrates how their value might be enhanced by focusing more clearly on policy objectives.

Of the other non-cash benefits which the CSO allocates, only housing subsidies have generated any specific controversy. Webb and Sieve (1971) have argued that the proper measure of this subsidy is the amount by which the actual rent of any local-authority dwelling falls short of the rent which the dwelling would command in the private rented sector. However, rents in that sector are subject to some degree of control and, more importantly, the nature of the housing market has been fundamentally affected by the fact that one-third of dwellings are in the local-authority sector whilst only one-seventh are in the private and rented sector. Any search for a 'true market rent' is, therefore, largely an exercise in fantasy. The CSO procedure provides a good measure of the housing subsidy being received. (One minor quibble can, however, be made. The item labelled 'housing subsidies' in the CSO analyses is in fact a mixture of rent rebates or allowances and what are more commonly known to social policy analysts as housing subsidies – that is, it mixes in those subsidies which go to the household and those that go with the dwelling. This combination of the effects of different programmes is unfortunate, since it obscures the separate impact of either.)

Allocation and Valuation of Taxes

On the tax side of the CSO exercise, two assumptions in particular deserve attention. The first is that the incidence of the employer's national insurance contribution falls on consumers. Prior to the redistribution analysis for 1969 (*Economic Trends* February 1971) the CSO used the assumption that both the employer's and the employee's national insurance contributions were taxes on workers' wages, i.e. that if those contributions did not exist, a worker's take-home pay would be larger by the total amount of the national insurance contribution paid on his or her behalf. Although the CSO never, to the author's knowledge, indicated the grounds on which its collective mind had been changed, its current practice is to assume that the employer's contribution is passed on by those employers in the form of higher prices. The tax is, therefore, assumed to be borne by UK consumers to the extent that they buy commodities whose prices, or the prices of whose component parts, have been so increased. This change of assumption affects the measured incidence of taxes as between members of the workforce and others, reducing the apparent burden borne by the former whilst increasing that borne by the latter, but the CSO have not explicitly presented the results of the two assumptions, or indeed of others – such as that the tax is borne by profits, or by any combinations of the two or three, wages, prices and profits – side by side; nor, as mentioned above, have they explained the reasons for the change. It should be noted that academic opinion is still divided on the issue (Brittain 1971).

The second important assumption is that taxes on goods and services are fully passed on to consumers as higher prices. An alternative assumption might be that some of the tax is borne by profits or wages or both. If one opinion must be chosen the CSO one seems preferable, but again some sensitivity analysis would be interesting.

Stepping outside the boundaries of the CSO exercise as presently conducted, an alternative method of dealing with both indirect taxes and subsidies (in principle including goods where the subsidy is 100 per cent, i.e. zero-priced goods such as education and the NHS) has been suggested by Prest. He argues that instead of seeking to impute to different households the costs and values of these items, one should 'calculate disposable income for each income group and then deflate the change in disposable income between the two years by a price index appropriate to that group' (Prest 1968, p. 90).

This argument, which is supported by Levitt (1976), has a clear appeal to anyone who feels that the conventional notion of 'final' income (that is, disposable income adjusted by the imputed costs or values of indirect taxes, subsidies and benefits in kind) is too far removed from any usual perception of income; it would also make for better analyses of the distribution of real income or purchasing power.

Two sets of objections arise in relation to this suggested course of action, even if the required range of indices were to be made available each year. Firstly, the direct effects of government actions would be obscured by being included with all other causes of change in the price index facing each group. If one sought to calculate them separately one would return to the difficulty of needing to determine what proportion of any government levy was borne by consumers. Secondly, any analysis of distributive impacts which began with the general government revenue and expenditure accounts would, unless revenue from indirect taxes chanced to equal expenditure on subsidies and benefits in kind, be left with a revenue-expenditure imbalance (as in the current CSO analyses – though with a different cause), which would distort the picture being presented.

Reviewing this argument, there is a very good case for adopting Prest's suggestion, but as part of an annual examination of the changes in the distribution of purchasing power, rather than as part of an attempt to assess the redistributive impact of government activity. It is manifestly unreal to accept the argument that those purchasing power changes which are not caused by Government activity are of no concern to the government; to accept this would be akin to arguing that the government should have no concern with income maintenance. Yet this view is implicit in the positions of those who look at questions of distribution or redistribution without examining differential price changes. Hence it would be a major improvement if the CSO analyses could be extended to include a line labelled 'real disposable income', though the question of whether the price base should be the previous year, five years or ten years would doubtless cause further argument. However, it would be foolish to ignore the fact that government activities are differently perceived to private activities: they are usually justified with reference to arguments of either (or both) efficiency or social justice, and hence are subject to greater examination with respect to their performance on those criteria. Therefore, the presentation should continue of the gains or losses to different family or income types from these government activities, though it can be questioned whether the concept of 'final income' is necessary to this process (see below, pp. 42–43).

Comparisons

Next we must consider the most appropriate distribution with which to compare the distribution of income after the allocation of taxes and benefits. The CSO analyses are so presented as to make the concept of original income the apparent base for comparison. The majority of tables and charts arrange households with respect to their position in the distribution of original income (see Chapter 2, p. 18). But the concept of original income is simply one point in the flow of resources in society; it depends on prior actions of the government and will influence future actions. It can certainly not be thought of as the state of affairs that would have existed had government intervention not taken place. As Prest argues:

> It was difficult enough to swallow the assumption that the distribution of pre-tax income would remain unchanged whilst various tax or expenditure substitutions took place. It is inconceivable that it would remain unchanged if all government revenues and expenditures were abolished. (1968 p. 88)

For example, some forms of government spending, such as the salaries of Civil Servants, are included in original income; and others, such as spending on road maintenance, are a necessary part of the environment in which employment income is generated. More important, however, is the question of whether the concept of original income provides a realistic input to policy formulation. It appears to be unrealistic to argue, for example, that without governmental benevolence the majority of retirement pensioners would have little or no income – which is essentially the inference of the CSO presentation. Most retirement pensioners have paid national insurance contributions during their working lives in the knowledge that they would receive the national insurance retirement pension. The appropriate measure of the effect of government is not the amount of pension they receive, but the difference between this and what would otherwise have been the case. Clearly, most people would have sought to make some private provision, possibly, as in the United States, by stronger trade-union pressure for better occupational welfare. Those who find this point unconvincing should consider what will happen if the CSO exercise is still being carried out in its current form when the new pensions scheme comes into full operation. Those whose employers and unions have opted out of the state earnings-related scheme will be shown as having most of their income from 'private' sources; those who have opted in will be shown to have low original incomes but they will seem to benefit considerably from state activity. Particularly since the state regulates the conditions under which contracting-out from the state scheme is allowed, this would clearly be a ludicrous distinction, yet it is only that implied in the present analyses. The distinction between pensions and work-income is probably of more importance for any analysis of redistribution than any distinctions within pensions.

The use of the concept of original income, therefore, gives a distorted impression of the effect of government activity.

The weaknesses of the concept of 'final' income have already been discussed. Nonetheless, the information about the distributional effects of individual items, such as housing subsidies and VAT, is valuable. Neither gross income nor disposable income suffers from the drawbacks discussed: they make no implicit pretensions about being 'prior to' or 'after' all government activities; and they are perhaps the points on the cycle of resource-flows which come closest to the common-sense perception of the income-status of a household. Hence, there is a strong case for making either gross or disposable income the base concept in these analyses. They are also more appropriate as vantage-points from which to measure policy effectiveness: in so far as government policy alters original income, it presumably does so (at least when the policy has any distributional intent) in order to move towards a particular pattern of distribution of gross or disposable income. Similarly, if the distributional impact of any subsidy or indirect tax policies plays a part in their formulation, it must be with respect to the change which any such policy would make in the existing distribution of disposable income or purchasing power. It would, consequently, be useful to know, for example, what proportion of the disposable income of various income groups or family types comes from particular income sources (both government and private); if direct taxes were being levied these proportions would come to more than one hundred and would be balanced by a negative figure for direct taxes. Similarly one would examine the distributional impact of benefits in kind, indirect taxes and subsidies by seeing their relative effects on disposable income. If desired, the overall effects of particular sets of government activities could be described using the terms 'net cash benefit' and 'net benefit'. Such a presentation would not only give a more valid picture of redistribution; it would also give a much fuller picture of the target-effectiveness of any particular programme.

Circularities

The practical value of the CSO analyses can also be criticised for the paucity of information they yield on circularities within the tax and benefit system – a central theme of this book – on the way in which the system gives with one hand and takes away with the other. There may seem to academics and administrators to be good reason for this circularity but, as has recently been said, 'Try explaining it to your uncle.' Piachaud (1979) made this point when discussing the possibility of giving people the option of not collecting the child benefit due to them, but of having a cut in their tax liabilities instead – an optional child tax credit, as it were.

An examination of the CSO analyses over the last two decades illustrates the increasing amounts of direct tax being taken from low income households. The development can also be seen in the fact that whilst the proportion of GDP represented by income tax and the national insurance contributions of employees and the self-employed increased from 13 per cent in 1961 to over 18 per cent in 1976, the proportion of these taxes paid out of wages and salaries increased from just over 50 per cent to 85 per cent. So not only has the direct tax 'take' gone up in the last fifteen years, but the share of it borne by wage and salary earners has increased massively, so that their payments accounted for over 15 per cent of GDP in 1976, as against $7\frac{1}{2}$ per cent in 1961. (*National Income and Expenditure, 1967–1977* (HMSO 1978), Table 9.7, and equivalent tables in earlier years.)

Hence much of the cost of better public services is being paid for by average and below-average wage earners, something which has only recently penetrated the 'received wisdom' of social policy. If the CSO analyses are to help in investigating this phenomenon of circularities we need to know not alone what numbers and types of households are making net gains and losses of various magnitudes but, more crucially, what is the relationship between gross and net gains and losses. It is often said that income redistribution in Britain represents much effort for little output – the availability of these sort of data would illuminate the processes of redistribution, and allow one to assess the validity of such statements.

The earlier CSO analyses gave some information on the number of households making net gains or losses sufficient to move them up or down by one or more ranges of income, but these data have not been published in more recent years. The Royal Commission on the Distribution of Income and Wealth adapted the device in its seventh report to show the percentage of households moving up or down by one or more deciles due to redistribution in 1976 and 1977. The picture that emerged each year was of a considerable degree of rank order constancy in the distribution; for example, almost half of the sample households were in the same decile in the distributions of original and of disposable income, whilst more than 40 per cent had changed by only one decile, (RCDIW 1979, Table 3.2). These are only 'net change' data, of course, so one is unable to draw any conclusions from them about the relationship between gross and net taxes and benefits. They do, however, suggest that an investigation of that relationship would be worthwhile.

Conclusions

In recent years a number of improvements have been introduced into the CSO analyses: they are now set more clearly in the context of total government revenue and expenditure; the impact of factors other than household type and income level, such as the number of workers in the household and its life-cycle stage, has been examined; separate articles on specific aspects of the analyses have been published; and deciles and quintiles are now being used instead of (rapidly outdated) income ranges. These are worthwhile changes which it would be unfair not to acknowledge. Furthermore, the CSO data have the advantage of being based on information about patterns of service usage, unlike some American data. Finally, there is obviously a limit to the amount of information which can be accommodated in an analysis which is already unique in being published annually.

Nonetheless, the criticisms of the CSO analyses are sufficiently important to force one to take an agnostic, though not an atheistic, view of their validity. Many, if not most, of the specific procedures used by the CSO are reasonable, but we need to know the consequences of alternative methods in disputed areas and of a range of methods in the relatively uncharted areas of unallocated taxes and expenditures. Given these data, the external as well as the internal validity of the existing analyses can be checked.

The absence of a policy context for the exercise is likely to prove more difficult to remedy. It seems unlikely that, in the foreseeable future, governments will commit themselves to specific distributional targets, or that the distributional consequences of policies will ever be more than, at most, a secondary consideration to some primary purpose such as revenue raising or income maintenance. Nonetheless, distributional data have an important part to play in illustrating policy consequences and hence in influencing policy reformulation. Essentially, that is the modest practical case for better and more relevant data on income redistribution.

References

Aaron, H. and McGuire, M. 1970, 'Public goods and income distribution', *Econometrica*, vol. 38.

Atkinson, A. B. (ed) 1976, *The Personal Distribution of Incomes*, London, George Allen & Unwin.

Barg, S. 1974, *Statistical Studies of Income Redistribution*, unpublished M. Phil. thesis, University of York.

Boreham, J. & Semple, M. 1976, 'Future development of work in the Government Statistical Service on the distribution and redistribution of household income' in A. B. Atkinson (ed) pp. 269–99.

Brittain, J. A. 1971, 'The incidence of the social security payroll tax', *American Economic Review*, vol. 61, no. 1 (March), pp. 110–25.

Brown, C. V. 1971, *Impact of Tax Changes on Income Distribution*, London, Political and Economic Planning.

Brown, C. V. 1972, *Impact of Tax Changes on Income Distribution: 1972 edition*, London, Institute of Fiscal Studies.

Brown, C. V. 1973, *Impact of Tax Changes on Income Distribution: 1973 edition*, London, Institute of Fiscal Studies.

Field, F., Meacher, M. and Pond, C. 1977, *To Him Who Hath: a study of poverty and taxation*, Harmondsworth, Penguin Books.

Gillespie, W. I. 1965, 'The effect of public expenditures on the distribution of income' in R. A. Musgrave (ed), *Essays in Fiscal Federalism*, Washington D.C., Brookings Institution.

Harrison, A. 1976, 'Discussion' in A. B. Atkinson (ed) pp. 345–8.

Jackson, P. M. and McGilvray, J. W. 1973, *The Impact of Tax Changes on Income Distribution: The 1973 Budget*, London, Institute of Fiscal Studies.

Le Grand, J. 1978a, 'The distribution of public expenditure: the case of health care', *Economica*, vol. 45 (May), pp. 125–42.

Le Grand, J. 1978b, 'The distribution of public expenditure on education', mimeo, London School of Economics, November.

Levitt, M. S. 1976, 'Discussion' in A. B. Atkinson (ed), pp. 334–45.

Maynard, A. 1976, 'Discussion' in A. B. Atkinson (ed), pp. 305–10.

Merrett, A. J. and Monk, D. A. G. 1966, 'The structure of UK taxation 1962–63',

Bulletin of the Oxford University Institute of Economics and Statistics, vol 28, no. 3 (August), pp. 145–62.

Musgrave, R. A., Case, K. E. and Leonard, H. 1974, 'The distribution of fiscal burdens and benefits', *Public Finance Quarterly*, vol. 2, no. 3 (July), pp. 259–311.

Nicholson, J. L. 1974, 'The distribution and redistribution of income in the United Kingdom' in D. Wedderburn (ed), *Poverty, Inequality and Class Structure*, Cambridge, CUP, pp. 71–91.

Nicholson, J. L. 1977, 'How should indirect taxes be allocated when estimating the redistribution of income' in A. J. Culyer and J. Wiseman (eds), *Public Economics and Human Resources*, Paris, Cujas.

Nicholson, J. L. and Britton, A. J. C. 1976, 'The redistribution of income' in A. B. Atkinson (ed), pp. 313–34.

Peacock, A. 1974, 'The treatment of government expenditure in studies of income redistribution' in W. L. Smith and J. M. Culbertson (eds), *Public Finance and Stablization Policy: Essays in Honour of Richard Musgrave*, Amsterdam, North Holland, pp. 151–67.

Peacock, A. and Shannon, R. 1968, 'The welfare state and the redistribution of income', *Westminster Bank Review*, August, pp. 30–46.

Pechman, J. A. and Okner, B. A. 1974, *Who Bears the Tax Burden?*, Washington DC, Brookings Institution.

Peretz, J. 1975, 'Beneficiaries of public expenditure: an analysis for 1971/72', mimeo, June, London, CSO.

Piachaud, D. 1979, 'Who are the poor, and what is the best way to help them?', *New Society*, 15 March, pp. 603–6.

Prest, A. R. 1968, 'The Budget and interpersonal distribution', *Public Finance*, vol. 27, pp. 80–98.

RCDIW 1979, *Report No. 7 – Fourth Report on the Standing Reference*, Royal Commission on the Distribution of Income and Wealth, Cmnd 7595, London, HMSO.

Roskamp, K. W. 1968, 'The Budget and interpersonal distribution: comments on the papers of professors Bela Csikos-Nagy and Alan R. Prest', *Public Finance*, vol. 27, pp. 99–105.

Ruggles, P. 1979, *The Allocation of Taxes and Expenditures to Households in the United States*, unpublished Ph.D. thesis, Harvard University.

Ruggles, P. and O'Higgins, M. 1981, 'The distribution of government expenditures among households in the United Kingdom', *Review of Income and Wealth*.

Webb, A. L. and Sieve, J. E. B. 1971, *Income Redistribution and the Welfare State*, London, Bell.

4 Tax Expenditures and Fiscal Welfare*Chris Pond

Introduction

Taxes and public expenditure, as the previous two chapters have demonstrated, can be used to redistribute income in a socially desirable way. This chapter pursues the same theme. It is concerned not so much with the contradictions between taxation and social policy, as with their characteristics as complementary systems of welfare and public expenditure. The first part of the chapter discusses the concept of 'fiscal welfare' and its usefulness in analysing the tax system in relation to the analogous apparatus of social welfare. Taxation is considered here as an *instrument* of social policy rather than merely as a source of finance. The chapter then turns to consider the concept of 'tax expenditures' which has had a considerable influence on tax policy in the United States and which is receiving increasing interest in the United Kingdom. Again, taxation is seen less as a means of financing public expenditure and more in its role as an agent in administering expenditure equivalents. Finally, some of the implications of both tax expenditure and fiscal welfare for social policy are examined.

It should be stressed at the outset that the two concepts of fiscal welfare and tax expenditures, although closely related, should be treated separately. By no means all elements of fiscal welfare, in the form of allowances and reliefs, can be counted as tax expenditures. Nor are all forms of expenditure administered through the tax system a response to particular needs equivalent to those at which social policy is directed. Care is therefore needed both in definition and use of the concepts. Nevertheless, it is valuable to identify the

* Chris Pond would like to acknowledge the helpful comments on this chapter received from Lesley Day and Adrian Sinfield as well as from his co-editors and colleagues at the Civil Service College. Responsibility for any remaining errors or ambiguities remains, of course, his own.

analogies between social and fiscal welfare and between explicit public expenditure and tax expenditures.

Fiscal Welfare

It is now almost a quarter of a century since Richard Titmuss (1958) presented his seminal paper on the 'social division of welfare'. While the implications of this framework for analysis are familiar to many specialists in social policy, economists concerned with public finance or the workings of the labour market, and for whom the significance is quite as important, have tended to ignore Titmuss's classifications. His argument was simple enough:

> Under separately administered social security systems, like family allowances and retirement pensions, direct cash payments are made in discharging collective responsibilities for particular dependencies. In the relevant accounts, these are treated as 'social service' expenditure since they represent flows of payments through the central government account. Allowances and reliefs from income tax, though providing similar benefits and expressing similar social purpose in the recognition of dependent needs, are not, however, treated as social service expenditure. The first is a cash transaction; the second an accounting convenience. Despite the difference in adminstrative method, the tax saving that accrues to the individual is, in effect, a transfer payment. In their primary objectives and their effects on individual purchasing power there are no differences in these two ways by which collective provision is made for dependencies. Both are manifestations of social policies in favour of identified groups in the population.

Titmuss identified three complementary and analogous forms of welfare provision: 'social welfare' – the social services and cash benefits normally identified as the core of the 'welfare state'; 'fiscal welfare' administered in the form of allowances, reliefs and exemptions from tax liability; and 'occupational welfare' dispensed by employers to improve the well-being of their staff and to improve relations in industry. There is evidence that all three forms of welfare continue to grow in importance, though the balance between them may change over time (Sinfield 1978). This chapter is primarily concerned with the first two categories.

The burden of Titmuss's argument was that to consider any one form of welfare provision in isolation presents a partial and distorted picture. The similarities between the different systems may readily be illustrated through a consideration of their operation in the event of an individual finding himself or herself in any one of several 'states of dependency'. An individual who finds himself un-employed, for instance, is eligible either for national insurance or supplementary benefit; such benefits are not currently taxable and in the early days of unemployment the individual may be eligible for further support through tax rebates; he may also be eligible for redundancy payments. On losing his job, the individual therefore receives support administered through three complementary systems of welfare: social, fiscal and occupational. Similar parallels may be drawn between the forms of income maintenance provided to the individual on retirement. In addition to the basic retirement or sup-plementary pension, the state provides increased allowances against tax on any earnings. Meanwhile, the pensioner may receive an occupational pension, any contributions to which would have been allowable against tax. Again, the three systems of welfare interact.

The operation of social and fiscal welfare is again apparent in a third common state of dependency – the case of families with children. The Tax Credit Green Paper (Cmnd 5116), describing the situation in 1972, referred to

> the overlap between the two systems which exists in the area of cash benefit for families with children and the Inland Revenue's dealings with the same families ... People in the tax field can benefit from tax allowances. All families with two or more children can claim family allowances, which are then subject to income tax and to a special tax deduction (the 'clawback'). A futher set of increases for children is available to national insurance beneficiaries. Low earners with children can claim family income supplement. Between them these systems provide substantial help for those who are bringing up children on low incomes.

The proposals for a Tax Credit Scheme were themselves an attempt to integrate the complementary systems of family support operating with the same objectives but through different mechanisms. The scheme itself, which will be considered in some detail in Chapter 12, was abandoned with the change of government in 1974. But the explicit recognition of the two systems survived, embodied in the Child Benefit Scheme, which represented the transition from fiscal welfare (in the form of child tax allowances) to social welfare (in the form of a tax-free cash benefit).

In the field of housing, too, policy recognition has been conferred upon the parallel systems. As Willis and Hardwick (1978) have commented,

> The fact that tax relief is the equivalent of a direct subsidy to the owner occupier who is a taxpayer was recognised in 1966 when the 'option mortgage' scheme was introduced, under which a house purchaser who was not liable to income tax (or not liable at the standard rate) could get a mortgage at less than the normal rate of interest. In short the non-taxpayer was offered an explicit subsidy which corresponded broadly to the indirect subsidy enjoyed by the standard rate taxpayer who was paying the normal rate of interest and getting tax relief on it.

The list of examples in which the two systems of welfare overlap is indeed considerable, and many are examined in detail in the chapters in Part II of the book.

In the process of building his classification, Titmuss was concerned to establish the status of his three forms of welfare provision as essentially complementary systems with similar objectives. But there are clearly very real differences between the elements of the 'welfare trinity' in terms both of level and mode of provision (Sinfield 1978). Later in this chapter, we present some estimates of the aggregate level of 'tax expenditure' which includes many 'fiscal benefits'. But attempts to assess the level of provision, either in aggregate or at the level of the individual recipient, is an exercise in social accounting for which only part of the data is available. Direct expenditure on public welfare is more easily itemised and, as Chapters 2 and 3 indicate, despite limitations, we can at least make brave attempts to allocate these to particular types of household. In the case of fiscal or occupational welfare, we cannot begin to estimate the impact on individual households in the same way and the assessment of the aggregate effects is almost equally formidable. Such exercises are rendered more hazardous by the fact that the balance between the systems tends to change over time.

The qualitative differences between the three forms of provision are intuitively easier to identify. The social security system is geared to the recognition of subsistence, or near-subsistence, needs and is often administered subject to a means-test. Provision through the fiscal and occupational welfare systems is rarely subject to the same stigma that attaches to dependence on the social security apparatus. To the extent that different groups are subject to the separate forms of provision, this can serve to create 'a differential recognition of needs'.

Adrian Sinfield (1978) has explained this characteristic of the welfare trinity in terms of its historical development:

> Although there may now be increasing overlap and sometimes planned integration, public welfare has often been the latest to be developed or expanded. Its role has consisted of extending to new groups some limited support of a kind which others have already been receiving through fiscal or occupational benefits.

Tax Expenditures

The framework of analysis so far described considers many of the allowances and reliefs embodied in the tax system to be a form of fiscal welfare, a means of achieving social policy objectives through the tax system. From the point of view of the recipient, the effect is the same (in financial terms) whether the subsidy is paid in cash or as a tax allowance. Moreover, from the point of view of the state it may be argued that the effect on the Public Sector Borrowing Requirement is also the same. Tax allowances may be a form of public welfare; they are also a form of public expenditure.

Although the concept of 'tax expenditures' has until recently gained little explicit official recognition in the UK, the past decade has seen its official acceptance within the system of budgetary control in the United States. The concept was pioneered by Stanley Surrey who, as Assistant Secretary to the US Treasury, pointed out that 'through various special exemptions, deductions and credits, our tax system does operate to affect the private economy in ways that are usually accomplished by expenditures' (Surrey 1973). These 'tax expenditures' he estimated, represented about a quarter of the Federal Budget, but were outside the normal procedures of budgetary scrutiny. The desire to include tax expenditures in the same framework of control as direct expenditures has resulted in the development of a Tax Expenditure Budget which, though far from exhaustive, (Goode 1977) provides estimates of the costs of the major tax relief programmes.

In Canada, too, the principle of tax expenditures has received official recognition. Although the government refuted the proposals for a comprehensive income tax by the Carter Commission on the grounds that some exemptions were economically or socially desirable, it has now developed a 'Tax Expenditure Account' to assess the cases of such exemptions (Government of Canada 1979).

Though official recognition of the concept has been slower to develop in the UK, the 1979 Public Expenditure White Paper (Cmnd 7439) did include, for the first time, a list of the estimated costs of allowances and reliefs against direct taxation. The White Paper also acknowledged that:

> Public expenditure ... presents only part of the picture. For an improved understanding of the role of fiscal policy it is necessary to look also at certain of the reliefs embodied in the taxation system. Such reliefs can have broadly the same effect on the Government's borrowing requirements as public expenditure. Although their distributional and incentive consequences will be different, there is a case for saying that, where a tax relief benefits a particular group of taxpayers, or a particular sector of the economy, it should be taken into account along with direct public expenditure related to those taxpayers or that part of the economy.

Care is needed in defining exactly what is meant by the term 'tax expenditures'. The US Treasury adopted a twofold classification:

(a)   the extent to which the tax base deviates from 'widely accepted definitions of income', and
(b)   the extent to which it deviates from 'the generally accepted structure of an income tax' (Surrey 1973).

The first of these criteria present difficulties enough. Are capital gains to be treated as 'income'? What about the 'imputed income' of owner-occupied housing or consumer durables? Should fringe benefits be fully integrated into an individual's tax liability? Before these questions can be answered we need a consistent definition of what constitutes 'income'. Such a definition was provided by the Minority Report of the Royal Commission on the Taxation of Profits and Income in 1955 which argued that 'no concept of income can be really equitable that stops short of the comprehensive definition which embraces all receipts which increase an individual's command over the use of society's scarce resources' (Cmnd 9474). This is close to the definition taken as the starting-point in the US assessment of tax expenditures, based on the Haig–Simons definition of income. Essentially such a definition would treat income as the amount that an individual could consume in a given period without reducing his stock of net wealth (Goode 1977). It would include all forms of money income plus income in kind (from fringe benefits or imputed income), gifts, winnings and real capital gains. Some commentators include legacies in this definition of income. On the other hand, allowances intended to 'refine' the concept of income, such as interest charges on capital borrowed to finance income-yielding assets or expenses connected with work, are not classed as 'tax expenditures'.

Tax expenditures might therefore be defined as any deviation in 'taxable income' from this concept of comprehensive income. But it is still necessary to identify, in the words of Surrey, 'which income tax rules are special provisions representing Government expenditures made through the income tax system to achieve various social and economic objectives and which income tax rules are just tax rules' (Surrey 1973). In other words, it is argued that those allowances and reliefs which are part of the structure of the income tax, such as the personal allowances and reliefs, should be excluded from the definition of 'tax expenditures'. In the United Kingdom, these allowances are intended to fulfil two functions. First, they are intended to exempt those on the lowest incomes from tax altogether. Secondly, the structural allowances provide an additional element of progression below the higher rates of tax (which affect less than 5 per cent of taxpayers). (Field, Meacher and Pond 1977.)

This is the second major difficulty in definition. For while the basic allowances are structural to the UK tax system, they are by no means the only way in which the objectives of exempting the poor and graduating tax rates could be achieved. Exclusion of those on low incomes could just as effectively be achieved through the use of tax credits or various forms of initial or vanishing exemption (Levy 1960; Seltzer 1968). Indeed there would appear to be a strong case for reforming the personal allowance system on the grounds that it allows taxation to conflict with social policy objectives. The tax threshold, made up of these personal allowances, is now well below the official 'poverty line' leading to many of the conflicts which feature throughout this volume (Chapter 5). And as the Royal Commission of the Taxation of Profits and Income noted in their Second Report:

> It seems to us clear that the practice of looking to personal allowances and earned income relief to provide effective exemptions has had the effect of distorting the tax structure at the lower end of the scale, in that the starting point of liability is lower than it could reasonably be expected to be if the needs of subsistence are borne in mind. Yet an artificial depression of the starting point is always to be expected if exemption can only be

achieved by increasing the figure of the personal allowances. For the circumstances that make it right to raise the starting point are not by any means the same as those that justify any general reduction in taxation. (Cmnd 9105)

To the extent that the personal allowances are part of the structure of the UK income tax, it might be argued that they should not be treated as tax expenditures. But to the extent that they achieve their structural objectives at a cost which is greater than might otherwise be necessary, we may justifiably consider at least part of the allowances as tax expenditures. Indeed, the proposition that the 'structural allowances' should be excluded at all from the definition is open to challenge. Such a definition may be irrelevant when considering their effects on living standards or on central government revenue. Moreover, as has been made clear by the child benefit scheme, personal tax allowances can be converted into explicit expenditures not linked to the tax system.

As Willis and Hardwick (1978) have noted, in the most comprehensive study of tax expenditures to be carried out for the UK, the problems of deciding what is part of the 'generally accepted structure' are compounded by the fact that such a definition will vary from time to time and from place to place. In some countries, capital gains are treated as income and their whole or partial exclusion from the tax base may be counted as a tax expenditure; in others such gains are not subjected to income tax because they are not treated as income. The same difficulties arise with the treatment of imputed income from owner-occupation.

Despite these difficulties, Willis and Hardwick have made a courageous attempt to estimate the extent of tax expenditures in the United Kingdom. The effective tax base was more than halved by tax expenditures: in 1973/4, only 45 per cent of total (aggregate) gross income was subject to tax. Structural allowances and deductions accounted for 32 per cent of total gross income, while non-structural deductions accounted for 15 per cent. The authors estimated that if only the non-structural deductions had been taxed at the (then) standard rate of tax of 30 per cent, tax revenue from individuals would have increased by almost a third. Adjusting the estimate for the fact that some people would still have an income too low to be subject to tax suggests that tax revenue would still rise by about a quarter if only the non-structural reliefs are withdrawn.

Estimates for the United States (for 1977) suggest that the adoption of a Comprehensive Tax Base would increase total revenue by 43.5 per cent (Minarik 1977). The two estimates presented above are not consistent, but comparative figures for the late 1960s showed taxable income to be 43 per cent of total personal income in the UK, 45 per cent in the United States, 24 per cent in France and 79 per cent in West Germany (Sinfield 1978). Professor Atkinson (1979) has estimated that the revenue gain of moving towards the type of comprehensive income tax considered by the Meade Committee would, by 1979, have been of the order of £5000 or an increase in income tax revenue of about 25 per cent which would be sufficient to offset a rise in the tax threshold of 50 per cent.

The Implications for Social Policy

The estimates of the cost of allowances and reliefs provided in the public expenditure White Papers of January 1979 and March 1980 suggest that the cost in terms of revenue foregone in this way is quite substantial. It is not possible merely to add the separate items to arrive at an estimate of overall cost, since many are interdependent. The withdrawal of one would affect the amount of revenue foregone through others. Moreover, this is a static analysis taking no account of the change in people's behaviour (such as the size of house they would buy) if the allowances were withdrawn. The magnitude of the figures involved is by no means insubstantial, however. Estimated income tax foregone through the exemption of interest on loans for the purchase or improvement of owner-occupied housing is put at £1110 millions in 1978/9 – of the same order as central government expenditure on roads and transport or loans to the nationalised industries. (For a comparison of cash and tax expenditures on housing see Chapter 6.) The married person's allowance alone accounted for £6600 millions in revenue foregone in 1978/9, which was very nearly equivalent to central government expenditure on health and the personal social services. Nor is the list of allowances for which costs are provided in the White Paper exhaustive. Indeed, the Meade Committee (1978) have suggested that 'an outstanding feature (of the UK income tax) is the great variety of personal allowances' and that 'the arbitrary and detailed complexity of this structure of allowances may well be regarded as constituting something of an anomoly'.

The impact of such tax expenditures on social policy should be assessed not only in terms of their distributive effect, but also of

their effect on the tax system as a source of finance. The acceptability of social expenditure appears to be very sensitive to the
acceptability of the taxation which finances it.

Distributional impact

The two previous chapters have been concerned with the allocation
of taxes and benefits to households of different income and family
composition. Yet an important element missing from the analyses
carried out by the CSO is the distributive impact of implicit
subsidies through tax relief. Such relief does of course register in
the average tax payments of households, but a separate analysis of
the distribution of the reliefs itself would be enlightening. (See
Chapter 2.)

The impact of the tax expenditures on individual households is
generally regressive. They are regressive in terms of 'vertical equity'
(between households at different levels of income) because the types
of expenditure or income excluded tend to be of a greater importance to high-income groups and because the value of the relief
is normally related to the highest marginal rate of tax paid. Those
already exempted from tax gain nothing. Estimates by Willis and
Hardwick (1978) suggested that, for single people and married
couples, the expenditures were mildly regressive – representing 3.5
per cent of the total net income of the lowest group and 5.6 per cent
for the highest – but the picture was not consistent. Part of the reason
for this was that the authors were forced to include child allowances,
which are not classed as 'expenditures' in their definition and which
are relatively more important to lower-income families.

Estimates for the United States show a similarly regressive effect.
Surrey (1973) estimated (for 1972) that the poorest 18 per cent of
families enjoyed only 0.2 per cent of the tax benefits. Meanwhile,
the top 1.2 per cent of families enjoyed 42 per cent of the total
benefits. It is questionable whether policymakers would sanction subsidies with this type of effect if they were presented as direct cash
payments. The impact is one of selectivity in reverse. The existence
of the tax expenditures also has an impact on horizontal equity, in
the sense that households with the same characterisitcs are treated
differently. Tax liability varies not only by *level* of income but by
source and by pattern of expenditure.

Effect on the tax system

Viewed as 'fiscal subsidies' the tax expenditures appear to be inequitable in both a vertical and horizontal sense. The other side of this coin is, of course, the effect that such subsidies have on the progressiveness of the tax system. Even a quarter of a century ago, the Minority Report on the Royal Commission on the Taxation of Profits and Income warned of the inequitable effects created by the erosion of the tax base through

> the introduction of successive concessions which have the effect of constantly shifting the tax burden in a manner which is no less far-reaching for being unobtrusive ... neither the public nor the legislature nor the Courts are conscious of the extent to which the tax system, behind a facade of formal equality, metes out unequal treatment to the different classes of the taxpaying community. (Cmnd 9474)

The 'formal facade' of the British tax system in the late 1970s was of a steeply progressive structure. Yet in 1978/9 even the top 1 per cent of income recipients were subject to an effective (average) rate of tax of less than 50 per cent, despite nominal (marginal) rates rising to 83 per cent and 98 per cent. Perhaps even more striking, the effect of the various allowances was to reduce the number of taxpayers subject to tax at *any* of the higher rates to 808,000 (3.8 per cent of all income taxpayers). The proportion was reduced further in the June 1979 Budget. (Inland Revenue 1978; HM Treasury 1979.)

An important consequence of this for social policy is that, whatever the reality, it is people's perceptions of the tax system that determine their response to demands for additional social expenditure and if it is felt that tax rates are already too high, there will be increased reluctance to sanction increased expenditure.

In one sense, of course, tax rates *are* very much too high in the UK. Marginal rates, especially for those at the bottom of the income tax scale, remain significantly higher than in most European countries (although effective average rates are about mid-range). Paradoxically, a large part of the reason for this is the size of the tax expenditures. By reducing the tax base, the allowances make it essential to apply higher marginal rates of tax to raise a given level of tax revenue. Willis and Hardwick (1978) estimated that for the same income tax yield the basic rate of tax could have been reduced from 30 per cent to 23 per cent if only the non-structural reliefs had been withdrawn and to 20 per cent if imputed income and income in kind were also included in the tax base. It is for this reason that the Meade Committee (1978) stressed the need 'to resist erosion of the tax base through a multiplication of exemptions and reliefs'. This is additionally important since the disincentive effects of a tax (the 'substitution effects') are thought to be most responsive to *marginal* rates of tax. The Meade Committee went on to stress that 'There will almost inevitably be some clash between the criteria of economic efficiency (which requires low *marginal* tax rates) and of vertical redistribution (which will require high average rates of tax on the rich).' It will be noted that, as a result of its relative generosity in the provision of tax expenditures, the UK tax system achieves the worst of both worlds. The ability of the system to raise a high level of revenue with which to finance social expenditure is reduced through erosion of the tax base and the disincentive effects of high marginal rates which it creates. Meanwhile the system is poorly equipped to achieve objectives of vertical redistribution because of the effect of tax expenditures on average rates of tax. (For a further discussion of this point, see Chapter 9, p. 164.)

It is not sufficient, however, to refer only to an erosion of the tax base through the effect of allowances. The structural allowances are intended to achieve a measure of progressiveness in the tax system while exempting the poorest households altogether. Meanwhile, the non-structural allowances serve to reduce the progressiveness of the income tax. In the United States, too, Surrey (1973) has noted that 'The income tax law is indeed a curious structure, harboring both a progressive income tax system and tax expenditure grants for the well-to-do. The grant system serves to undercut the progressive income tax system to leave us with a complicated mixture which is both a bad tax system and a bad grant system.'

What seems to have been happening in the UK is that the tax base has been changing shape: the decline in the tax threshold has pulled increasing numbers of low-income families into tax liability, broadening the tax base at the lower end of the income scale. Meanwhile, the non-structural allowances have reduced the amount of taxable income at higher levels. The effect of this change in the value of allowances has been to increase sharply the tax burden on those with lower incomes from work, so that in many cases net income from work is only marginally (if at all) above the official supplementary benefit 'poverty line' (see Chapter 5). This in turn has tended to act as a constraint on the ability of policymakers to raise benefit levels. For instance, the Royal Commission on the Distribution of Income and Wealth (Cmnd 7175) received evidence from the Supplementary Benefits Commission concerning the inadequacy of living standards afforded by SB, but noted 'It is a matter of social policy that State benefits for those not in work are generally lower than earnings from work ... if Supplementary Benefits were raised there could be a possibility, especially for heads of large families, of paying people more for not working than for working and this would raise questions of equity and incentives.' This problem is exacerbated by the current exemptions from tax of short-term benefits.

Budgetary control

An aspect of tax expenditures which has caused considerable concern is the lack of budgetary control which is applied to their introduction and administration. As Stanley Surrey has noted in relation to the USA,

> It can generally be said that less critical analysis is paid to these expenditures than to almost any direct expenditure program one can mention. The tax expenditures tumble into the law without supporting studies, being propelled instead by cliches, debating points, and scraps of data and tables that are passed off as serious evidence. A tax system that is so vulnerable to the injection of extraneous, costly and ill-considered expenditure programs is in a precarious state from the standpoint of the basic tax goals of providing adequate revenues and maintaining tax equity.

Moreover, once a tax expenditure has been introduced, it tends to represent an open-ended commitment over which policymakers have little control. An increase in building-society interest rates, for instance, has the effect of immediately raising government 'expenditure' on mortgage interest relief.

By contrast, direct expenditures tend to come under strict scrutiny and control. It is for this reason that the United States Treasury has now established its 'Tax Expenditure Budget' in order to bring such forms of expenditure into the same forum of Congressional discussion. And although the initiative in the UK Public Expenditure White Papers to itemise the cost of the main allowances and reliefs is to be welcomed, it can hardly be said that the expenditures are integrated with overall public expenditure planning process.

The willingness of policymakers to sanction tax expenditures appears to stem from a belief that such forms of assistance involve less government interference than cash subsidies and that they confer less stigma on the recipient. These are indeed both notable characteristics of tax expenditures as they currently operate in Britain and the United States. However, they have nothing to do with the fumdamental nature of tax expenditures as opposed to cash expenditures; they merely reflect the difference in administration of the two types of subsidy. The lower level of government interference in the provision of tax expenditures compared with explicit expenditures reflects more the casual way in which tax expenditures are administered and the relatively rigid way in which direct subsidies are proferred.

This is not merely a comment on the control of public expenditure. The implications for social policy are well summarised by John Due (1977):

> Expenditures of this nature may be regarded as objectionable in principle in two ways: they are not subject to annual budgetary review, and their disguised nature may result in much higher levels than Congress would ever vote outright. Since the deductions reduce tax revenue, a higher tax rate is necessary to raise a given sum of revenue, with the possibility of greater adverse effects on incentives in the economy. Under usual theories of governmental decision-making, the likely result is that tax rates are somewhat higher and other government expenditures somewhat lower than they would be if the deductions were not provided.

The real issue for social policy therefore is that of priorities in public expenditure. Tax expenditures reduce revenue, exerting downward pressure on programmes of social expenditure. Yet if tax and direct expenditures were considered side by side, policymakers might choose a very different set of priorities.

The failure to treat the two forms of expenditure in the same way has created some odd effects on social policy decision-making. The switch from child tax allowances and family allowances to child benefit has, for instance, resulted in an increase in 'public expenditure' without affecting the government's borrowing requirement. Similarly, the recent switch from relief for life-assurance premiums to cash subsidies will show up on the public expenditure side of the budget, although the additional cost will be close to zero. Indeed, as Willis and Hardwick (1978) note, there may be administrative savings. Expenditure on the option mortgage scheme comes under annual budgetary review, while that part of the subsidy to owner-occupiers that remains as tax relief continues to be exempt. As the House of Commons Expenditure Committee (1976) noted in their deliberations on the 1976 White Paper, 'it would assist rational assessment of Government policy if tax reliefs in relation to housing, children or investment were considered in conjunction with housing subsidies, family allowances or investment grants.' The Committee went on to comment, 'it becomes difficult to form a coherent political discussion when ... the two halves of the argument are in different places.'

Conclusion

The tax system is not merely a means of financing social expenditure or of achieving a desired distribution of income. As this chapter has demonstrated, it is itself an instrument of social policy. Many of the reliefs and allowances provided through the tax system may be considered as 'fiscal benefits' analogous to cash benefits or public services. A comprehensive analysis requires that fiscal welfare should be included alongside the social welfare to which it is complementary. Both systems have the effect of increasing the economic resources available to individuals or households, and thereby their standard of living. Explicit public expenditure provides only part of the welfare package.

The analogy also has meaning when viewed in terms of government spending commitments and revenue requirements. The provision of an allowance or relief has the same effect as the provision of cash benefits or public services on the government's borrowing requirement. Revenue is lower, or tax rates higher, than would be the case if the exemption from tax did not exist. Yet in the UK at least, recognition of this fact, or of its implications, remains in its infancy. In other countries tax expenditures are not much more fully integrated with systems for the control of public spending.

The implications for social policy are significant. In the absence of similar mechanisms for the monitoring and control of tax expenditures, there is a danger that these tend to be higher and explicit social expenditure to be lower than would otherwise be the case. At the same time, the reduction in the tax base which results from the existence of the exemptions involves the need for higher marginal tax rates. These, in turn, may have an effect on incentives and economic efficiency which reduce the resources available for social expenditure, while increasing resistance to such expenditure in response to perceptions of the heavier tax burdens indicated by high marginal rates. Tax allowances also tend to have a regressive effect on the distribution of income and the tax system.

This is not to suggest that tax expenditures are in themselves undesirable. The criticisms summarised above may also be levelled at some types of explicit public expenditures. It is important, however, that the magnitude and effects of tax expenditures are carefully examined both by social policy analysts and by those concerned with the finance and control of public expenditure.

References

Atkinson, A. B. 1979, 'A tax strategy for the 1980's', *New Society*, vol. 48, no. 873.

Due, J. 1977, 'Personal deductions' in J. A. Pechman (ed), *Comprehensive Income Taxation*, Washington DC, Brookings Institution.

Field, F., Meacher, M. and Pond, C. 1977, *To Him Who Hath: a study of poverty and taxation*, Harmondsworth, Penguin Books.

Goode, R. 1977, 'The economic definition of income' in J. A. Pechman (ed), *Comprehensive Income Taxation*, Washington DC, Brookings Institution.

Government of Canada 1979, *Tax Expenditure Account*, Department of Finance.

HM Treasury 1979, *The Government's Expenditure Plans 1979-80 to 1982-83*, Cmnd 7439, London, HMSO.

House of Commons Expenditure Committee 1976, Fourth Report, HC 299, London, HMSO.

Inland Revenue 1979, *Inland Revenue Statistics*, 1979, London, HMSO.

Levy, M. 1960, *Income Tax Exemptions*, Amsterdam, North Holland.

Meade, J. R. (Chairman) 1978, *The Structure and Reform of Direct Taxation*, London, George Allen & Unwin/Institute for Fiscal Studies.

Minarik, J. J. 1977, 'The yield of a comprehensive income tax' in J. A. Pechman (ed), *Comprehensive Income Taxation*, Washington DC, Brookings Institution.

Pechman, J. A. (ed) 1977, *Comprehensive Income Taxation*, Washington, Brookings Institution.

Proposals for a Tax Credit System 1972, Cmnd 5116, London, HMSO.

Royal Commission on the Distribution of Income and Wealth 1978, *Lower Incomes*, Report no. 6, Cmnd 7175, London HMSO.

Royal Commission on the Taxation of Profits and Income 1955, *Final Report*, Memorandum of Dissent, Cmnd 9474, London, HMSO.

Royal Commission on the Taxation of Profits and Income 1954, *Second Report*, Cmnd 9105, London, HMSO.

Seltzer, L. 1968, *The Personal Exemptions in the Income Tax*, New York, National Bureau of Economic Research.

Sinfield, A. 1978, 'Analyses in the social division of welfare', *Journal of Social Policy*, vol. 7, Pt 2.

Surrey, S. 1973, *Pathways to Tax reform: The Concept of Tax Expenditures*, Harvard Harvard University Press.

Titmuss, R. M. 1958, 'The social division of welfare: some reflections on the search for equity', reprinted in *Essays on 'The Welfare State'*, 3rd ed, London, George Allen & Unwin.

Willis, J. R. M., and Hardwick, P. J. W. 1973, *Tax Expenditures in the United Kingdom*, London, Heinemann Educational Books/Institute for Fiscal Studies.

Part II
Fiscal Aspects of Social Policies

The first part of the book illustrated the interaction between taxation and social policy, as two, largely complementary, systems. The four chapters in this second part explore the links between the two systems in more detail. Four central aspects of social policy have been chosen: social security, housing, pensions and family policy. Each illustrates the concept of 'fiscal welfare', (introduced in Chapter 4) and its relationship with social and occupational welfare in the context of a particular policy area. Each also reveals the importance of 'tax expenditures' in these areas. If the two systems are largely complementary in their effects, there are also conflicts between the two: the frustration of policy objectives; unintended or perverse distributive effects; and constraints on future policies.

The effects of such interaction between the two systems are most prominent in the area of social security. In Chapter 5, David Piachaud describes how the extension of the income tax system after the War combined with the wider use of means-tested assistance to the 'working poor' to create the poverty trap. The chapter shows how the tax threshold – the starting point for income tax – has fallen so that it now stands at a level below the official poverty line. The effect of this reduction of thresholds has been exacerbated by the high starting rate of income tax in the UK which is higher than in most comparable countries.

David Piachaud warns however that the fall in the tax threshold need not, in itself, have resulted in falling living standards, so long as cash benefits – such as family allowances or child benefit – had been increased to compensate. This has not happened. He also argues that an increase in the tax threshold is a better way of over-coming the 'poverty trap' than a reduced rate band although as the TUC have pointed out, an increase in the threshold may soon be eroded by inflation: a continuing solution to the poverty trap may have to come through a structural change in the tax system. Alternatively an increase in benefits is likely to be more redistributive than either a reduced starting rate band or a higher threshold. This policy debate, together with that on the taxation of short-term benefits or the merits of a negative income tax also discussed in this chapter, are likely to echo through the years ahead.

The debate is no less heated in the area of housing policy. In Chapter 6, Christine Whitehead illustrates the results of operating a housing policy with scant regard to any consistent set of objectives. The criteria by which public assistance has been awarded appears to vary by tenure group, resulting in inequities and distortions in the housing market. The author explains how public intervention in housing can be justified, in economic as well as social terms, and shows that (sometimes inconsistent) fiscal policies now have a major influence on housing policy.

A similar inconsistency in the application of policy instruments or the pursuit of objectives manifests itself in pension provisions, discussed by Mike Reddin in Chapter 7. Here all three members of the 'welfare trinity' (social, fiscal and occupational) are well represented. But lack of co-ordination has resulted in generous provision for some groups co-existing with inadequate provisions for others. Pension schemes, contributions and pensions themselves have been treated in a variety of ways under the tax system: not only are different kinds of pension schemes (private or state) treated differently; other forms of savings are subject to different tax regimes both from pensions and from each other.

Two aspects of family policy and taxation are considered by Ruth Lister in Chapter 8, the treatment of married women and the effects on the horizontal distribution of income. The author argues that at present the tax system hinders progress towards equal opportunities for women by treating married women as dependents of their husbands. The dramatic increase in women's economic activity rates throughout the post-war period, and especially amongst married women, renders such treatment inappropriate. The definition of the tax unit should, the author argues, reflect greater recognition of sexual equality. Ruth Lister's chapter also illustrates the changing impact of taxation on families with children. Chapter 5 showed the decline in the tax threshold for a 'typical family', and the rate of decline has been substantially faster for families with children than for those without. The increase in child benefit has not been sufficient to offset the long-run decline in child tax allowances.

The essays in this part of the book suggest that insufficient recognition of the links between the tax system and social policy, and the inconsistent application of policy instruments, have resulted in contradictions and the frustration of objectives. This is not merely an administrative matter. It appears that the two systems, as channels for the allocation of resources, have tended to reflect underlying social and economic inequalities. For while it is true that the interaction of fiscal and social policy has often resulted in contradictory outcomes, it has also, in many cases, tended to reinforce the existing distribution of resources.

5 Taxation and Social Security
David Piachaud

Income taxation and social security are both instruments – in some respects the most important instruments – used by government to establish a more equitable distribution of incomes. In broad terms, both the assessment of the income tax due *from* a person and of social security due *to* a person are based on personal circumstances in relation to personal needs. Income tax may be discussed in terms of ability to pay and social security in terms of needs. But ability to pay is merely the converse of needs. In other ways, too, income tax and social security are inextricably intertwined. Much of social security is paid for out of income tax and income tax is paid on much of social security receipts. The national insurance contributions may themselves be treated as a form of 'tax'. Thus the relationship of taxation to social security raises many questions which are not only intricate but also important for government policies on income distribution.

In this chapter the relationship between taxation and social security, ability to pay and needs are discussed, first, for those who are in work and, secondly, for those out of work. In the third section of this chapter a more fundamental question is discussed. Many writers, most forcefully Milton Friedman, have challenged the very existence of social security and proposed that in its place the income tax system should be extended to include some form of negative income tax. This final section will therefore try to explore the relative merits, in principle and practice, of redistributing income through social security or through negative income taxation.

Income Tax and People at Work
It is in the field of social security that the interaction between taxation and social policy is most evident. The overlap between the two systems is largely the result of the post-war extension of the income tax system to large numbers of manual and clerical workers

who were previously exempt together with the extension of cash benefits (normally subject to a means-test) to those with low employment incomes.

Table 5.1 illustrates the first of these phenomena, the spread of income tax. The table shows the value of the tax threshold – the level at which tax starts to be paid, both in relation to average male manual earnings and to the supplementary benefit level. The figures are given for a married couple with two children.

Table 5.1

	Tax threshold (Tax-free income)			*Standard rate threshold*	*Effective standard rate*
	as % of average earnings	*as % of SB level*	*First rate payable*	*as % of average earnings*	
1955/6	96.0	224.6	9p in £	179.3	33p in £
1965/6	70.5	137.5	15p in £	109.8	32p in £
1979/80	46.8	96.9	25p in £	62.6	30p in £

Notes: 1. Tax Thresholds for 1979/80 are presented in the form of earnings at the tax threshold *plus* tax-free child benefits, or 'tax-free' income. This method allows the switch from taxable family allowances to tax-free child benefits to be taken into account.
2. SB level is short-term rate with average addition for housing in November.
3. Average earnings are average male full-time earnings in October, with an estimate for 1979/80.

The tax threshold for a two-child family was approximately the same as average male earnings in the mid 1950s. By 1979 it had fallen to less than half average earnings. For a single person the tax threshold has fallen from about a third of average earnings to about a quarter. For many households, the tax threshold lies at an income below the supplementary benefit level (including housing costs) for that household. It is not surprising therefore that there has been increasing concern over the decline in tax thresholds. This development has arisen in part through fiscal drag – the erosion by inflation of the real value of tax allowances – and, most recently, partly because of the transition from child tax allowances to child benefits paid in cash. In the table above, child benefits are taken into account by presenting 'tax-free income' in 1979/80.

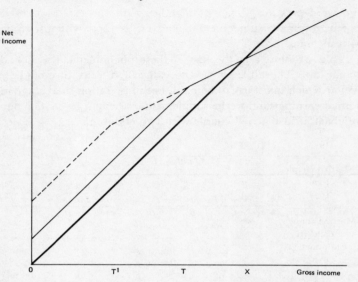

Figure 5.1   The effect of replacing family allowances and child tax allowances with tax free child benefits

The effect of replacing the combination of family allowances and child tax allowances with tax-free child benefits is illustrated in Figure 5.1. Before the change, no tax was payable up to the tax threshold OT; thereafter the amount of tax increased with income so that at income OX the tax exactly equalled the family allowance (for simplicity, only one tax rate is shown in the diagram). With the introduction of child benefit and the abolition of child tax allowances the tax threshold falls to OT'. Nevertheless, all those with incomes below OT gain from the change, those with incomes below OT' gaining the full amount of the increase in child benefit over the old family allowance rate. The level of child benefit in the illustration is such that those with incomes above OT gain nothing from the change.

The fact that the tax threshold has fallen does not necessarily mean that the poor are worse off; indeed as the illustration shows the tax threshold can fall while the poor become better off. Thus we are led to the conclusion that tax thresholds are in themselves of little or no significance in relation to poverty. What matters is the net effect of benefits and taxes. This is illustrated in Table 5.2. Tax

Table 5.2

	Tax threshold as percentage of average gross earnings	Net earnings after tax, national insurance contribution and child benefit (family allowance) as percentage of gross earnings at:		
		½ average earnings	⅔ average earnings	average earnings
Single person				
1970	28.6	77	74	71
1977	24.9	76	72	68
Married couple				
1970	40.9	84	79	74
1977	38.3	84	78	72
Married couple, 2 children (aged under 11)				
1970	58.4	97(97[a])	88	81
1977	47.9	96(105[a])	87	78

[a] Including family income supplement.

Source: RCDIW (1978). Tables Q1 and Q6 and author's calculations.

thresholds in 1977 were substantially lower, relative to average earnings, than in 1970. By contrast there was a much smaller decline in net earnings (including benefits) as a proportion of gross earnings. Of course for those who received no child benefit nor any other social security benefit a reduction in the burden of tax is the most direct way in which net money income can be increased. For those receiving benefits, however, tax thresholds are not what matter – indeed if an increase in the tax threshold is at the expense of a higher benefit it is the worst off who lose. In analyses of changes in taxes and benefits therefore it is essential that the *net* effects be examined.

One of the effects of the fall in the tax threshold (or tax-free income) has however been the fact, as noted above – that tax is payable on incomes which are below the supplementary benefit level. This is illustrated, for November 1979, in Table 5.3.

It will be seen that the gap between the tax threshold and the supplementary benefit level for a two-child family stood in 1979 at over £7 a week. This is in contrast to 1973, when the relationship between the two levels of income was the reverse of what it is today.

In the case of a married couple with four children, the gap between the two has widened to almost £20 a week. Supplementary benefit is not of course payable to families with an income from full-time work, although family income supplement is. We can see from the table that, in the case of the two-child family, the tax threshold is even further below the eligibility limits for FIS than for SB.

Table 5.3

	Tax threshold (Tax-free income)	Supplementary benefit[a]	Family income supplement limit of eligibility
Single person	22.40	26.00	n.a
Couple, no children	34.90	37.40	n.a
Couple, two children[b]	42.90	51.40	60.50
Couple, four children[c]	50.90	71.75	69.50

[a] Short-term supplementary benefit rates with average addition for housing; children aged 5–8.
[b] Children aged 4 and 6.
[c] Children aged 3, 8, 11 and 16.

One consequence of this overlap between the income tax system and the social security system is the problem of the so-called 'poverty trap'. It can be seen from Table 5.3 that families with children who are eligible for family income supplement (and therefore probably for a number of other means-tested benefits such as rent and rate rebates and free school meals) may at the same time be liable to pay income tax. Indeed, it was estimated that in 1979 about three-quarters of all FIS recipients were above the tax threshold: this proportion compares with 20 per cent in 1974. (Hansard, 1979.) The total numbers of families involved in this overlap of income tax and FIS in 1979 was estimated at 59 000. Such families stand to lose at least 65p and perhaps more than a pound out of each additional pound earned; for a substantial number of families there is in effect virtually no increase in net income over a considerable range of earnings.

The problem of the poverty trap has been exacerbated by another phenomena illustrated in Table 5.1. Over the post-war period, a number of modifications have been made to the structure of marginal tax rates, principally the abolition of the reduced rates payable on lower levels of earnings. From the table it can be seen that in 1955/6 the two-child family which started to pay income tax just below the average earnings began to pay at a marginal rate of only 9p in the pound. By 1979//80 the tax threshold had fallen to less than half average earnings and the marginal rate at which tax became payable on entry to the tax system was 25p in the pound. This is in contrast to the standard rate payable which has changed little throughout the post-war period.

Concern with the marginal rate at which income tax starts to be paid has been second only to concern about the level of tax thresholds. For example the Chancellor of the Exchequer in his Budget statement in 1978 said: 'I have been particularly impressed by the argument that the rate at which people become liable to enter income tax is too high. It is, indeed, the highest in the world' (Hansard 1978).

So impressed was the Chancellor that he introduced a lower rate of tax, at 25 per cent compared to the then standard rate of 34 per cent, on the first £750 of taxable income. One of the most influential organisations urging the case for a reduced-rate band was the General Council of the Trades Union Congress whose reasons were: 'that a reduced rate band will have a continuing beneficial effect on the 'poverty trap' and that it concentrates the cash benefit of the reduced tax revenue on average and below average incomes' (TUC 1978).

Is this true? It is convenient to consider, first, whether a reduced-rate band concentrates the cash benefit on those with lower incomes and, second, the impact of a reduced-rate band on the poverty trap.

We shall consider the introduction of a reduced-rate band under two assumptions: (a) that it is done at zero net cost; and (b) that it is done with a positive net cost, that is to say, with a sacrifice of tax revenue. The analysis is confined to the great majority paying standard rate or less; but it holds good for those paying higher rates of tax on the assumption that thresholds for higher-rate tax bands remain unchanged. The assumption of zero net cost is illustrated in Figure 5.2(a). Before the introduction of the reduced-rate band, tax started to be paid at gross income OT and net income increased as shown by the line OBF. If a reduced-rate band were then introduced retaining the same tax threshold, the net income schedule would then follow the line OBEH. Such a schedule would however be incompatible with our assumption of zero net cost since all households with income above OT would gain. Therefore it is inevitable that if the schedule is to have the same shape as OBEH, representing a reduced

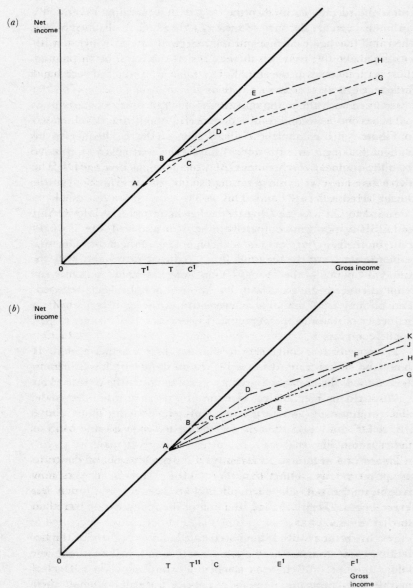

Figure 5.2   The effect of the introduction of a reduced-rate band (a) at zero net cost, (b) with positive net cost

and standard rate of tax, then the tax threshold must be lower, OT',
with the new net income schedule OADG. As is clear from the
diagram, the new schedule means less tax is paid by those with
income above OC' but it is at the price of more tax being paid by
those with incomes between OT' and OC'. The reduced-rate band
introduced at zero net cost has therefore *not* benefited those on the
lowest incomes, indeed the opposite has occurred.

The second assumption, of a decline in tax revenue, is illustrated
in Figure 5.2(b). Now the reduced-rate band can be introduced
without making anybody worse off, so that it is possible to move
from the original tax schedule (OAG) to a new schedule OADJ. The
alternative however exists of raising the tax threshold without introducing a reduced rate band. This would allow the tax threshold to
be raised to OT". Comparing the two possible tax schedules OADJ
and OBH it is quite clear that those with incomes below OC' would
gain more from an increase in the tax threshold than from a
reduced-rate band; for example, those with incomes between OT
and OT" would cease to pay tax altogether whereas with the
reduced-rate band their tax burden would only be partially reduced.
Thus again it is clear that a reduced-rate band is of more benefit to
the better off than to the worse off.

The comparison that has been made is between the introduction
of a reduced-rate band and an increase in the tax threshold. It
should be added that either of these policies give more benefit to
those on low incomes than does a reduction in standard rate. This
is illustrated in Figure 5.2(b) where the schedule OAK shows the
effect of reducing standard rates; only those on incomes above
OE' or OF' gain more than they would from a reduced-rate band or
higher threshold.

The second argument in favour of a reduced-rate band concerns
the poverty trap. The Chancellor stated, 'Most taxpayers now
caught in the poverty trap will find its impact that much less
severe because their tax will be nine percentage points lower than
now' (Hansard, 1978).

Yet, while the reduced-rate band cut the marginal rate of the tax
paid by many taxpayers (in 1978 estimated at 4 million of the low
paid), it meant that the tax starts to be paid at a lower level of
income than need otherwise be the case. Some people had their
marginal rate reduced by 9 per cent but others had it increased by
25 per cent over what it could have been if the same resources had

been devoted to raising the tax threshold. Thus it is impossible to generalise about the effect of a reduced-rate band on the poverty trap. For an individual the effect depends on income and on household circumstances. In aggregate the effect depends on the number of individuals at different levels of income. Given the distribution of incomes, it is clear that many more people have a reduced marginal rate than are 'unnecessarily' paying tax at all, but, on the other hand, it is at the lower levels of income that the marginal losses of benefits that give rise to the poverty trap are most severe.

Thus, whether the reduced-rate band will have 'a continuing beneficial effect on the "poverty trap"' is uncertain and unknown. But it is quite clear that it is not true that a reduced-rate band 'concentrates the cash benefit of the reduced tax revenue on average and below average incomes' if the alternative is an increase in the tax threshold. Raising the tax threshold is more favourable to those on low incomes than introducing a reduced-rate tax band (which is why the tax threshold was raised and reduced-rate band abolished in the 1970 Budget). On the other hand, as seen earlier, increased benefits, even if accompanied by a lower tax threshold, are more redistributive still. If those benefits are also made taxable, then redistribution in favour of those on low incomes can be increased still more.

Finally in this section we should note that national insurance contributions are themselves a tax: their 'threshold' is far below income tax thresholds and the lack of any allowances and an upper ceiling on contributions means that for most they are proportional to income but for those with the highest earnings they represent a declining proportion of earnings. While they are not directly comparable, it could be said that national insurance contributions have a much more adverse effect on those with low earnings than does income tax.

Social Security and People Out of Work

Of some £15 billion spent on social security in 1978/9, 8.5 per cent went on benefits for the unemployed and 4.5 per cent for the short-term sick. Yet it is on these two groups that most attention has been focused and around whom most controversy has raged. In particular, attention has been focused on whether or not the level of benefits encourages people to become unemployed or sick and discourages them from finding or returning to work.

One factor in determining income out of work relative to income in work is the tax treatment of social security benefits. Short-term national insurance benefits – unemployed and sickness benefit – and supplementary benefits are not liable to income tax. This contrasts with the treatment of retirement pension, widow's pension and invalidity benefit, all of which are taxable.

What then is the case for and against taxing short-term benefits and what are the practical problems? (Here it is convenient only to consider short-term national insurance benefits. Some of the same considerations apply to supplementary benefits; but since these are already income-tested, making them liable to tax would have much less impact than taxing short-term National Insurance benefits.)

There is, first, a case in equity for making short-term benefits taxable. The broader the tax base and the more forms of income that are taken into account, the fairer the system (see Chapter 4). Some of those receiving short-term benefits have, at the same time, substantial other incomes and, in terms of ability to pay, there is no reason why they should not be taxed on their benefits. A second argument for making short-term benefits taxable goes as follows: most people are only unemployed or sick for quite a short period of time so that even if they have little income while out of work, taking their income over a period of, say, one year (as is done for tax purposes), they are in general not badly off. Therefore, it is argued, there is no reason to exclude one component of income received for one part of the year from an annual tax assessment.

A third, more complex, argument in favour of taxing short-term benefits arises from the possible incentive effects. The most important factor when assessing the effect of unemployment benefit on the level of unemployment is the replacement ratio – the proportion of net income in work that is or would be received when out of work. Replacement ratios would of course be affected if unemployment benefit were taxed. The first point to be noted about replacement ratios is that they offer no explanation for recent changes in the level of unemployment. In the last five years when unemployment has doubled, replacement ratios have fallen slightly. Changes in replacement ratios may, nevertheless, affect the level of unemployment.

From a cross-section study using the 1972 General Household Survey, Nickell (1979) estimated that the increase in replacement ratios resulting from the introduction of the earnings-related supplement in 1966 implied a rise of about a tenth in the level of male unemployment. Atkinson and Flemming (1978) have discussed one factor which may bias Nickell's result:

> In each case the net income attributable to a man 'in work' is that associated with a full year's earnings and the income when unemployed is calculated without any regard to tax rebates or the effect of unemployment on subsequent tax liabilities. However, in deciding how hard to try for a job, or how choosey to be about one offered, an unemployed person might reasonably ask what it is worth to him to start work this week rather than next. In this connection taxes have a very different impact, as a result of the tax base being total annual earnings excluding unemployment benefit ... marginal net earnings for a week's work are considerably lower than average net earnings, and it is the former which really ought to be compared with the tax-free unemployment benefits when deciding not *whether*, but *how long* to stay unemployed.

Thus Atkinson and Flemming argue that the disincentive problem may be potentially more serious than earlier studies, using average replacement ratios, suggested. While proposing improvements in benefits for the long-term unemployed, Atkinson and Flemming argue for the taxation of the short-term national insurance benefit – the additional revenue to be used for the improvement of benefits.

Arguments against taxing short-term benefits depend on considerations of the impact on the incomes of those out of work. Short-term benefits are already substantially below long-term benefit rates. The highest replacement ratios occur when earnings-related supplement is being received and if there is a real disincentive problem, which is arguable, then this might be as well tackled through alterations in the earnings-related supplement as by taxing short-term benefits. Furthermore, the replacement ratio depends on the net income in work as much as it does on the net income out of work; increasing the former is preferable to reducing the latter if the replacement ratio is to be reduced.

On balance, there is a good case for taxing short-term benefits although this cannot, without severe consequences, be an isolated policy change. If accompanied by an increased tax threshold or increased benefit levels to those in and out of work such a change would have much to commend it. Yet while this may be desirable in principle the practical problems are formidable.

It has been estimated that some 10 000 additional civil servants would be required in order to tax short-term benefits. To understand why, it is necessary to consider some of the workings of the PAYE system. PAYE is a cumulative withholding system whereby tax on any week's earnings are related to a tax code, based on personal tax allowances and on income up to that point in the tax year. The basic difficulty of taxing short-term benefits is that PAYE relies on each earner having an employer which is precisely what those who are unemployed have not got. Various ways round this are possible but all are administratively complex.

First, it would be possible to treat each spell of sickness or un-employment as a period in which the person's 'employer' is the Department of Health and Social Security. Thus on becoming sick or unemployed the last employer would fill out a form, similar to the P45 now provided on leaving a job, certifying the income in the year to date and the tax code. When a new employer was found or the spell of sickness ended, the DHSS would have to fill in another such form to be given to the employer. While in principle this method would work quite satisfactorily, in practice, with some 5 million claims for unemployment benefit and 10 million claims for sickness benefit each year, the administrative problems would be colossal both for the Civil Service and for employers.

A second possible approach would be for DHSS to notify the Inland Revenue of all payments of sickness or unemployment benefits. This notification would then require the Inland Revenue to recover the tax due. In addition to the paperwork involved, the recovery of tax would raise a further problem. In any one year some two-thirds of taxpayers pay their correct tax through PAYE and make no tax return. If most of those who had received unemployment or sickness benefit during the year had a liability for tax at the end of the year, the costs of assessment and particularly of tax collection would be greatly increased.

A third approach would be to tax short-term benefits at source, which would in effect mean paying lower rates of benefit, and allowing those with low incomes to claim back the tax. This would how-ever create severe problems for those on low incomes since by definition they are in need of the income when they are out of work and it would serve little purpose to pay them the over-deducted tax at the end of the tax year. If those receiving the reduced (taxed) benefit were still eligible for supplementary benefit then the result would be to increase dependence on SB in the short term, however it was resolved at the end of the tax year; once again the burden on the administration would be increased.

Thus it is hard to see how, in practice, short-term benefits can be taxed in a manner that is equitable, that avoids undue hardship, and that does not involve a very heavy administrative cost.*

Social Security and Negative Income Taxation

The most forceful and influential critique of the very existence of state social security schemes is that of Milton Friedman. He states:

> The humanitarian and egalitarian sentiment which helped to pro-
> duce the steeply graduated individual income tax has also pro-
> duced a host of other measures directed at promoting the
> 'welfare' of particular groups. The most important single set of
> measures is the bundle most misleadingly labelled 'social security'.
> (Friedman, 1962)

Friedman's criticisms of social security are on three main counts.

Social security involves the 'nationalisation of the provision of required annuities'. Just as the government may require car insurance
but leaves provision to the private market, so the government could
require insurance for old age but not nationalise its provision. If
there are economies of scale in the provision of annuities the government may be able to undersell competitors but in that case it will
get the business without compulsion. (In passing, he mentions that
one political cost of the 'nationalisation' of social security is that
'the bulk of the experts become employees of the nationalised system,
or university people closely linked with it. Inevitably they come to
favour its expansion'.)

More radically, Friedman questions whether individuals should be
compelled to use some of their current income to purchase annuities
to provide for their old age. The choice is posed between freedom –
'if a man knowingly prefers to live today, to use his resources for
current enjoyment, deliberately choosing a penurious old age, by
what right do we prevent him from doing so?' – and, on the other
hand, paternalism and dictatorship, however benevolent. Friedman
concedes that there may be a case for government intervention if the
improvident would impose costs on others, requiring private charity
or public assistance, but Friedman believes that only 'a few people
might become charges of the public'.

---

* Since this chapter was written, the government has announced a commitment to
tax short-term benefits from 1982.

Friedman's most fundamental criticism is that social security involves redistribution to the beneficiaries which 'is independent of their poverty or wealth; the man of means receives it as much as the indigent'.

While castigating social security, Friedman does see a place for governmental action to alleviate poverty and he proposed a negative income tax. Such an arrangement 'gives help in the form most useful to the individual, namely, cash' and 'makes explicit the cost borne by society'; at the same time it reduces but does not eliminate the incentives of those helped to help themselves. Most important, however, is that it is 'directed specifically at the problem of poverty', in that people are helped because they are poor not because they happen to be a member of any particular group in society. The negative income tax that Friedman put forward was based on the federal income tax using an annual assessment of income (the rates Friedman uses for illustration are long since out of date).

Is it therefore desirable that the tax system, extended to include a negative income tax (or one of its many variants), should supersede the social security system?

Friedman's criticisms of social security are highly questionable. Friedman's argument, that even if the government compels the purchase of annuities it should allow private provision, begs the crucial question. The government would still have to decide what level of provision was to be required. Would the government, for example, require annuities to be inflation-proofed? (If so, on British experience, they would be unobtainable.)

The question of how many would fail to provide for themselves and thus become public charges is an empirical question. In Britain 2 million out of 7 million pensioner households now receive supplementary benefit so that nearly one-third might be said to have failed to provide adequately for themselves in old age. It is scarcely convincing to argue that government social security has inhibited the development of private pensions if one considers the tax treatment of occupational pension schemes and, more recently, the contracting-out terms for occupational pensions in the new pension scheme. Thus if nearly one-third now require supplementary benefit even with national insurance pension provision, it seems highly probable that a much higher proportion would have required public relief had it not been for national insurance.

Friedman's objection to the arbitrary nature of the redistribution resulting from social security is based on a narrow conception of redistribution and the alleviation of poverty. Social security now redistributes income over a variety of time periods: pensions involve redistribution over the life cycle and inter-generationally; unemployment benefits redistribute from those in the labour force to those out of the labour force; short-term benefits redistribute to those who are without earnings often for only a few days or weeks. There is no reason to believe that a negative income tax based on an *annual* assessment of income would be sufficient to alleviate *short-term* poverty. Nor is there any reason why redistribution should be confined to one time period; the development of social security suggests that most people accept and approve of redistribution over weeks, years, lifetimes and inter-generationally.

Once one accepts the obligation on government to alleviate poverty, as Friedman does, there are inevitably complex value judgements to be made. Friedman is contemptuous of the value judgements of paternalists; yet even a residual relief of poverty through a negative income tax involves value judgements as to the appropriate time period (as discussed), judgements about the relative treatment of families of different sizes and, of course, of the poverty level to be guaranteed. Friedman's 'pure' negative income tax does not eliminate the need for such value judgements. To relate a negative tax to the single criterion of initial annual income is simple in principle but inequitable in practice. Is it fair, for example, to provide the same minimum poverty level to an elderly person as to an able-bodied man who has the offer of a job? Restricting the level of income guaranteed by a negative income tax to the most basic minimal level would in practice mean consigning all those who society thought more deserving to the same level as those society regards as least deserving.

Social security by redistributing income on criteria other than the level of pre-tax income – criteria such as old age, widowhood, unemployment or invalidity – makes it possible for those satisfying these criteria to be raised above an unconditional minimum poverty level guaranteed by society to anyone. (In Britain no such unconditional minimum poverty level exists.) There are states which *usually* give rise to income loss – even if *some* of those who are, for example, elderly or unemployed have adequate initial incomes. (See Beckerman 1979.) By identifying these states of income loss, many of which are not privately insurable, it is possible to provide for those in such states above a minimal poverty level. To provide for those in such states only when initial income fell below a certain level would in effect mean means-testing all social security. This would undermine the contractual nature of most social security schemes and give rise to the most fearful anomalies and inequities. In any case, by financing social security out of earnings-related contributions and by taxing social security benefits, the social security system is itself, to a modest degree, redistributive.

A negative income tax scheme for the United Kingdom which guaranteed an income equivalent to average supplementary benefit levels to everyone who had zero pre-tax income would require a standard rate of income tax of around 60 per cent. (See Chapter 11.) In order to maintain the incomes of those meeting certain criteria at current supplementary benefit level while maintaining far lower rates of tax it is necessary to specify those criteria and identify which individuals meet them. This is precisely what social security does. Thus, as the Meade Committee concluded from its review of the whole range of possible approaches to redistributing income, there are major advantages in identifying (or tagging) certain groups and making specific social security provision for them. (Meade 1978.)

Negative income tax in one of its many possible forms may become a useful adjunct to existing redistributive mechanisms, but it is inconceivable that it could replace the basic social security system. This is not to say that social security cannot be or should not be modified and improved with better identification of contingencies giving rise to income loss, but it does suggest that social security and tax will continue to coexist.

References

Atkinson, A. B. and Flemming, J. S. 1978, 'Unemployment, social security and incentives', *Midland Bank Review*, Autumn, London.

Beckerman, W. 1979, 'The impact of income maintenance payments on poverty in Britain, 1975', *Economic Journal*, June.

Friedman, M. 1962, *Capitalism and Freedom*, Chicago, University of Chicago Press.

Hansard 1978, 11 April, Col. 1204, London.

Hansard 1979, 26 July, Col. 419, London.

Meade, J. E. (Chairman) 1978, *The Structure and Reform of Direct Taxation*, London, George Allen & Unwin/Institute for Fiscal Studies.

Nickell, S. 1979, 'The effect of unemployment and related benefits on the duration of unemployment', *Economic Journal*, March.

RCDIW (Royal Commission on the Distribution of Income and Wealth) 1978, *Lower Incomes*, Report no. 6, Cmnd 7175, London, HMSO.

Trades Union Congress 1978, *Economic Review*, London.

6 Fiscal Aspects of Housing
Christine Whitehead

Introduction

Although British governments have generally made clear and consistent statements about their housing objectives, actual policy has usually arisen more as a response to immediate problems (by no means always specifically related to housing) than as part of a coherent approach to meeting these objectives. The result, in the late Tony Crosland's much quoted phrase, is 'a dog's breakfast' (Crosland 1975) which cannot be rationalised either in terms of these objectives or of the more general aims of the fiscal system.

The aim of this chapter is to do no more than describe the ways in which taxation and public expenditure policies interact with housing policy to produce this complex and messy relationship, and to examine a few of its implications for the achievement of social policy with respect to housing. Our analysis falls into two sections. In the first, we spell out the objectives of housing and fiscal policies and their inter-relationships. In the second, we describe the current fiscal framework in which the social policy towards housing has to operate.

Fiscal and Housing Objectives

The objectives of housing policy
Perhaps the most succinct statement of these objectives is to be found in the Conservative government's White Paper 'Fair Deal for Housing' (Cmnd 4728 1971) where they were stated as:

(i)   a decent home for every family at a price within their means,
(ii)   a fairer choice between owning a home and renting one,
(iii) fairness between one citizen and another in giving and receiving help towards housing costs'.

The Labour government's Housing Policy Review (Cmnd 6851

1977) listed eight distinct objectives, including the traditional aims as stated above but added, on the supply side, a better balance between investment in new dwellings and in improvement of existing units; and, on the consumer side, reasonable stability in housing costs, increased scope for mobility, freedom from interference in the way tenants use their homes and improved access to more suitable accommodation for those in housing need.

The interaction between housing and fiscal policy

Fiscal policy is one means the government uses to achieve these specifically housing aims. Thus, for example, subsidies might be provided to assist low-income households with their housing costs, or similar tax treatment might be accorded to new building and improvement to help achieve the 'correct' balance between different types of investment.

However, the interaction between housing and fiscal policy also works in the other direction. Because housing is a major part of both investment and consumer expenditure, housing policy can be seen as one tool to be used in the achievement of the more general goals of fiscal policy, including the maintenance of full employment of resources and their more efficient allocation, the stability of the price level, the steady growth of national output and the fairer distribution of national income and wealth. But in the main, the interaction between housing and fiscal policy has been concerned less with macro-stabilisation than with allocational and distributional aims.

In meeting these objectives certain characteristics are normally required of the tax system employed (Meade 1978), in particular, neutrality and equity or fairness.

(i) Neutrality within the fiscal system requires that taxation and transfers should not distort the workings of the private market, except as part of a purposive choice to meet other objectives. Within housing policy neutrality can, for instance, imply the housing objective of a fairer choice between tenures. Similarly, neutrality between housing investment and other investments might be a fiscal objective. One important element in achieving neutrality is the choice between work and leisure and between taxed and non-taxed work. Here the trade-off between housing and general fiscal objectives can become particularly problematic. Housing objectives, for instance, require that those without income be provided with suitable accommodation.

This may reduce the incentive to work especially if the benefit is withdrawn rapidly as income rises (as with the present rent and rate rebate system), resulting in a high implicit marginal tax rate.

(ii)   Equity demands that the fiscal system should be horizontally equitable, i.e. that it should treat those in similar circumstances similarly, and that it should also be vertically equitable, i.e. capable of redistributing income from the rich to the poor. Horizontal equity corresponds to the housing objective of 'fairness between one citizen and another' cited above, while housing may be one means of achieving the objective of redistribution.

The two requirements of neutrality and equity are often mutually incompatible. This is particularly important where redistribution is undertaken in kind (in this case housing) rather than in cash as this inherently biases the consumer's choice between goods (see, e.g. Lees 1961). For this reason assistance specifically tied to housing would appear to be inferior to redistribution via the more general tax system which allows freer choice. However, for pragmatic reasons it may be deemed a suitable instrument. Moreover, housing objectives have been formulated taking account of the existing redistributive effects of the fiscal system, which have been inadequate to ensure suitable accommodation for all.

Market imperfections

These two characteristics of a good tax (and implicitly of a good transfer) system define a base from which positive policies, aimed at modifying incentives and reallocating resources more in line with government priorities, can be generated. Such policies would be unnecessary if the private market worked effectively and the tax structure achieved a desired income distribution, without distorting the allocation of resources (Musgrave 1959). If these conditions were met, it is argued, people would then have a free choice about how they spent their money and employed their resources. With respect to housing, this would mean that all households had the right to buy as much, or as little, housing as they liked, provided by private suppliers at its market price (see, e.g. Pennance 1969 and Stafford 1978).

If these conditions do not occur there will be a case for government intervention either to modify incentives or directly to produce and allocate housing (e.g. Allan 1971; Sandford 1978; Le Grand

and Robinson 1976 and Lansley 1979). Causes of such imperfections
include:

(i) *Externalities* – where benefits or costs are borne by those not
involved in the decision to consume or produce, the market price
will not reflect social costs and benefits. For example, if I do not
maintain my property and I suffer a loss because the value of the
property falls, I think this loss is worthwhile, taking account of
maintenance costs. However, my neighbours also suffer losses because
the poor repair of my house brings down the value of their property
and reduces the benefits they get from it. This is an external cost.
Similarly, external benefits arise from the good repair of surrounding
houses (see Davis and Whinston 1961). Historically, the external
costs of insanitary and unsafe and fire-prone housing may be regarded
as a major reason for government intervention in the housing market
(see, e.g. the Inquiry into the Sanitary Conditions of the Labouring
Population of Great Britain 1842, cited in Cmnd 6851 1977, Technical Volume 1). This type of argument provides a case not only for
minimum standard legislation but also for such subsidies as repair
and improvement grants, especially when the quality of one unit
affects that of others.

(ii) *Imperfect supply conditions.* If supply is not available at the alternative cost to society of the resources involved (i.e. their value in their
next best use) the market will neither provide nor allocate effectively.
This is a problem with housing provision because it is heterogeneous
(i.e. one unit is not like another if only because of its specific loca-
tion), because supply cannot be varied rapidly (Lansley 1979) and
because conditions in the construction industry are not fully com-
petitive (e.g. Bowley 1967). All these factors are likely to result in
lower supply than is socially desirable, and sometimes considerable
market power for private suppliers of new and existing housing. To
correct both of these deficiencies requires government involvement,
for example, through provision and through rent and access controls.

(iii) *Incorrect investment decisions.* Private decision-makers decide
whether or not to invest by looking at their own resultant costs
and benefits, including the alternative cost as measured by the rate
of interest. But the prevailing rate of interest is often regarded as incorrect from society's point of view because of imperfections in the
finance market, and because, as mortals, people may give less weight
to future benefits and costs of using scarce resources than does the

community as a whole. These imperfections are thought to result in under-investment in housing and may provide a rationale for such policies as interest rate relief on housing investment, improvement grants and government provision of housing.

One conclusion to be drawn from the above analysis is that the fiscal system should not be neutral with respect to housing but should be modified positively, to offset imperfections in the private market.

However, there is another set of reasons why government may wish to make sure that people get more housing than they would choose themselves, even when resources are correctly priced from the point of view of private decisions. These include:

(i)   the fear that individuals do not fully perceive the benefits of housing to themselves, because their housing decisions are irregular and the information available to them is poor (e.g. Collard 1968).

(ii)   the view that housing is such an important part of community welfare that at least a minimum standard should be provided even though individuals, given their incomes, would not choose to spend enough to meet that standard (e.g. Culyer 1971; Burrows 1977).

(iii)   the possibility that the extent of general redistribution of income via the fiscal system is inadequate to meet the vertical equity requirement. Housing may then be regarded as a particularly suitable additional way of increasing redistribution, especially if the community sees reasonable quality housing as a minimum social requirement (i.e. (ii) above). (See Sen 1973, for a discussion of the theoretical bases of social welfare functions which take these points into account.)

This second group of reasons for government intervention requires that society in one way or another (by subsidy or direct provision) helps individual members to consume more housing than they would freely choose given their incomes and privately determined resource costs. This can be done through direct controls but, in the main, in free market societies, the most effective measures are likely to be fiscal.

The importance of housing

The above arguments imply a case for government intervention, additional to that provided by an efficient general tax system. Although they exist across a wide range of good (see, e.g. Le Grand

and Robinson 1976 and Collard 1972), housing has been singled out
for particular attention by governments for a number of reasons.
First, it is a large item in the household budget (housing costs
account for about 15 per cent of average household expenditure and
considerably more for low-income households, see Table 6.1) so distortions and inequities bear particularly hard on individuals.
Secondly, housing investment is a large proportion of total investment, accounting for about 4 per cent of gross domestic product,
and usually well over an eighth of total investment. Taken together
with the strong feeling that housing is a necessary good, the provision
of which could, at the limit, be regarded as a social service to be
made generally available at least at a minimum standard, governments of all types have felt it necessary to intervene.

Table 6.1   Expenditure on housing by household income

Household income	Under £30	£30 and under £60	£60 and under £100	£100 and under £150	£150 and under £200	£200 or more	All
Proportion of expenditure on housing	23	19	15	15	13	12	15

Source: Family Expenditure Survey 1978.

Historically, most intervention was in the form of minimum
standards, starting at least as early as the Middle Ages for fire and
other building regulations in some localities. Nationally, there was a
spate of legislation in the nineteenth century of which the Public
Health and the Artisans' and Labourers' Dwellings Improvements
Acts of 1875 were perhaps the most important. There was then a
growing realisation that many could not afford to pay the price of
minimum standard accommodation (see, for instance, the evidence
presented to the Royal Commission on the Housing of the Working
Class in 1884-5, and the discussion of housing conditions in the
Royal Commission on Housing in Scotland, Cd 8731 1917).
There being, at the time, little acceptance of the idea of general
income supplementation nor any available administrative structure
for its distribution, the main policy tools available were fiscal – via
supply subsidies and direct provision, both of which became significant elements of government housing policy in the inter-war years.

Specifically income-related subsidies were finally also introduced, but not until 1972, as part of the Housing Finance Act.

Consequently fiscal policies now form a major element of housing policy. But, as will be clear from the next section, the piecemeal way in which these mechanisms have been built up, together with the inherent trade-offs required between meeting different housing objectives, as well as the trade-offs between housing and more general fiscal policy, mean that the resultant system can hardly even be rationalised, *ex post*. It certainly cannot be regarded as the most effective way of providing a decent home for every family at a price within their means or achieving the more detailed range of housing objectives now seen as a necessary part of social policy.

The Fiscal System and Housing

The fiscal means used to implement social policy include elements of both the tax and the expenditure systems. They compromise tax reliefs and direct transfers to cover both current and investment spending and public expenditure allocated mainly through local authorities and housing associations to increase the supply of socially owned housing. We look at each in turn.

The Tax System and Fiscal Concessions for Housing

Owner-occupation

An owner-occupied dwelling is both a consumption good and an investment good. Consequently it is difficult to determine how housing should be treated for tax purposes, if the system is to be neutral. In practice it is not treated consistently as either an investment or consumption good although the reason for this does not seem to be explicable in terms of the objectives described in Section I (see Hughes 1979). There are at least four areas where owner-occupation is treated differently from other goods: mortgage interest, imputed income, capital gains and stamp duty.

Mortgage interest relief is available to all owner-occupiers who borrow to purchase their principal home. As relief is given on interest paid each year at the marginal tax rate, the amount of relief obtained is determined by the income of the owner-occupier, the size of the mortgage, the interest rate charged, the type of mortgage and when it was issued. For instance, interest payments decline over the life of annuity mortgages (the normal type of building-society mortgage) but remain constant with insurance-based endowment mortgages.

The maximum mortgage on which relief is obtained has, since 1974, been limited to £25 000. It is no longer available on mortgages for second homes taken out since 1974, or after six years on existing mortgages of this type.

About 80 per cent of transactions in owner-occupied houses involve some loan finance, of which about 80 per cent of the value is provided by building societies. However only about 55 per cent of households have a mortgage outstanding.

Over the last few years the total amount of relief has increased rapidly in money terms from £235 million in 1969/70 to £687 million in 1974/5 (see Cmnd 6851 1977, Technical Volume 1 Table IV 20). Total relief was estimated at £1110 million in 1978/9 and £1450 million in 1979/80 (Hansard 12 December 1979).

The increase has occurred as a result of the rapid rise in house prices and the average value of a new mortgage, the increase in the number of mortgages, the increase in the mortgage interest rate since 1973 and especially in 1979, and the increase in money incomes, taken together with relatively constant tax thresholds over the early part of the 1970s, which have drawn large numbers of people into the tax system.

At the top end of the income scale the proportion of assistance due to relief in excess of the basic rate varies considerably from year to year as a result of changes in the tax thresholds, especially in relation to inflation. In 1978/9 for instance it accounted for about one-tenth of total relief but this proportion fell significantly in 1979/80 as a result of the tax changes introduced by the Conservative government.

To help those at the bottom end of the income scale, the option mortgage scheme was introduced in 1968. This allowed mortgagors to choose to pay a lower rate of interest on their mortgage instead of receiving relief. In this way the vertical equity of the system was increased by enabling lower-income households, who either did not pay income tax at all, or insufficient at the standard rate to claim full relief, to obtain similar assistance to other mortgagors. About 20 per cent of all mortgagors used the option mortgages scheme at the peak of its popularity in 1972 but the proportion has been falling consistently and is now about 14 per cent in terms of numbers and slightly less in terms of value (see Whitehead 1979).

The rationale of mortgage interest relief is straightforward if housing is treated as an investment good: interest is one cost of acquiring an investment and therefore should be deducted from gross revenue to determine net taxable income (see Chapter 4).

Historically, tax relief has always been available on interest. However in 1969 the general right of individuals to obtain relief on interest was removed and relief restricted principally to loans for the purchase or improvement of property. (Although the general right was reintroduced in 1972 it was removed again in 1974.) Consequently mortgage interest relief has come to be treated differently from all other expenditure by individuals. One rationale for this is that, as the major investment most people make, it should continue to be treated like investment elsewhere in the economy. More generally, investment neutrality might be regarded as more important than neutrality between different types of consumer expenditure. However, one might expect that if mortgage interest is treated as a cost of investment, the return on that investment in the form either of income or of capital gains would be taxed. This is, however, not the case.

When income tax was introduced it included a tax on income from property (schedule A). This covered imputed income on the then tiny number of owner-occupied properties as well as income from tenanted units. Imputed income was that which the occupier was assumed to receive from the use of the dwelling and which he could have obtained in cash if he were to let the dwelling. The costs of running the investment: repair, maintenance, management, etc., could be offset against the tax and a minimum allowance was automatic.

However, schedule A tax was abolished in 1963 for a number of reasons. First, there had been no revaluation of the rental value base since 1936, so little relation between the tax and the concept remained. Secondly, in part because of the lack of a revalued base, the revenue was small (about £25–30 million). Thirdly, owner-occupation had become the most important tenure and many felt that it was wrong to tax imputed income from this source when that arising from other assets (such as cars, household durable goods or works of art) was not taxed. It is certainly true that there is no history of such taxation outside housing, so this could be seen as an argument for its abolition. However owner-occupied housing also continued to receive relief against costs as if it were an investment good, while not paying taxes on that income. Tax treatment was thus no longer neutral and the resultant system must be regarded as horizontally inequitable, between investment goods, between the choice of goods consumed by individuals and between consumption and savings (Kay and King 1978 and Yates 1979).

The possible revenue foregone through the absence of schedule A has been variously estimated at £930 million in 1974/5 (Willis and Hardwick 1978) and £1500 million in 1976 (Meade Report 1978, Appendix 23.1). If a tax on imputed income were to be reintroduced and housing treated as an investment good, the tax would formally fall especially heavily on those without mortgages (usually the middle-aged and the elderly) who have no interest costs to set against their liability.

Owner-occupied housing is also exempt from the other major tax levied on many investments, that of capital gains. Capital gains tax was introduced in 1965 as a tax on the realised increase in monetary value between purchase of an asset and its sale. It was drawn up to exclude any gain on the taxpayer's sole or main residence, at least partly because the gains are more monetary than real. As such it would have imposed a serious burden on households who would anyway have to buy another house at a similarly enhanced price. However, this argument does not distinguish housing from other goods. When someone sells a painting and pays capital gains tax he cannot repurchase the painting, so why should it be necessary for him to be able to purchase the same house? Nevertheless the practical consequences for house owners were regarded as socially unacceptable. Thus, although there have been estimates made of the effect on different groups of its imposition (see, e.g. Townsend 1979 and Robinson 1980), if it were ever implemented it would be in such a different form (e.g. excluding inflation, allowing roll-over provisions, etc.) that the actual effect would be very different, and possibly quite small. (See, e.g. Meade 1978, where the assumption is made that tax would only be levied on 'real' gains.) However, the fact remains that once again owner-occupied housing is treated differently from other assets.

These three reliefs make up the majority of the special assistance formally given to owner-occupation through the fiscal system. The argument for each separate tax may seem quite cogent: mortgage interest relief should be allowed against costs because housing is an investment good; there is no precedent within the British tax system for levying tax on imputed income; there are few real gains involved in the sale of owner-occupied accommodation so spending power has not increased and tax should not be levied.

But as a result of all these elements taken together, owner-occupied housing is clearly treated differently from other goods. If it is seen as an element in the individual's expenditure it is treated differently because tax relief in not generally allowable. If it is regarded as an investment good it is treated differently because, although costs are allowed, neither income nor realised capital gains are taxed. Thus, owner-occupied housing obtains special fiscal benefits.

In one respect, however, owner-occupied housing is treated more harshly than other assets. Stamp duty is levied on conveyancies of over £20 000 at a rate of 0.5 per cent of the price rising to 2 per cent on the whole price over £35 000. With these thresholds it affects a significant proportion of transactions including many first-purchaser sales. The take has been increasing rapidly in the 1970s and is estimated at nearly £150 million in 1979/80. As such, the tax is quite an important cost of moving which does not arise when exchanging other assets (Whitehead 1980).

Owner-occupation is treated similarly to other assets under capital transfer tax (Chapter 9). However, as capital transfers between spouses are anyway exempt, owner-occupation in the main is not subject to tax (for when the house is transferred to others it will not normally be to the owner-occupier).

New building and improvement of dwellings in all tenures is zero-rated, in line with the view that housing is a socially desirable and necessary investment, which should be given assistance in relation to other expenditure. However, repair work is subject to VAT at the standard rate, as are services such as solicitors and estate-agent fees. Levying VAT on repair work reduces the incentive to undertake these repairs (until ultimately non-taxed improvements become necessary). This would appear to go against the objectives of neutrality and balance as well as making it more difficult to meet the objective of a decent home for every family.

Because rates are property taxes levied on rateable values based on the estimated net market rent, they can be regarded as a tax on housing (and other property). If this view is accepted, rates partly offset the other fiscal benefits given to owner-occupation and mean that rented property is taxed differently from other expenditure (see Cmnd 6851 1977, Technical Volume 1, Chapter 4). Rates would also seem to conflict with the housing policies designed to increase the availability and consumption of housing, particularly as they are strongly regressive between households (see Cmnd 2582 1965; Sandford 1978). Alternatively they can be regarded as a general tax for financing local expenditure unrelated to housing policy as such. However, this interpretation does not change their non-neutral and inequitable nature.

Some effects of fiscal concessions to owner-occupation. Taking the tax system as it is, mortgage interest relief and the option mortgage subsidy clearly increase with income, as reliefs inevitably increase with the amount borrowed up to the £25 000 limit. The amount borrowed is in turn strongly related to both consumption of housing and to income. The relationship between distribution of income and the amount of relief is shown in Table 6.2 taken from the Housing Policy Review. The table shows that mortgage interest relief increased fairly consistently with income in 1974/5, offsetting to some extent the progressiveness of the tax system. (Later figures are only available in less detail but show a similar picture.) The effect is particularly noticeable in the highest income bracket because of

Table 6.2   Distribution by income range of tax relief on mortgage interest and option mortgage subsidy, 1974–5

Income of head of household and wife	Number of households (thousands)	Total tax relief and subsidy (£m.)	Average subsidy or tax Relief (£)
Under £1000	100	6	59
£1000–£1499	170	12	73
£1500–£1999	380	34	91
£2000–£2499	590	61	104
£2500–£2999	720	73	101
£3000–£3499	850	110	129
£3500–£3999	640	82	129
£4000–£4999	910	135	148
£5000–£5999	370	66	179
£6000 and over	380	139	369
Total	5100	718	141

Source: Table IV, 34, Cmnd 6851 1977. Technical Volume 1.

the effect of higher-rate relief. Assistance is also concentrated in the early part of the mortgage (helping people to buy more housing in the expectation that money incomes will rise to cover the additional costs as the proportion of annual outgoings covering the repayment of principle increases). Moreover, help is concentrated on younger age groups. Older households are less likely to take out new mortgages, partly because they move less, partly because they have less opportunity to borrow, and partly because they have less need to do so.

It has been argued that the increase of tax relief with incomes can be seen as a positive choice by government for dealing with what is believed to be an over-progressive income tax system. Chapter 9 shows that this view of the British income tax is largely illusory. Moreover, there is little reason why this should be done specifically in relation to housing, as the effect depends on whether one has a mortgage (only about 55 per cent of households do have housing debt outstanding), the length of time it has been outstanding and past moving behaviour. The effect, therefore, is arbitrary and creates inequities and inefficiencies not only in the housing market but in investment, consumption and saving as a whole. If government requires a less progressive tax system it might be better to alter that structure directly than to use a roundabout way of achieving the result for a minority of the population. The picture is not greatly different in structure (although it is, of course, in absolute terms) if a definition of assistance more in line with a neutral tax system approach (Hughes 1979; Robinson 1980) is used to calculate the formal benefits.

One reason given for the special assistance to owner-occupied housing is that it increases the supply of new and improved accommodation and thereby helps meet housing objectives and offsets some market imperfections. It even suggests a justification for helping those at the top end of the market as it is also argued that the best way to obtain more housing is to help consumers near the top of the market to buy more housing. The units they vacate will then filter down the system to other households who will similarly be enabled to pay for more accommodation.

Besides this increased demand for housing arising from the assistance given to owner-occupiers, building-society interest rates are usually below the market clearing price (perhaps reflecting the argument that general interest rates do not reflect the social long-term value of investment). This is due partly to the concessions given to building societies through the composite tax rate. (This is the tax rate paid by building societies on behalf of their investors which is calculated in such a way that societies gain perhaps 0.5 – 1 per cent in comparison to the costs faced by their competitors.) Further, building societies have normally regarded it as their social duty to keep mortgage rates down, even at the expense of building up queues (e.g. Boleat 1979). Sometimes this practice has been backed by government, as in 1974, when a special loan was made to allow societies to hold down the mortgage rate at a time of great volatility in general interest rates.

However the view that increasing demand, or reducing interest rates, will help investment depends on the supply of housing being elastic. In fact, in the short run the effect of, say, an increase in tax relief, is to allow people to spend more on housing. Supply cannot be expanded rapidly (the annual net output of new houses is usually between 1 and 1.5 per cent of housing stock) so the initial effect is to increase house prices.

In the longer run, builders may be able to respond to this higher price by increasing output so that some expansion of investment is obtained. (See White and White 1977 and Follain 1979.) Housing appears to be unlike most other goods in that expanding output increases the cost of each additional house built. This is, in part, because supply of land is limited, but also because construction is a relatively labour-intensive activity. Productivity increases are therefore lower than elsewhere (see Cmnd 6854 1977, Technical Volume 1, Chapter 3). As a result at least some of the increasing purchasing power goes, even in the longer term, into higher prices. Indeed, some argue that the effect of increased demand in increasing investment is extremely limited and most increased demand will be 'capitalised' into increased land prices (see Kay and King 1978).

If additional investment is not forthcoming, fiscal benefits of the type described above cannot help additional households to enter owner-occupation. For, if supply is relatively inelastic, potential owner-occupiers seeing the fiscal and interest rate benefits they can obtain by becoming owner-occupiers will simply bid up prices. The main effect will then be to increase the capital gains obtained by existing owners. Similarly, existing owner-occupiers will also wish to consume more housing for the same reasons. One consequence of this is the low density of occupation among many owner-occupiers (see Cmnd

6851 1977, Technical Volume 1, Chapter 2). Another is to increase further the price faced by first-time purchasers.

To the extent of the relative benefits available and, perhaps more importantly, the continuing expectation that owner-occupiers will continue to do well in the future, the choice between owner-occupation and other tenures is distorted. There are a large number of studies of the comparative benefits available to those already in each tenure (e.g. Odling-Smee 1975, Cmnd 6851 1977, Hughes 1979 and Lansley 1979, Robinson 1980, for a wide range of estimates using different assumptions). All have concluded that the position has not been neutral in the past. However there is little evidence on the extent of the current distortion, as estimates of the differences between those already in each tenure do not reflect the position of those trying to gain access which is what affects tenure choice. Historically, however, it is accepted (see Nevitt 1966) that the special treatment given to owner-occupation has been a major cause of the decline of the private rental sector. Further, most commentators still regard owner-occupation as the best investment available to individuals (Kay and King 1978) implying continuing distortion as resource costs are not declining.

The rental sectors

Unlike the owner-occupier, the landlord in the private rental sector is treated like any other commercial enterprise for fiscal purposes. He invests in a dwelling, receives reliefs against costs, including interest, and pays tax on income and capital gains. This last, if he is in business as a landlord, he can roll over if the money is reinvested in housing (i.e. tax is not paid until the benefit is fully realised).

As a result the private landlord is clearly in a worse fiscal position than the owner-occupier. He is however treated similarly to the owners of other commercial investments, except in one sense. Housing is treated as a perpetual asset. So landlords cannot obtain general depreciation allowances, or other special allowances based on depreciation, which have been introduced from time to time to assist investment. Housing is by no means the only asset treated in this way, but it is one area where tax changes might improve the incentive to undertake investment, especially on improvement.

The main problem in the private rental sector is not specifically fiscal, but the effect of rent controls and security of tenure. Rent controls in many cases reduce potential income to a point where it may not be worthwhile for a landlord to continue his investment (see Cmnd 6851 1977, Technical Volume 3, Chapter 9). When vacant possession is obtained, if there is a possibility of sale to the owner-occupied sector, the owner is likely to take the opportunity. This does not necessarily mean that the landlord is making a poor rate of return on his property, if he bought since rental control was introduced; only that the return he can make on sale rather than letting is greater (largely as a result of the concessions available to owner-occupiers). See (e.g. Paley 1978).

Overall, the tax system clearly does not favour rental housing relative to other investment as it does owner-occupiers. It hardly touches the local authority as a supplier of housing. The authority does not pay income tax, as its financial regime currently requires that there is no profit. Nor is it liable to capital gains tax – although this is not an important concession, as hitherto the authority has not realised such assets without reinvestment.

Neither private nor local-authority tenants receive special fiscal incentives for current expenditure. They simply pay rent out of incomes which have already been taxed, and realise no capital gains, except in terms of lower rents (discussed below). They are eligible for relief against interest on loans for housing improvements but few can or do make use of this provision.

The comparative position of tenants and owner-occupiers depends not only on their relative position with respect to the tax system, but also on the public expenditure they receive directly or indirectly through rent and cost reductions. These matters are discussed in the next section.

Public Expenditure on Housing

Central government spending on housing takes two main forms: direct transfers to consumers to help with their current or investment housing expenditure and assistance to suppliers in the public sector (local authorities and housing associations) which is passed on to tenants through the increased availability of housing and through their rent policies. The extent of these expenditures can be seen in Table 6.3.

Direct transfers to assist current expenditure
   To tenants. A national scheme of direct housing subsidies to tenants

is of recent origin. Rebates for local authority tenants and allowances for private unfurnished tenants were introduced in 1972 as part of the Housing Finance Act. Furnished tenants were brought into a similar scheme in 1973 and further modifications were made in 1974. The original scheme was introduced against a background of central government determination to raise rents to 'fair rent' levels and therefore to reduce the general public-sector subsidy. In practice, however, this subsidy also increased, as a result of rising housing costs, general inflation, and government policies to control prices and incomes.

Table 6.3   Public expenditure on housing (Great Britain)

	£m. at current prices	Indices (1977–8 = 100) at constant prices	
	1978–9	1973–4	1978–9
Public sector housing			
Subsidies:			
From central government	1353	59	106
From rate fund	245	83	114
Rent rebates	403	94	101
Investment:			
Local authorities:			
land purchases	63	237	99
new dwellings	1229	70	87
acquisitions	65	155	96
improvements	605	150	131
other	68	104	102
New towns investment	195	79	96
Sales	−202	115	134
Private sector housing			
Improvement grants	121	399	184
Lending to private persons:			
Gross	229	333	118
Repayments	−330	99	96
Option mortgage subsidy	148	63	96
Rent allowance to			
private tenants	93	58	103
Total public expenditure on			
housing	4823	88	103

Source: Table 9.23, *Social Trends* 1980.

The amount payable in rebate or allowance is based on the calculation of a needs allowance which takes account of family circumstances (this allowance is higher than that for supplementary benefit because of the costs of being employed); the income of the tenant and in part that of his dependents; and the rent payable, excluding such items as service charges and rates. In the case of furnished tenants the rent is that designated by the local authority as 'reasonable'.

If income is equal to the needs allowance, the tenant receives a rebate or allowance equal to 60 per cent of his rent. The subsidy is reduced by 17 per cent of any additional income and increased by 25 per cent of any shortfall. In this way the disincentive effects are reduced and proportionately more help is given to the very poor.

Many rebates and allowances are claimed by households where there are working members. Supplementary benefit or supplementary pensions (whichever is relevant) are available for those who are not presently employed. Here the full rent is included (plus rates) for the needs estimate, against which income is offset to calculate eligibility. Help to poorer households is therefore greater. However, one pound of supplementary benefit is lost for each pound of income above a very low limit. If a tenant is eligible for both supplementary benefit and rent rebates he may choose to apply for whichever helps him the most.

About 45 per cent of local authority tenants receive income-related housing assistance, 25 per cent from supplementary benefit and 20 per cent from rent rebates (Hansard 24 and 26 July 1979). Take-up of rent rebates is estimated at about 80 per cent and the majority of those receiving help are elderly (see Table 6.4). The cost of rent rebates (including the rent element of supplementary benefit) in Great Britain in 1978/9 was about £403 million although it is thought that this figure overestimates the true cost of housing assistance.

The cost of rent allowances (to the private sector) was about £93 million in 1978/9, most of which went to tenants in unfurnished accommodation. Assistance is again heavily concentrated among the elderly (Table 6.4), but take-up is much lower (55 per cent for those in the unfurnished sector – 65 per cent in money terms – and 10 per cent for furnished tenants). Cullingworth (Chapter 8 1979) discusses the reasons for low take-up.

To owner-occupiers. Owner-occupiers in receipt of supplementary benefit are eligible for financial help with their housing costs. The

Table 6.4 Help with housing costs: by household type and tenure, (Great Britain, 1977)

Numbers and percentages

	Individual aged under 60	Small adult household	Small family	Large family	Large adult household	Other small household	Individual aged 60 or over	All types
Receipt of help by type of tenure								
Local authority tenants:								
Both rent and rate rebate	13	6	8	8	6	27	23	14
Rent or rate rebate	3	1	2	3	2	10	8	5
Supplementary benefit	15	5	15	15	9	23	54	21
None of these	69	88	75	74	83	40	15	60
Total	100	100	100	100	100	100	100	100
Number in sample	215	404	697	508	702	730	679	3935
Renting privately unfurnished/ from housing association								
Both rent allowance and rate rebate	2	1	3	..ᵇ	3	14	13	8
Rent allowance or rate rebate	1	1	2	..ᵇ	1	12	12	6
Supplementary benefit	3	4	9	..ᵇ	10	18	41	19
None of these	94	94	86	..ᵇ	86	56	34	67
Total	100	100	100	100	100	100	100	100
Number in sample	95	130	153	36	102	242	291	1049

Owner-occupiers with mortgage								
Rate rebate	1	1	2	3	1	18	.. [a]	2
Supplementary benefit	1	1	1	2	1	3	.. [b]	1
Neither of these	98	98	97	95	98	79	.. [b]	97
Total	100	100	100	100	100	100	100	100
Number in sample	134	726	1343	444	561	119	35	3362
Owner occupiers without mortgage								
Rate rebate	18	2	5	9	8	26	33	20
Supplementary benefit	2	1	1	2	2	5	17	7
Neither of these	80	97	94	90	90	69	50	73 [c]
Total	100	100	100	100	100	100	100	100
Number in sample	132	259	218	86	404	925	618	2642
All tenures [a]								
Number in sample	576	1519	2411	1074	1769	2016	1623	10988

Source: Table 9.21, *Social Trends*, 1979.

[a] Excluding those renting furnished or with a job or business.

[b] Small base number.

[c] Slight underestimate owing to the exclusion of households were the amount of rate rebate was not known.

amount claimable is equal to the interest element of the mortgage payment plus an allowance for repairs. As such, help is greatest during the early years of a mortgage. However the majority of owner-occupiers receiving supplementary benefit have no mortgage; about 7 per cent of owner-occupiers without a mortgage receive supplementary benefit as against about 1 per cent of those with a mortgage. Over 75 per cent of people receiving help are pensioners (Table 6.4).

The rationale for making supplementary benefit payable only on the interest is that assistance should be given to help people cover necessary expenditure, rather than to acquire an asset. However the distinction between interest and capital is no more than formal – the payment of either helps asset acquisition and which is paid depends mainly on the form of the mortgage and when it was originally taken out. More practically, building societies will usually allow households in short-term difficulties to hold over capital payments until their finances have recovered. Another problem is that the elderly receive very little help as the regular assistance for repair and maintenance is extremely limited, although special grants for large expenditure are available on occasion (see Townsend 1979).

To all sectors. Rate rebates based on similar principles to rent rebates and allowances, are paid to about 2.7 million ratepayers, a take-up rate of perhaps 70 per cent (Hansard 24 and 27 July 1979). This is the main form of help to older owner-occupiers – see Table 6.4. About 20 per cent of all owner-occupiers without a mortgage receive this subsidy, as against only 2 per cent of those with mortgage (reflecting the structure of lifetime earnings).

The objective of the types of direct transfer provided by supplementary benefit and rent and rate rebate schemes is probably twofold: to allow people to obtain a minimum standard of housing and to redistribute income in an hypothecated fashion. The main problems are those of all means-tested benefits: take-up is not complete and some of those who need help most (those in the private rental sector) are least likely to obtain it. Further, when taken together with transfers for other purposes, they result in a very high marginal 'tax' rate (the loss of benefit for each additional pound earned) and add significantly to the problems of the poverty trap (Atkinson and King 1980).

In terms of fiscal objectives, although the system clearly does provide an element of vertical equity, its operation does not provide full horizontal fairness. Within the rental sector both differential take-up and variations between subsections in what can be claimed are important. The difference in the nature of the good obtained by owner-occupiers and tenants makes equity between them difficult even to define, but the actual system is inconsistent and can result in hardship, especially among elderly owner-occupiers.

Direct transfers for investment

The most widely available form of direct transfer for investment purposes is the improvement grant. Currently standard grants are available to all owners in the private sector for the provision of basic amenities and further grants are available at the discretion of the local authority for certain other types of improvement and sometimes for repairs necessary at the same time. The current Housing Bill extends the scheme to public sector tenants as well as increasing discretion on the rate of grant to the private sector.

In 1978 about 217 000 grants were approved in the UK (as against the peak of 456 000 in 1973). About half of these went to the local authority sector, over one-third to owner-occupiers and only 6 per cent to private landlords. Within the private sector grants appeared to account for about 40 per cent of the total cost of improvement undertaken on grant-aided dwellings (Howes 1979).

Private improvements are usually made either at the time when a unit changes tenure (normally from private rental to owner-occupation but sometimes through municipalisation) or, if already in the owner-occupied sector, at the time that the house is sold. In the main, take-up would seem to be concentrated among younger age groups and probably higher social classes as evidenced by significant gentrification especially in the early 1970s. (See Expenditure Committee 1972–3 and Cmnd 5529 1974.) Even with relatively generous grants very few elderly owner-occupiers, the group most likely to be living in substandard conditions, make use of improvement grants (National Dwelling and Housing Survey 1978 and Table 6.5). But, most important from the point of view of housing policy, there is a poor level of take-up in the private rental sector even though tenants have a right to make landlords undertake repairs and improvements (see Table 6.5 for evidence on dwelling quality). As a result, the private tenant and the elderly owner-occupier, generally the poorest members of the community, obtain the least assistance. (See Paris and Blackaby 1979.)

Table 6.5   Quality of accommodation by tenure (percentages)

		At least one amenity lacked	No bath/shower	No inside WC
(a)	By tenure			
	Owned: outright	7.0	3.5	5.4
	with a mortgage	1.4	0.5	1.2
	Rented: from council	3.5	0.4	2.7
	from housing association	7.0	3.7	4.0
	from private landlord:			
	unfurnished	21.2	13.6	16.8
	furnished	7.7	2.0	3.0
	All households	5.8	2.7	4.4
(b)	By age of head of household			
	Age of head of household			
	Under 23	5.6		
	23–34	9.0		
	35–44	7.5		
	45–54	11.3		
	55–64	17.9		
	65 +	48.7		

Source: National Dwelling and Housing Survey, Tables 6 and 10.

Improvement subsidies are currently available to local authorities in much the same forms as that for new building – i.e. a subsidy to cover 66 per cent of loan charges on expenditure approved by government (with some additional constraints). Expenditure which does not attract subsidy is likely to be higher for improvement schemes than for new units, so improvement is more expensive for the local authority, especially as the standards required are often similar to those for new building.

Area improvement policies were first introduced in the 1969 Housing Act in the form of General Improvement Areas (GIAs) to be followed in the 1974 Housing Act by Housing Action Areas (HAAs). Both allow higher rates of grant and wider coverage together with greater local powers to force improvement. Progress has been slow both in defining areas and in terms of the results within each area (see Roberts 1976).

Improvement grants to the private sector seem to be aimed mainly at the provision of minimum standards, especially because of their emphasis on basic amenities. However, they would appear often to go to households who could anyway afford to do the work and who gain also from any resultant capital appreciation. Administrative complexities and the requirements for additional work, often made by local authorities, clearly limit take-up (see Lomas and Howes 1979) and this probably affects lower-income households disproportionately.

Improvement grants in the public sector go to increase standards to a relatively high level, which might lead to the saving of future costs. However this must be at the expense of helping many other households to obtain minimum standards.

Finally, except to a small extent in GIA and HAA schemes, no subsidy is given for environmental factors. Yet this is clearly an important area where one would expect private decisions to result in under-investment (see Robinson 1979) suggesting a strong case for government assistance.

Direct transfer to first-time purchasers
Finally, first-time purchasers obtain a direct transfer to help them enter owner-occupation. Under the 'Homeloan' scheme, brought in on 1 December 1978, first-time purchasers are eligible for a loan of up to £600, interest free for five years, together with a cash bonus of up to £100. In order to qualify, people have to save for at least two years, so payments will not start until late 1980. At the time of its introduction the assistance was worth about 5 per cent of the average price of a dwelling bought by a first-time buyer. However, inflation has eroded its value significantly so that the requirement to save for at least two years may be costly when compared with trying to buy as quickly as possible. It is not clear precisely who will be helped by the scheme. Some marginal buyers may be able to become owner-occupiers when they could not have done so otherwise, but the majority of assistance will probably go to speed up entry for those who would anyway have become owners.

Another problem is the possible effect on house prices. As the amounts and numbers of people involved are likely to remain small there will probably be little effect but, because supply is not completely elastic, some benefit will go to existing owner-occupiers via higher prices. There will also be some slight stimulation of supply, due to increased demand, even though only about 40 per cent of first-time purchasers buy new units. Over all, however, the scheme is very limited and its impact on prices is unlikely to be important.

In general, direct transfers are more clearly aimed at achieving minimum standards and helping poorer households than are the available tax reliefs. But, especially with respect to improvement grants, the connection is often still rather tenuous. Furthermore, the general problems of income-related benefits, particularly that of take-up, severely limit their effectiveness in meeting desired housing objectives.

Indirect transfers via public sector subsidy

The final area relating fiscal and housing policy is that of indirect transfers. Central government provides subsidies to local authorities, new towns and housing associations for investment and current expenditure which are passed on to tenants in the form of increased availability and lower rents.

For local authorities this subsidy currently covers a proportion of the loan charges incurred by both new and past housing expenditure. The subsidy to housing associations is in the form of a capitalised payment but is based on similar principles. Subsidy is only payable on reckonable expenditure (i.e. that which central government defines as necessary). Local authorities then raise the difference between the subsidy and annual expenditure through rent or rates. If a rate fund contribution is made (for some items it is legally required) this is eligible, like other rate expenditure, for rate support grant. The new Housing Bill introduces a different basis for subsidy, the central government paying most or possibly the whole of the difference between deemed costs and deemed rents. (Smith 1977.)

The transfer to the tenant can be seen as equal either to the difference between his rent and the (historic) cost incurred in providing that accommodation, or as the difference between rent and market value. The second definition appears more appropriate in economic terms, as long as the local authority is regarded as owning the property (e.g. Grey *et al.* 1978; Rosenthal 1977). However, in terms of public expenditure, and therefore fiscal policy, the first more clearly reflects reality and is the figure used in official publications.

The distribution of assistance by income group can be seen from Table 6.6, taken from the *Housing Policy Review* (which can be compared with Table 6.2 for owner-occupiers). It suggests that in terms of general subsidy (i.e. that transferred through lower gross rents) the poorest households obtain the least assistance but that over the rest of the range the subsidy is almost a lump sum. Direct transfers in the form of rebates then make overall assistance redistributive over the lowest ranges. A similar picture emerges if a more formal economic definition of subsidy is used. (Hughes 1979.)

Table 6.6.   Local authority and new town housing subsidies, 1974–5

Income (*head of household and wife*)	Number of households (*thousands*)	Total general subsidy (*£m*)	Average general subsidy (*£*)	Average rebate (*£*)[a]	Total rebate (*£m*)	Total all subsidies
Under £1000	1230	148	120	46	56	204
£1000–£1499	660	87	132	48	32	119
£1500–£1999	510	78	152	28	14	92
£2000–£2499	660	90	137	7	5	95
£2500–£2999	660	97	147	–	–	97
£3000–£3499	430	67	154	–	–	67
£3500–£3999	260	38	148	–	–	38
£4000–£4999	240	39	164	–	–	39
£5000 and over	50	7	154	–	–	7
All ranges	4700	651	139	23	107	758

[a] Average over all tenant households in the range, not just over the number of households receiving rebates.

Source: Table IV 35, Cmnd 6851 1977. Technical Volume 1.

One way of rationalising the current system is to say that tenants as a whole receive the benefit of capital gains, because local authorities are required not to make a profit, in the same way as owner-occupiers. The benefits are then distributed via the rent pooling system which, in the main, appears to result in rents rising less than in proportion to quality. Thus, those in better quality accommodation obtain more of the capital benefit. These gains are not realisable or transferable, as they are in the owner-occupied sector, unless the tenant is able to buy his council house. When such sales occur there is a once-and-for-all transfer to the specific purchaser equal to the discount on market value that he receives. There may or may not be any public expenditure effect involved, depending on how long the property has been in the local authority's hands, its cost and past rental income. If the price is greater than historic cost, some benefit of the realised capital gains goes to other tenants and some to central government. (Again this is under review in the new Housing Bill.)

Subsidies to rent can thus, in part, be rationalised in terms of comparability with owner-occupation: lower rents implicitly equate to the capital gains available and tax is not charged on the resultant imputed income any more than it is for owner-occupiers (Whitehead 1977). But the connection between the two sectors is limited by the extreme differences in financial arrangements between the sectors and by the existence of choice of housing in the one and administrative allocation in the other.

Further, in the main, vertical equity is not achieved via general subsidies to the local authority sector. Rather the subsidy acts as a lump-sum payment, only rationalisable on the argument that all members of society should be assisted to consume more housing. But this reading is contradicted by the lack of any equivalent assistance to the private rental sector, where many of the poorest households live and where the quality of accommodation is certainly lowest.

Effect on investment

The effect of subsidy on investment and purchase by local authorities is unclear, as it is not known whether these units could have been provided in other ways. However, the extent of subsidy can be expected to have increased the total amount of accommodation available. Until 1977, local authorities had full discretion to build as many units as they liked as long as they met Parker Morris standards and building-cost limits. Since then housing investment plans and cash limits have been introduced, which reduce local authority discretion. By these provisions, local authorities are required to define their priorities in terms of needs and then keep, in fairly global terms, to a total agreed by central government. Thus, total investment becomes an element of central government housing policy.

It is clear that Parker Morris standards are far in excess of defined minimum standards, and indeed are often in excess of those found in the private sector. They can perhaps be partially justified on the basis of their future social value. Yet there is little evidence that any account has been taken, either on cost or benefit grounds, of the difference between building at high standards or of building at lower but acceptable standards and improving later. It must be assumed that high standards have to be traded against further units which might help the needy more effectively.

The subsidies to local authority investment apparently meet the requirement of neutrality and balance between new building and improvement. But, in practice, the proportion of costs given assistance varies, biasing choice towards new building. Moreover, the inflexible standards required for improvement reduce its value as a way of providing a range of qualities for different needs. Because the basis of the assistance available is so different, it is impossible to compare the sectors.

Overall, indirect transfers via local authority rent and investment policies do benefit many lower-income households. However, they also benefit, often by similar or greater amounts, many who are not in these groups. Also, the majority of those housed in the sector clearly live at standards which, although probably desirable, cannot readily be justified except in terms of private benefit.

Indirect transfers to private rental occur via rent controls from landlord to tenant rather than from the government. But they do not involve expenditure by the Exchequer except to the extent that tax revenue is lost. They are, therefore, excluded from this discussion. Thus, the only official assistance available to private rental tenants is via the allowance scheme and yet many of the poorest households and those in the most housing need are still housed in the private rental sector.

Conclusions

This survey of the fiscal aspects of housing policy suggests that, although the policy is extremely expensive (public assistance to housing in the form of income tax relief on mortgage interest, option mortgages, rent rebates and allowances, improvement grants and public-sector housing subsidies accounted for nearly £3400 in 1978/9), there is no very strong rationale for the majority of this expenditure.

Undoubtedly the effect of assistance has been to increase expenditure on housing and thus consumption in total. Partly as a result of this, Britain's housing conditions are generally better than those found in countries with higher average incomes (Cmnd 3651 1977). However, the cost in terms of diverting resources from other services has never been fully assessed. What, for example, is the relative cost of building to a high standard rather than investing less now and improving later? It is thus not clear whether our emphasis on housing above high minimum standards and, in particular, on giving considerable formal assistance to the vast majority who could in any case afford such standards, is in line with overall social objectives. Moreover, a major part of any effect from increasing assistance in the private sector clearly goes not to increased investment but into rising prices, redistributing wealth to existing owner-occupiers and landowners. Nor is it clear that fiscal policies related to housing help to offset market imperfections, particularly as subsidies are not directed at environmental factors, and the private rental sector, where the most obvious problems are found, receives the least assistance.

In terms of redistribution, only direct transfers appear to help low-income households more than others. General assistance acts as near lump-sum payments in the local-authority sector increases with income for the owner-occupied and is non-existent in the private rental sector.

Fiscal neutrality and 'appropriate' incentives are not obtained: between consumers, between different types of investment, within housing, between housing and other assets, or between consumption, saving and investment. Horizontal inequalities between tenures are particularly common and, especially for people living in the private rental sector, assistance helps to exacerbate the strong vertical inequities of the system. Even where the system achieves its objectives, as in the provision of decent housing for those in the two main sectors, at a price they can afford, the success is not unqualified. It may be, for example, that the majority would have afforded adequate housing anyway and the cost to the public exchequer and thus to other services is out of all proportion to the social benefit obtained. Furthermore, the system leaves unaided many of those, who on any objective grounds, would appear to need help the most.

However, if only because the majority do appear to gain, the system will be extremely difficult to dismantle. Reform will have to be achieved in a piecemeal fashion in the same way as the system evolved, but with a difference. The direction reform is to take must be clearly defined and understood. Each element of change must be a clear step towards the final goals of obtaining reasonable housing for all, horizontal and vertical equity and the appropriate incentives to invest and consume. It is probably only when government is prepared to overhaul the general fiscal system in the light of strategic social objectives that housing aims can start to be met at a reasonable cost both to individuals and to the public purse.

References

Allan, C. M. 1971, *The Theory of Taxation*, Harmondsworth, Penguin Books.

Atkinson, A. B. and King, M. A. 1980, 'Housing policy, taxation and reform', *Midland Bank Review*, London, February.

Boléat, M. 1979, *The Building Societies Association*, London, Building Societies Association.

Bowley, M. 1966, *The British Building Industry*, Cambridge, CUP.

Burrows, P. 1977, 'Efficient pricing and government intervention' in M. V. Posner (ed) *Public Expenditure*, Cambridge, CUP.

Collard, D. 1968, *The New Right: A Critique*, Fabian Tract 387, London, Fabian Society.

Collard, D. 1972, *Prices, Markets and Welfare*, London, Faber and Faber.

Committee of Inquiry into the Impact of Rates on Households, (the Allen Report) 1965, Cmnd 2582, London, HMSO.

Crosland, A. 1975, Speech to the Housing Centre Trust, June 18 1975, partly published in *Housing Review*, September/October 1975.

Cullingworth, J. B. 1979, *Essays on Housing Policy*, London, George Allen & Unwin.

Culyer, A. J. 1971, 'Merit goods and the welfare economics of coercion', *Public Finance*, no. 4.

Davis, O. and Whinston, A. 1961, 'Economics of urban renewal', *Law and Contemporary Problems*, vol. 26.

Expenditure Committee 1972–3, *House Improvement Grants*, Tenth Report of the Expenditure Committee, HC 349–11, London, HMSO.

Fair Deal for Housing 1971, Cmnd 4728, London, HMSO.

Follain, J. R., Jnr. 1979, 'The price elasticity of the long-run supply of new housing construction', *Land Economics*, vol. 55.

Grey, A. *et al.* 1978, *Housing Rents Costs and Subsidies*, London, CIPFA.

House Improvement Grants: Government Observations on the Tenth Report from the Expenditure Committee 1974, Cmnd 5529, London, HMSO.

Housing Policy: A Consultative Document 1977, Cmnd 6581, London, HMSO.

Howes, E. 1979, 'Private sector improvement: more facts and figures', *CES Review*, no. 6.

Hughes, G. A. 1979, 'Housing income and subsidies', *Fiscal Studies*, vol. 1, no. 1.

Kay, J. A. and King, M. A. 1978, *The British Tax System*, Oxford, Clarendon Press.

Lansley, S. 1979, *Housing and Public Policy*, London, Croom Helm.

Lees, D. 1971, *Health through Choice*, Hobert Paper no. 14, London, Institute of Economic Affairs.

Le Grand, J. and Robinson, R. 1976, *The Economics of Social Problems*, London, Macmillan Press.

Lomas, G. and Howes, E. 1979, 'Private improvement in Leicester', *CFS Review* no. 6.

Meade, J. E. (Chairman) 1978, *The Structure and Reform of Direct Taxation*, London, George Allen & Unwin/Institute for Fiscal Studies.

Musgrave, R. A. 1959, *The Theory of Public Finance*, New York, McGraw-Hill.

National Dwelling & Housing Survey 1978, Department of the Environment, London, HMSO.

Nevitt, A. A. 1966, *Housing, Taxation and Subsidies*, London, Nelson.

Odling-Smee, J. C. 1975, 'The impact of the fiscal system on different tenure sectors', *Housing Finance*, Institute of Fiscal Studies Publications no. 12, London, Institute of Fiscal Studies.

Paley, B. 1977, *Attitudes to Letting in 1976*, Office of Population Census and Surveys, London, HMSO.

Paris, C. and Blackaby, R. 1979, *Not Much Improvement*, London, Heinemann.

Pennance, F. G. 1969, *Housing Market Analysis and Policy*, Hobart Paper no. 48, London, Institute of Economic Affairs.

Roberts, J. 1976, *General Improvement Areas*, Farnborough, Saxon House.

Robinson, R. 1980, *Housing Tax-Expenditures, Subsidies and the Distribution of Income*, Paper given at LSE Urban Economics Seminar.

Rosenthal, L. 1977, 'The regional and income distribution of the council house subsidy in the United Kingdom', vol. XLV, *Manchester School*.

Royal Commission on Housing in Scotland, Cd. 8731 1917, London, HMSO.

Sandford, C. T. 1978, *The Economics of Public Finance*, 2nd ed, London, Pergamon.

Sen, A. 1973, *On Economic Inequities*, Oxford, Clarendon Press.

Smith, M. 1977, 'Local authority housing finance', *CES Review* no. 2.

Stafford, D. C. 1978, *The Economics of Housing Policy*, London, Croom Helm.

Townsend, P. 1979, *Poverty in the United Kingdom*, Harmondsworth, Penguin Books.

White, M. S. and White, L. J. 1977, 'The Tax-Subsidy to Owner-Occupied Housing: Who Benefits?', *Journal of Public Economics 3*.

Whitehead, C. M. E. 1977, 'Neutrality between tenures: a critique of the HPR comparisons', *CES Review* no. 2, December.

Whitehead, C. M. E. 1979, 'Option mortgages', *CES Review* no. 6.

Whitehead, C. M. E. 1980, 'Stamp duty', *CES Review* no. 8.

Willis, J. R. M. and Hardwick, P. J. W. 1978, *Tax Expenditures in the United Kingdom*, London, Heinemann.

Yates, J. 1979, 'The distributive impact of subsidies arising from the non-taxation of imputed rent in Australia 1966–68', *PSERC Discussion Paper* 79/04, University of Sheffield.

7 Taxation and Pensions
*Mike Reddin**

A Proper Cause for Concern

Taxpayers and tax systems are not fixed entities: frequently they adapt themselves one to another. One formulation of this interaction might be called the 'pursuit model'. Taxpayers mend or bend their ways in order to avoid a predatory tax system. The tax system responds to these evasive moves, blocking exits, becoming more observant and learned in the ways of the evader. The hunted learn the ways of the hunter, the hunter anticipates the ways of the hunted. The hunter has no wish to *kill* (Goose-and-Golden-Egg syndrome) but, at very least wishes to keep the hunted within sight.

In another formulation, but pursuing the same analogy, the tax system may seem concerned with 'domestication'. The aim is to tame the beast (the taxpayer), encourage certain forms of behaviour, reward these behaviours persistently and then sustain a collusive relationship of mutual backscratching. There is more than a trace of each model in the inter-relation of tax and pension systems in Britain today. It is not simply that taxes bear upon pensions: pensions in turn bear upon tax systems. If tax reliefs encourage styles of economic behaviour, such behaviours themselves impose continuing demands on tax systems – if only for continuity. If wage levels become increasingly set – especially where marginal rates are judged high – with an eye to the tax system then, viewed from downstream, and allowing for the time-lag for adjustments to work through, it is likely that both wages and benefits are increasingly tax-adapted systems. Whatever their current effects, moderating or stimulating short-term behaviour, taxes affect the longer term. Tax arrangements generate assumptions: they evoke long-term expectations, particularly where they have already operated for many years. They may become endemic, *natural*

* The author wishes to express thanks for advice and comment from colleagues, Della Nevitt and Brian Abel-Smith, from Ron Hartley, and from Mike Brown of the Company Pensions Information Centre.

to the general context of provision. As such they tend either to pass barely noticed (escaping appraisal as to their continuing merits) or appear so inherently 'in the scheme of things' as to be deemed immovable. Where the scale and pervasiveness of tax and tax relief is substantial tax considerations can themselves become the fulcrum of policy; in this case, the tax tail comes to wag the pension policy dog.

Further, taxes are, broadly speaking, in the lap of the political choice-makers. This contrasts markedly with other major 'uncontrollable' vagaries of pension provision, such as changes in mortality, occupational mobility, incomes, inflation, and investment returns. To have at least one variable (taxation) which can be controlled encourages us to keep it stable. However, this very 'controlability' means that it may be called upon to compensate for changes in the other variables. These two pressures – to be both stable and adaptable – are given added weight by a third consideration, namely that *several* variables affect the survival of pension systems (especially those which are based on savings, i.e. funded schemes). In the face of changes which place unexpected burdens on the pension fund, it will help if there is some 'slack' among the variables. That there are *several* variables tends to minimise the importance of any one; conversely, if any one dimension takes 'a turn for the worse' the remaining variables achieve proportionately greater significance. Recent poor investment returns and the imposition of pension vesting (the right to retain pension benefits on change of employment) thus increasing fund obligations have made the 'tax variable' rise in stature.

Fourth, the new explicit partnership of state and occupational pension schemes, with the latter extremely sensitive to tax considerations, makes this state of 'tax-dependency' ever more acute. As the pension futures of millions are committed to occupational schemes, most of which are financed and survive on the basis that their tax treatment will continue as at present, then tax/pension relationships grow in importance. The willingness of the state to 'endanger' its private partners by changing their fiscal environment may be correspondingly reduced. If current arrangements are inequitable they are now further consolidated: if change is needed it is harder to achieve.

One further dimension cannot be neglected: funded pension schemes are not *just* pension schemes. They hold massive sums of capital and play an increasingly significant investment role in industry, property and, not least, as major lenders to government. With this *ancillary* role – ancillary to their notional prime function of pension provision – their prosperity and survival achieve double significance. The funds can make a major contribution to the retirement incomes of substantial numbers of citizens; they simultaneously lend to government and to industry; their potential behaviour in this latter role undoubtedly affects governments' willingness to affect the climate in which they operate. The point is a simple one: relations between the state and pension funds, particularly via taxation, will not be founded exclusively on a concern for pensions *per se*.

The Actual and the Potential

The discussion which follows is concerned as much to explore the possibilities for tax/pension interactions as to describe their present format: thus it does not confine itself to current happenings. Current arrangements are not the product of total wisdom nor are they likely to be the final word in tax – pension relationships (despite our acknowledgement of their resistance to change) and hence the need to be alert to the range of potential interactions. Whether or not such alternative arrangements might actually be introduced by a UK government is not central to the argument which follows. However, two points can usefully be made about the relevance of such a speculative approach. Firstly, nobody has a monopoly of answers to the political guessing game called 'what will they think of next?'. This debate, and its conclusions, are not already totally circumscribed. Secondly, the *actual* outcomes of policies are often distinct from those intended: we need to note the potential consequences of moves which, whatever their intent, can have outcomes very similar to those explored here.

The sheer range of component parts of tax and pension systems mean that there are a multitude of variants which can be developed within and between the systems. Changes can be rung on the tax deductability of contributions, the tax treatment of pension benefits, the tax reliefs to funding systems, the tax context within which pension benefit formulae operate, and so on. In each case we can decide not only whether or not taxes will be imposed or relieved, but the rates at which we can do so, the range over which they will operate (e.g. within income bands), whether to tax income in different ways at different stages of working life and retirement or whether to vary the tax burden as between different parties (e.g. employer and employee). Any description of current arrangements ought to stimulate thoughts of possible *re*formulation. Thus the legitimacy of any description, of a 'naming of parts', is that it may make us consider the potential of the components in other formulations.

Direct Taxation, Pensions and Interdependence

Most of what follows concerns relations between direct taxation systems – primarily income taxation – and pensions. The pensions in question are retirement pensions provided through the state scheme of national insurance and pensions provided via occupational pension schemes. We shall also touch on those pensions (best described as individual retirement annuities) increasingly purchased by the self-employed and those working for employers with no 'company' scheme. Supplementary pensions via the supplementary benefit scheme, paid for from general taxes will be ignored (as will the treatment of occupational pensions as 'resources' in means-testing). But it is the mainstream of state insurance and related private provision which will be our deliberate focus.

Public/private distinctions

The state retirement pension scheme is that described in the Social Security Pensions Act 1975 and brought into operation from April 1978. In return for a wholly earnings-related contribution from employees and employers it offers an earnings-related 'two-tier' benefit, replacing 100 per cent of earnings up to a 'basic amount' (the equivalent of the former flat-rate pension benefit) plus 25 per cent of earnings above this basic amount up to an income ceiling of seven times this sum. The scheme builds up gradually to achieve full benefit levels over the next twenty years. It is run on a Pay-As-You-Go (PAYG) basis, using the contributions and taxes of current national insurance contributors and taxpayers to finance current benefits.

It has one important and unusual characteristic. If an employer (whether in the public or private sector of the economy) operates an 'acceptable' pension scheme then the employees can be *contracted-out* of part of the state scheme. The employee and employer's contribution to the state scheme is reduced and employees must be offered an occupational pension benefit comparable to the additional component (the 25 per cent part) of the state scheme.

If the state scheme can be described in this way, nonetheless distinctions between public and private domains are at times misleading. The 'state scheme' stands clearly demarcated as the national 'universal' retirement pension scheme – modified by contracting-out. But then there are the 'public' schemes, the pension provisions for both central public service (Civil Service) and local government employees, and 'public sector' (nationalised industry) employees. Third, there are 'private' schemes – generally for those working in the private sector of the economy. This sector is not constant – companies and whole industries move between the public and private sectors – and the boundary is not always clear-cut. (For example, the Government Actuary's survey of occupational pensions defines the university teachers' scheme as a 'private sector' scheme). Characterised in terms of their finances, these sectional distinctions range from the state scheme's Pay-As-You-Go to the public sector's mixture of PAYG and others 'notionally' or 'partially' funded and the 'private schemes' which are almost entirely funded.

The discussion which follows recurrently notes two main dimensions of tax – pension relationships. First there is the varied treatment of three phases of the classical funded pension process – *inputs* (contributions), *earnings* (accrual via interest and capital gain) and *outputs* (benefits). Second there are those aspects which distinguish the tax treatment of public (state) and private (occupational) pension systems.

Points of Taxation and the Duration of Reliefs

The first matter to note is that the three phases mentioned are not necessarily distinct in time. We find situations of simultaneous input to and output from the same schemes, e.g. the employee is receiving a company pension towards which the employer is *still* actively contributing. Further, the *earnings* period of a funded scheme is continuous. Accrual begins from the date of the first contribution to the fund, and continues year by year, earning interest and achieving capital gains. This occurs not just on the new inflow of contribution income but successively upon the earnings of the earnings of the earnings, a process sustained right through the period of benefit payment. New 'contributions' may cease but the fund is not disbursed overnight; it continues to *earn* until the 'exhaustion' of the capital fund itself, a point which, on a perfect actuarial calculation, would be coincident with the date of death of beneficiary or survivor.

We find further examples of overlapping phases when, as not infrequently happens, a man retires from Company A at age 60 and starts to receive its pension, but then enters new employment with

Company B. He is now simultaneously a beneficiary (from Company A) and a contributor (to Company B and the state scheme). So, the phases and their associated tax treatments are not discrete and some are inevitably simultaneous. With this in mind we can nonetheless observe the different ways in which tax systems have impact on these component parts.

Inputs

The employee's contribution
The employee who contributes to a pension scheme that is approved for the purpose of tax relief by the Inland Revenue (i.e. an 'exempt approved' pension scheme) is granted full tax relief on the sum involved. This means that the contribution is deducted from earnings prior to taxation of the remainder. The value of such relief is thus equivalent to the amount of tax which would otherwise be payable. If tax of 30 per cent would normally apply then relief reduces the 'costs' of an employee's contribution by 30 per cent: it means that the employee can contribute £5 at a real net cost of £3.50. With a marginal tax rate of 60 per cent the value of relief is increased accordingly: the £5 contribution costs just £2. In practice, with a standard proportionate rate of income tax of 30 per cent for some 95 per cent of the population, the value of employee's tax relief will be a simple function of the magnitude of their contribution.

We should not minimise these recurrent characteristics of the British income tax system; that the value of its reliefs is greater the larger the absolute sum involved (e.g. the higher the pension contribution paid), and *proportionately* greater the higher the marginal rate of tax. Such characteristics assume particular significance when we speculate on the likely prospects for change in fiscal policy. Those with the highest gains from tax reliefs are typically those with the highest incomes and probably the strongest self-interest in their continuance. Yet, because income taxation is now a virtually *universal* phenomenon amongst earners, so is tax relief. Thus even at the lowest rates of tax, 'savings' of 30 per cent will mean a great deal and will apply to virtually all pension-scheme members.

Further, it is with the employee's contribution that we find the most 'discriminatory' tax treatment as between the state scheme and occupational alternatives. Whereas the 'private' contribution is wholly tax deductible, the 'public' contribution is not. This contrast is most revealing in the case of 'contracting-out' from the state scheme under the provisions of the Social Security (Pensions) Act 1975. Part of the employee's contribution to the state scheme is reduced by 2.5 per cent if the company scheme is contracted-out. In effect this means a choice between paying a *non-deductible* 2.5 per cent or a *deductible* 2.5 per cent: on accountable earnings of £100 this means a 'choice' between £2.50 or (with a 30 per cent marginal rate) just £1.75. Alternatively the contracted-out company scheme could ask the employee for £3.75 which, with tax relief, would only involve the same net cost (of £2.50) as the state scheme would otherwise demand.

As a final note on the contributions of the employee, we have to acknowledge the very generous tax treatment afforded those withdrawing from occupational schemes prior to retirement and who allowed some measure of contribution refund. In such cases the refund of the employee's contribution – having enjoyed full relief previously at the relevant marginal rate – is taxed at the nominal rate of 10 per cent. Perhaps this generosity has been intended in some way to compensate for the staggering benefit losses experienced by that vast majority of job-changing employees. If so, it offers a further insight into the potentials of tax systems as 'compensatory mechanisms' – a facet which has not been made explicit in British tax policy.

The employer's contribution

In marked contrast, the employer's contribution experiences no differential treatment between state and private schemes: in both cases pension contributions are deductible as 'business expenses' and as such are relieved of tax. In this sense there is no immediate tax incentive to be contracted-in or contracted-out, such as we noted for the employee. Similarly, whereas it may be more tax-efficient from the employee's perspective to receive remuneration in the form of an employer's contribution to a pension scheme (on which the employee will not be taxed), it will be neither more nor less costly for the employer to make payment as wage or pension contribution. Only in so far as the employee prefers the pension contribution and its associated benefits might the employer benefit in terms of lessened wage demands. In short, there are no conspicuous direct tax advantages for the employer in supporting a pension plan; there will have to be other factors which make it worthwhile.

There are however considerable distributional effects resulting from the employer's contribution *per se* which, because it is 'subsidised' through tax expenditures, must now be taken into account. The employer contributes to the state scheme, at a level determined by the rate of individual employee wages. The employer of the highly paid contributes more than the employer of the low paid. However, these contributions are not directly attributable to an individual employee's 'National Insurance Account'. They become part of the total resources generally available for state scheme benefits. Thus, beneficiaries who will have experienced widely different levels of earnings over working life and some, having been self-employed, who have never had an employer will benefit from these (tax-relieved) employer contributions.

The new pension formula from 1978 grants the lower paid a proportionately higher rate of return than the higher paid: presumably there is some transfer between the two groups. In part this stems from individual employee contributions, and from the Exchequer contribution, but also from the employer's contribution. The self-employed also share in these transfer benefits in the same way. Thus, the value of tax reliefs accorded to the employer which complement these 'contributory transfers' must have a related redistributive effect.

We should remind ourselves that the advantage of both contribution and relief are ultimately enjoyed only by those who receive pension benefit. Just as not all employees are in occupational schemes (perhaps half the work force) so not all company employees are likely to be members of the pension scheme (and of course not all members will remain with the firm or survive to enjoy full or even partial benefits). Thus, there are many *intra*-company distributions which are most likely to occur from the most mobile (women, the lower paid and manual workers) to the least mobile, (non-manual, higher-paid males). Each is underscored by the tax exemptions we have itemised. Once again, tax reliefs endorse existing patterns of distribution.

Accrual

Both the interest earned and the capital gains realised by pension fund investments are fully exempt from tax liability. This obviously plays an enormous part in reducing the *visible* contributory costs of funded pensions. Other factors serve to compound the impact of this tax-exempt status. Earnings (and therefore tax reliefs) are continuous throughout the life of pension funds, arising from both new savings (contributions) and the 're-cycled' profits of former savings: they are also spread over a period of perhaps sixty or seventy years. This must be the most substantial form of tax relief which exists within Britain today: continuation in its present format will certainly make mortgage relief look trivial. Further, the tax-exempt pension fund, in making 'pension-saving' so *cheap* discriminates substantially against other forms of saving (See Chapter 9).

If the opportunities exist to save towards retirement during working life then the current major differentiating factor between the attractions of one savings route or another is the tax system. With the exception of approved pension schemes and, to a lesser extent, life insurance, all forms of cash saving must be made out of post-tax income. To save £1 such gross income must be earned which, *after* deduction of income taxes and national insurance contributions, will leave £1 net. At January 1980 tax rates most people, with a marginal rate of 30 per cent tax plus 6.5 per cent national insurance contributions (or 4 per cent if contracted-out), must earn £1.57 to produce a 'saveable £1' (£1.51 for the contracted-out employee). This latter individual may also have to make a 5 per cent (gross) contribution to the company pension scheme: making it necessary to earn £1.60 to achieve the £1 for any alternative form of 'private savings'.

Non-pension savings must be made from post-tax income whether in the form of National Savings, building society or bank deposits, government stocks, Premium Bonds or equities. Tax treatment of the outcomes of such forms of saving are less consistent. This will depend in part on where the money has been placed and indeed on the size of the saving. Some savings, like building-society interest, will be taxed at source, while some will enjoy full tax relief providing that the holding is limited to a certain size, as will some forms of National Savings. Taxation of the earnings from money saved can be a continuing or one-off process; it may be determined by the ultimate *disposal* of savings. If in liquidating any saved capital a capital gain was enjoyed then the gain could be taxable. Further, the income realised from these savings will be designated as *investment* income and thus subject – if of sufficient amount – to the additional levy of the investment income surcharge.

In the fact of all these exigencies it is hardly surprising that individuals – whether in a purely personal capacity or as employees – look to that exceptional tax haven, the exempt-approved scheme. Here, as individuals via a retirement annuity, or as employees via a company scheme, they can make contributions from tax-free income. Furthermore, during the lifetime of their savings the exempt-approved saver will pay no tax on interest or capital gains accruing to the pension fund. And, when the products are paid out, the pensions will be taxed as *earned* rather than *unearned* income. All in all, the funded pension route to paradise has a remarkable tax status, not just in contrast to the state scheme but in comparison to all other forms of saving.

One final if obvious point must be made about the reliefs – and their consequent savings – they are mainly enjoyed by those whose pensions come from funded schemes. Pensions provided through 'Pay-As-You-Go' or 'notional funding' systems will simply have to pay their way much more visibly and much more directly than the funded sector. Funded schemes epitomise the low profile: they have low visibility of earnings (in terms of its source) and the general low visibility of fiscal reliefs. In so far as the funded schemes are 'unevenly' distributed amongst the working population, then so are these tax-derived benefits.

Outputs

Taxation and pension benefits
Taxation shapes the form and level of pension benefits and, as already noted, the tax treatment of pensions varies substantially as between state and private schemes. At times this arises because the private schemes offer different *forms* of income receipt than the state schemes – and some of these forms are tax-free. Thus lump sums do not exist in the state schemes but are widespread in occupational schemes; they are free of tax when paid at levels up to one and a half times final salary. (There is, of course, no theoretical objection to the state schemes having a lump sum option.) This means that occupational schemes provide tax-free an income which, if the same sum were de-livered as an annuity (as the state scheme *requires*) would be taxable. Thus a tax *advantage* is conferred simply because the state scheme fails or chooses not to provide an equivalent benefit format. However the main impact of taxation on pension benefits is more distinctive.

Pension formulae are almost all related to previous *gross* earnings – averaged over various periods. The fact that the Inland Revenue are prepared to 'allow', for tax purposes, private pension benefits of two-thirds of *final* salary (normally averaged over the last three or the best of the previous five years) has probably been a major incentive in the move towards final salary arrangements. For somebody with final gross earnings of £100 per week, it means that a private pension of up to £66 can be paid. (Under the graduated scheme of 1961–75 and the new pension scheme from 1978 the contracted-out 'equivalent' occupational benefits count towards the two-thirds limit. In contrast, the 'contracted-in' pensioner *could* receive full State pension – with the earnings-related component – *plus* occupational benefits of up to two-thirds final salary).

However, pre-retirement is generally a period when income is high (especially as many households will contain two earners). At the same time, tax relief is at its lowest as children have left home and the mortgage has been paid off. For many, the only tax relief at this time will be on pension or life-insurance contributions. Thus, take-home pay is at its furthest remove from gross pay. At a conservative estimate we might assume that the pre-retirement married male is bringing home only 75 per cent of his gross earnings. Thus his '66 per cent pension' (on £100 earnings) can be juxtaposed with his take-home pay of £75 giving him a private pension level at some 88 per cent of previous take-home pay.

With a company pension at 66 per cent of gross and with just a basic flat-rate state pension for himself and wife (at £37.30 per week from November 1979) the combined state and private pension equal 103 per cent of previous gross earnings, some 138 per cent of previous take-home pay. Thus at retirement the married pensioner could experience an increase in income from £75 per week to £103 – an extra £28 per week (ignoring, for the moment, taxation of this total).

In this example it has been assumed that the pensioner was contracted-out of the state scheme and had no entitlement to the new earnings-related pensions. However, it is highly unlikely that he would have spent his entire working life in contracted-out schemes and *theoretically* he could realise the 66 per cent limit, plus flat-rate, plus full earnings-related state pension. If his earnings had averaged £100 per week over the best twenty years of working life then, his pension could comprise the flat-rate £37.30 plus 25 per cent of income between £19.50 and £100, which means a further £20.12. Thus a total state pension of £57.42 is to be added to the company £66 giving a pension income of £123.42. This amounts to 123 per cent of previous gross earnings and 165 per cent of previous take-home pay. He would thus bring home as pensioner £48 more than pre-retirement.

It is these proportions that make the tax-effect so important in the relation between pension and tax systems: taxes reduce gross income to a net level whilst pensions are calculated with regard to that previous gross figure, in both state and private formulae. At the next stage, however, we have to note the impact of taxes upon these pension benefits – singly and in combination.

Pensions and age relief

Income received in old age is treated differently from income received earlier in life. The boundary line is precise – age sixty-five for both men and women – and is not related to any notion of retirement. (This clarity of vision within the tax system contrasts with the social security system whose boundary lines combine age, retirement and marital status and where the employee's obligation to make national insurance contributions ceases at sixty for women and sixty-five for men whilst the employer's liability continues.)

From the sixty-fifth birthday, there are higher rates of personal allowance and an exceptional system of 'marginal rates'. (Before 1979 there was, additionally, a higher exemption threshold before investment income surcharge became payable.) These components work to ease the tax liabilities of the aged and particularly of pensioners. For those who continue in employment beyond pension age the income tax concessions can be of considerable value, although this is not to suggest that they are particularly influential in encouraging or discouraging employment beyond age sixty-five.

Further, the man who works beyond the age of sixty-five (or woman beyond sixty) will experience a weekly saving of at least 6.5 per cent of income or 4 per cent if previously contracted-out (the contracting-out option ceases at state pension age) as a result of their having no liability for national insurance contributions beyond this age. They will still gain increments to pensions by deferring retirement. In addition, the age allowance will increase their tax threshold and thus decrease the average rate of tax on income they continue to earn. The age allowance for the tax year 1979/80 exceeded the normal single and married person's rate by £375 and £640 respectively. Thus a married man with a pre- and post-retirement income of £5000 per annum would enjoy a combined tax and national insurance contribution saving at age sixty-five of £517, an extra income of £9.94 per week. The level of the post-retirement tax threshold will go a long way to determine the received value of pension benefits.

Age relief and company pensions

One further 'complication' arises from the fact that many of the more generous occupational schemes display their largesse (at least for men) by way of an earlier retirement age, often at age sixty (the minimum age that the Inland Revenue will approve) and in so doing generate some interesting circumstances.

The occupational pension scheme normally incorporates a retirement condition which involves retirement from that particular company.* This of course does not mean that the individuals concerned have to cease work altogether. They might cease work for a Company A on the Friday – collect their company pension and lump sum included – and then start work for Company B on the following Monday. The combined income of lump sum, pension and new salary will make for an affluent year. A woman may also lay claim to her state retirement pension from that same date.

Age relief is such that it will be of no help to the company pensioner retiring at age sixty or who continues in employment beyond this age: it is only available as noted, for men and women, aged sixty-five. Thus, the tax system, operating at the usual rates over the years sixty to sixty-five, gives a lower 'take-home' return to the pensioner than an equivalent income received after age sixty-five. Those trying to plan a reasonably *even* income flow over the years from sixty onwards will need a higher gross income in the years sixty to sixty-five because of this effect. The search may be on for pensions which are not constant (disregarding up-ratings). Men with retirement at sixty may want high incomes from the company scheme from age sixty to sixty-five and then, with the arrival of the state retirement pension at sixty-five, could accept correspondingly less from the company for the remaining years of their lives. The Inland Revenue has recently been changing its rules to accommodate this type of scheme.

The earnings rule as tax system

For the working pensioner, who has formally 'retired' there is a secondary tax system. In order to receive the state pension the 65-year-old

---

* Under a recent arrangement negotiated by postal workers, the employee can reach age sixty, collect the occupational pension *and* continue in the full-time employ of the Post Office. Civil Servants at 60 can draw any accrued lump sum and continue work: any lump sum balance is payable at eventual retirement. The current extent of such occupational 'non-retirement' options is not known to the author.

male or 60-year-old female must indicate that they have 'retired' but this does not mean 'ceasing to work'. Essentially, it means that the 65-year-old male has to limit his earnings in order to receive the pension at full value. Beyond a certain level (currently at £52 per week) the pension starts to be reduced, first by 50p in the pound and then pound for pound. At current rates the single person's pension of £23.30 would thus be eliminated entirely if their earnings rose to £77 per week.* At this income level the pensioner would be well over the tax threshold and would need to consider the net income resulting from any aggregation of pension and earnings. With earnings prospects at or near this level it may pay not to 'retire', as by working they will earn increments to their state pension through deferment. Furthermore, age relief will reduce taxes and no national insurance contribution will be payable, so the calculation of economic break-even points – allowing for the risk of death – demands rather fine judgement. There will be an even more dramatic shift at age seventy (sixty-five for women) when the earnings-rule/retirement condition is withdrawn and the pension becomes payable regardless of continuing income or employment. The working 71-year-old male can receive a full pension, plus wages limited only by his capacity to earn. All will be potentially taxable depending on their aggregate level, but it certainly seems legitimate to extend our conception of 'tax systems' to cover devices like the earnings-rule, devices which only apply to State pensions.

Taxation and Public Sector Pensions

The significance of tax systems in the development of public sector schemes – the extent to which their peculiar forms of finance have been developed with at least one eye on the tax liabilities of government as employer – deserve more attention than they will receive here.

The major link between taxation and the public sector unfunded schemes (and the 'funded' schemes in so far as they are but notionally funded) is an obvious one. Tax revenues provide the income out of which both the wage and pension benefits of public sector employees are paid. We need to distinguish here between the public sector scheme for, say, electricity workers (a public corporation where there

---

* The earnings which are taken into account are not full gross earnings; certain factors are offset and these mean that typically earnings in excess of £85 per week would be needed to eliminate the pension.

is a saleable product and where wage or pension can be financed from trading income) and service sectors such as the Civil Service *per se* or teachers or doctors. The school teacher as public employee has a contributory pension scheme with contributions from the employer (the local authority). Taxes (from many sources) finance teachers' salaries and likewise the employers' superannuation contribution. The employee's contribution is tax deductible as for a private sector scheme. The employer enjoys 'tax exemption' although this is primarily attributable to the fact that the local authority is a 'non-taxable' agency. Our main interest here is with *tax* as the *employer's* income source – taxes which include (in the case of the local authority) receipts such as charges, rents and rates, and then central government grants derived from the full range of tax revenue sources (income, capital, excise, VAT, corporation, and so on). This special feature of the public schemes, where the employer's input is tax-derived, adds particular importance to the distributional effects. The distributive incidence of pensions will derive in part from the pool from which the pension scheme is financed. Where all or part of the scheme is effectively Pay-As-You-Go (from government's perspective) then it is the incidence of the taxes which are used to pay for the pension (in the year in which the pension is paid) which will contribute to these distributional effects.

Inputs and Outcomes: Which is Best to Tax?

If the inputs to pension schemes are normally non-taxable, then at least benefits seem prone to taxation. To tax the income from which savings are made would, if we were also to tax its products, be deemed an example of that unmentionable 'double taxation'. However, this 'infamous' practice is of course the norm for other forms of savings and applies most conspicuously to state pensions. However, we might usefully comment on considerations of whether to tax 'at one end or the other'. The very notion of a trade-off between taxing yesterday's contributions and today's benefits is rife with problems. Not least, we *know* about today's taxes, but none of the assumptions about future taxes are assured.

From the perspective of the Exchequer's tax receipts, to relieve tax on a £5 contribution may make sense if it will one day realise (via fund earnings) a taxable £25 pension benefit. (On the other hand, we currently deliberately ignore this *investment* income element, taxing

the entire product as if it were indeed deferred pay.) We have already
referred to one very conspicuous 'exempt' benefit – the lump sum
at retirement. Another 'delayed exemption' arises because of age relief.
Thus we are not dealing in precise before and after equivalents: the
£1 contribution may have 'avoided' tax at a certain rate;
subsequently, due to age relief it may avoid tax altogether or only
attract tax at a much lower rate.

Further, we have to allow for the simple passage of time between
'non-payment' in the past and the subsequent demand for taxes on
the realised income. There are two considerations here: one relates
to changes in the value of money over the years, the other to changes
in the tax system itself. To consider the latter first; it is probable that
over the life span of a pension scheme (at least fifty years) there will
be changes in tax legislation. Such changes could modify the tax treatment of pension benefits in unpredictable directions. The light taxes
of a previous contributory period may be more than offset by proportionately higher taxes when retirement is reached: alternatively,
the high taxes of youth might be recompensed by the total abolition
of taxes for the elderly.

Inflation has a dual potential: it changes the value of money received and taxes paid (or not paid) over time; it is unlikely that these
changes will be proportionate one to another. Further, unless tax
thresholds have kept pace with economic change incomes may have
become more or less subject to taxation via fiscal drag. Such a 'delay
mechanism', again relative to the contributory period, may make incomes received in later years less valuable (expressed in cash terms)
simply because they will be taxed more.

At very least, we can argue that the notion of foregoing taxes now,
on the assumption that they will be recouped later, is of dubious
credibility. Worlds change and so do taxes. The argument implies
a stable order unlikely in practice to span such periods of time. And
we must also note one other important characteristic of this situation:
'save now pay later' policies will heavily favour funded pension
schemes, effectively discriminating against PAYG systems: in the latter
we must pay now (from taxed income) for the (taxable) benefits of
others.

Taxation and the Exchequer Contribution
The state retirement pension is financed from several sources. The

national insurance contributions of the current workforce pre-
dominate (the employed and self-employed and employers), but a
substantial addition comes direct from the Exchequer. The Exchequer
contribution is fixed at 18 per cent of 'reckonable' contribution income.
This comprises both the actual contribution income received and an
amount equal to the contributions foregone as a result of contracting-
out: that is, 18 per cent of all the contributions that would have been
received if there were no contracting-out.

The taxes from which this Exchequer contribution is derived are
general – income, corporation, VAT, customs and excise duties,
capital transfer taxes, and so on – across the full range of government
tax sources. From our perspective there are two main points to note.
First, there is a general problem of describing the incidence of this
mixed bag of taxes – and thus the extent to which they can be presumed as progressive or regressive in aggregate. The evidence and
the limitations of that evidence have been considered in Chapters
2 and 3 of this book.

Pensions generally are not particularly beneficent redistributors.
The poor tend to start paying for them earlier in their lives and then
die younger (36 per cent of unskilled male manual workers are dead
before pension age). Thus, although the tax-derived Exchequer contribution has the potential to make a positively redistributive contribution to pension finance, its impact will be moderated by the simple
differentiating facts of mortality.

The second point, which further complicates these redistributive
analyses, relates to the contracting-out factor. Given the scale of contracting-out (some 10 million scheme members and their employers),
then the Exchequer contribution, calculated as described earlier, is
increased in relation to the actual level of contributory income received.

Taxes and Inflation-proofing

The inflation-proofing of pensions must, where it occurs, be one of
the most significant developments in pensions in recent years. It exists
as a statutory obligation in the new state scheme (although its basis
is not immutable as recently shown in proposals to change the index).
It is also similarly obligatory under the Pensions (Increases) Act 1971
which covers most of the public sector pension schemes. The private
schemes are affected in two ways. The contracted-out schemes will

provide a pension at least equivalent to the state scheme's additional component, what is known as the *guaranteed minimum pension*, (GMP). Once it is actually in payment this sum will be inflation-proofed by the state scheme. As to any 'excess' company pension entitlement (beyond the GMP) then its value post-retirement is not guaranteed beyond the promises and capacity of that particular company scheme. Finally, schemes (whether company or individual) which are not con-tracted-out are under no obligation to maintain the value of benefits once in payment.

There is one further point at which inflation-proofing can arise which must be explained before we can turn to consider the relevance of taxation to this whole issue. This occurs, as happens and obviously will continue to happen, when people *change* jobs and leave a particular company pension scheme. Again, if the scheme is contracted-out then, with some exceptions, the GMPs must be preserved – either by transferring them to a new employer (uncommon) or by buying the employee back into the state scheme (rather more common) or by preserving the pension benefits earned to date and holding them until retirement age (the most common procedure). Where benefits are pre-served in this way the company scheme must maintain their value up to the point of retirement, the state then taking over the inflation-proofing of the benefits once in payment.

The buy-back arrangement (by means of 'contribution equivalent premiums') is the most costly format from the perspective of the state. Having 'relieved' the contracted-out contributions (at, say, 30 per cent) they are now being received by the state scheme (with no reclamation of tax relief) at face value, despite any inflation in the interim years: in other words, 'contributions foregone' are now 're-paid' at their original face value. (The same phenomenon has been observed in recent years with the buy-back of pension rights under the 1961–75 graduated pension scheme; a buy-back at 1961 prices.) The costs of this arrangement are presumably met from the general income of the national insurance scheme (those contracted-in and -out) and the Exchequer contribution.

But the major inflation-proofing cost obviously arises post-retire-ment. What part do 'taxes' play in meeting these costs? The question is extremely difficult to answer and, in one sense, because the current scheme is only just coming into operation, any answer must be some-what speculative. Essentially, the state is meeting all the post-retire-ment costs of inflation-proofing both state pensions and contracted-out pensions up to guaranteed minimum pension level. But what source of income is it using to do so? Since the entire scheme of state pensions is run on a Pay-As-You-Go basis then the state must ultimately use current or future revenues to pay for current or future liabilities. The state has already 'foregone' taxes on the contributions and investments of the contracted-out schemes and their funded components: now it has to meet the liability for preserving their benefit values from *either* national insurance contributions (levied on the 'current' workforce – i.e. those who are working when pensions are paid out) or current general taxes, or both. Of course, in determining the contracting-out fraction – the amount by which contribution to the state scheme would be reduced in return for the scheme accepting liability for the pension benefit *per se* – this factor may have been taken into account. In other words, the contracted-out contribution is actually higher than would have been necessary if the state were not promising this inflation-proofing at the end of the day. However, this kind of 'equity' (where the contracted-out pay more than is strictly necessary – an argument made nonsensical when we acknowledge the effects of tax relief on their contributions – in order to 'cover' them for future inflation-proofing) is decidedly hard to pin down. The 'concession' or 'surcharge' is made on one generation; its costs/benefits are picked up by another. In practice, it seems that the costs of inflation-proofing are going to be borne by future generations of taxpayers. For good or ill, Pay-As-You-Go will be matched by Taxed-As-Someone-Might-Be. From a policy perspective the interest will be in who will bear those costs: nothing in the current pension formulae of the state scheme or its pension partners makes this predetermined.

Conclusion: The Reluctance to Change

Much of this argument has been designed to demonstrate the intimacy of the tax–pension relationship, particularly that between fiscal and occupational welfare systems. If much of the current viability of funded pensions hinges on their fiscal treatment, then it seems likely that governments will be most reluctant to make changes which in any sense threaten their position. Since their prosperity and viability are by no means uniform, this probably means ensuring that even the most weak and most precarious are not endangered. 'Partnerships' add to this reluctance.

A commitment to current practices and their continuity seems a dangerous handicap in a society in which changes *will* be needed. Current fiscal policy in the field of pensions tends to underwrite inequities, effects little if any redistribution and persistently rewards private acts whilst 'punishing' public behaviour.

Further Reading

Field, F., Meacher, M. and Pond, C. 1977, *To Him Who Hath: a study of poverty and taxation*, Harmondsworth, Penguin Books.

Government Actuary's Department 1978. *Occupational Pension Schemes 1975*, London, HMSO.

'Pensions and Company Finance' 1970, *Journal of the Institute of Actuaries*, vol. 96, pt II no. 404, September.

Reddin, M. 1976, 'National insurance and private pensions' in K. Jones, M. Brown and S. Baldwin (eds), *Yearbook of Social Policy 1976*, London, Routledge & Kegan Paul.

Williams, D. M. 1978, 'National insurance contributions – a second income tax', *British Tax Review*, no. 2.

8 Taxation, Women and the Family
Ruth Lister

'In marriage, husband and wife are one person, and that person is the husband'*

In this chapter we deal with two main issues: the treatment of married women in the tax system, which involves the question of what the tax unit should be, and the treatment of families with children. Linking the two is the critical question of the distribution of resources through the taxation and child support systems.

The Present Tax Treatment of Married Couples

Under Section 37 of the Income and Corporation Taxes Act 1970, 'a woman's income chargeable to tax shall . . . be deemed for income tax purposes to be (her husband's) income and not to be her income'. Thus a husband is responsible for his wife's tax affairs and his wife's income is aggregated with his when calculating the family's tax liability. In essence, not much has changed since the 1918 Taxes Act which defined married women as 'incapacitated persons' along with infants, lunatics, idiots and insane persons.

Since the end of the First World War, married men have received an additional married man's tax allowance, (MMA) which is paid regardless of whether their wives are also in paid employment and thus eligible for wife's earned income relief (EIR). EIR, which can be set against earned income only, has been the same level as the single personal allowance (SPA) since the end of the Second World War. The MMA is for *married* men; it cannot be claimed for a cohabitee as such. One of the more glaring anomalies of the present system is that, where the wife is the sole breadwinner, her husband can transfer his tax allowance to her so that she can set both the MMA and the EIR against her earnings, though this is often difficult to do in practice.

* Blackstone, T. 'Commentaries on the laws of England', quoted in EOC 1979.

There are two ways under present tax laws in which the effects of this unequal tax structure can be mitigated. Since 1971 it has been possible to opt for separate taxation of earned income, known as the wife's earned income election. The application must be made by both partners, who then each receive a single person's allowance and are taxed as individuals for earned income purposes. However, the wife's earned income election is not for the masses, since a couple whose combined income did not bring them into the higher tax brackets would lose money if they opted for separate taxation. Little more than 2 per cent of taxpayers were subject to the higher rates in 1979/80. The other possibility, separate assessment, can be applied for by either partner. In the words of the Inland Revenue leaflet:

> Separate assessment makes no difference to the total tax charged on the couple's income or to the total amount of the personal reliefs allowed to a married couple. Its effect is simply to divide both the tax bill and the allowances in proportion to their incomes, so that each individual is responsible for his or her own share of the tax. (Inland Revenue 1978)

Separate assessment is still very much the exception to the rule; it is complicated and expensive to administer and only 3 per cent of married women currently choose it (WNACCP/1979). This may be due to the lack of publicity for separate assessment and also the apparent reluctance of some local tax offices to implement it.

The 1978 Finance Act made some concessions to the growing demands for equal treatment of married women in the tax system. Tax rebates will now be paid direct to a married woman, except where she is assessed under schedule D or where there is liability for higher-rate tax on the couple's joint income; some of the discriminatory aspects of the minor tax allowances have been removed; and the Inland Revenue will reply direct to a married woman who has written to them, instead of to her husband as previously. Sir Geoffrey Howe has since announced that he intends to make two further changes. Under the first, the Inland Revenue will now write direct to a married woman about her tax affairs, whether or not she has first written to them. The second affects 'the excessive basic-rate adjustment' which, in the past, has meant a reduction in the wife's coding where a couple's joint earnings attract higher-rate tax. In future, the husband's coding will be reduced unless the wife's earnings are expected to be greater than the husband's or the couple prefer the reduction to be made in the wife's coding.

These changes, while welcome, leave unscathed the more fundamental sex discrimination which underpins the whole tax system. The
fact remains that a married woman is presumed not to exist as an
independent entity and that equal pay does not yet mean equal *take-
home* pay. A married woman earning the same as a married man takes
home £4.44 a week less than him (assuming they are both standard-
rate taxpayers). As the Equal Opportunities Commission has noted:
'The aim of seeking to improve women's position in relation to pay will
be continually thwarted if the pay that they take home is eaten into by
a discriminatory taxation system' (EOC 1979, p. 2).

Underlying the treatment of married women is a set of assumptions
about women and the family. These can best be understood by
separating out the principle of aggregation of income from the fact
that, when aggregated, it is treated as the husband's and that, in
addition, husbands are entitled to an extra tax allowance. The
rationale for the aggregation of income is explained in an OECD
report, which, in noting that every tax system has to decide on the
relationship between the tax paid by single and married taxpayers at
the same level of income, commented:

> For a long time, the major criterion for deciding on this point
> involved taking as a reference base the income level required to meet
> necessary expenditures and, so the argument usually ran, as married
> couples enjoy certain 'economies of scale', the non-discretionary
> income which they require is less than twice that of a single person
> with a similar pre-tax income. The logic of this position entails
> considering that the members of a family effectively pool their
> incomes and consider their expenditures as being met out of a
> common budget. (OECD 1977, para. 56)

The assumption underlying the treatment of the aggregated income
as the husband's is spelt out in the Meade Report: 'the idea that a
woman on marriage becomes a dependant of her husband, who is then
responsible for her welfare and for that of the family accounts for much
of the present treatment of the tax unit' (Meade 1978, p. 377). The
MMA was introduced partly for fear that aggregation of income
would otherwise act as a disincentive to marriage. But Hilary Land
(undated) has argued that the stronger reason appears to have been
that which was put forward again over fifty years later in the context of
the tax credits debate: 'a man with a wife to support has clearly a lower
capacity to pay tax than a single man'. In the words of the EOC, 'there
are few areas where Whitehall has clung so tenaciously to the

assumptions of the Victorian era' (EOC, 1977, p. 4). In fact, the same applies to the social security scheme which is also riddled with assumptions about the dependent status of married women. It is a source of anger to many that, because the government is exempt from the requirements of the Sex Discrimination Act, sex discrimination in the social security and tax systems can continue. Moreover, the Treasury does not even appear to recognise that the tax system flouts the spirit of the SDA. In correspondence, it has argued that 'we fully support the spirit of the Sex Discrimination Act and our view is that these rules do not generally discriminate between people on grounds of sex' (EOC 1979).

Returning to the real world of the Elizabethan era, the Meade Report commented that

> this notion of dependency of the woman on the man does in fact correspond with reality in many of the older married couples, where the wife, having from the start of the marriage stayed at home to care for the family and to bring up the children, has only a limited possibility of supporting herself at a later date by her own earnings. On the other hand, the notion is becoming less and less compatible with modern attitudes to the relationship between men and women, and in fact corresponds less and less closely with reality when an increasing number of married women work in paid occupations. (Meade 1978, p. 377)

The reality indeed is that the economic activity rate for married women has more than doubled in the last twenty-five years. It is now estimated to be over 50 per cent and Department of Employment projections for 1986 set it at 55 per cent. Even among the older age groups the pattern is changing and the highest activity rate is among women aged thirty-five to fifty-four of whom seven in ten are economically active. As the Department of Employment has noted: 'it is now normal for married women to work, and withdrawal from the labour market and return to it is the general pattern' (1975, pp. 2–3). Although, not surprisingly, the rates are lowest during the child-bearing years, even here growing numbers of mothers are taking paid employment. Between 1961 and 1971 the employment rate of mothers with pre-school children increased by 63 per cent. By 1976, a quarter of mothers with pre-school children were in employment and OPCS surveys suggest the proportion would be higher if better childcare facilities were available. It is true that most employed married women with children work part-time, particularly if the children are young.

Nevertheless, the great majority of them work between sixteen and thirty hours a week and there is enough accumulated evidence to puncture the myth that their earnings are no more than 'pin money' (EOC 1977; Hurstfield 1978).

The assumption that incomes are effectively pooled within the family is also open to question. What evidence there is suggests that the husband's income is not always shared fairly with the rest of the family so that his income is not necessarily a reliable indicator of the income available to the family as a whole (EOC 1977). The common-budget argument is no more valid for married couples than for any other type of household that may have a common budget. Many people reduce overheads by sharing accommodation and other expenses.

In effect, the state is imposing, through the tax system, one particular model of family life on families. It is a model which ignores the 'attitude, becoming increasingly accepted that men and women have a right to be considered as independent persons *vis-à-vis* the fiscal authorities', and, as the OECD report argued, they 'therefore should not be forced to adopt any particular attitude towards their habit of earning and spending even if, in practice, they do follow a unitary approach to them' (OECD 1977, para. 56).

Dissatisfaction with the tax treatment of married women is not new. Back in 1910, George Bernard Shaw was battling with the tax-man to whom he wrote the following letter:

I have absolutely no means of ascertaining my wife's income except by asking her for the information. Her property is a separate property. She keeps a separate banking account at a separate bank. Her solicitor is not my solicitor. I can make a guess at her means from her style of living, exactly as the Surveyor of Income Tax does when he makes a shot at an assessment in the absence of exact information; but beyond that I have no more knowledge of her income than I have of yours. I have therefore asked her to give me a statement. She refuses, on principle. As far as I know, I have no legal means of compelling her to make any such disclosure; and if I had, it does not follow that I am bound to incur law costs to obtain information which is required not by myself but by the State. Clearly, however, it is within the power of the Commissioners to compel my wife to make a full disclosure of her income for the purposes of taxation; but equally clearly they must not communicate that disclosure to me or to any other person. It seems to me under these circumstances that all I can do for you is to tell you who my wife is and leave it to you to ascertain her income and make me pay the tax on it. Even this you cannot do without a violation of

secrecy as it will be possible for me by a simple calculation to
ascertain my wife's income from your demand. (Quoted in the
Sunday Times (1978) with acknowledgement to the Society of
Authors on behalf of the Bernard Shaw Estate.)

The result of this letter was that the government accepted separate
filings and billed Shaw for any shortage.

More recently, articles in the *Sunday Times* and *Woman's Own*
resulted in 30 000 and 6500 people respectively registering their
protest against the current tax laws and, of over 2000 responses to an
EOC discussion paper, only 15 defended the status quo. The responses
presented 'a formidable dossier of dissatisfaction' (EOC 1979, p. 4),
which should help to persuade a sceptical Treasury that there really is
a strong desire for change. Sir Geoffrey Howe certainly appeared to be
convinced when, in the debate on the 1978 Finance Bill (before he
became Chancellor) he attacked the changes initiated by the Labour
government as 'cosmetic' and as 'a less than adequate response to the
growing chorus of dissent at the way the present tax system operates
between the sexes' (Hansard 1978b). Yet, so far, he has merely
announced more cosmetics (see p. 136), with the promise of a Green
Paper in 1980, which was accompanied by the ominous warning that
'radical changes should not be made in haste' (Hansard, 1980).

The Options for Change

This Green Paper was originally promised by the last government and
its subject was to be the tax treatment of the family including personal
tax allowances and the principle of aggregation. The key question the
Green Paper will have to tackle is: what should be the tax unit – the
individual or the couple? The Meade Report set out a number of
criteria, recognising that they are not all compatible:

1. The decision to marry or not to marry should not be affected by
   tax considerations.
2. Families with the same joint resources should be taxed equally.
3. The incentive for a member of the family to earn should not be
   blunted by tax considerations which depend upon the economic position of other members of the family.
4. Economic and financial arrangements within the family (e.g.
   as regards the ownership of property) should not be dominated
   by sophisticated tax considerations.
5. The tax system should be fair between families which rely upon
   earnings and families which enjoy investment income.

6. Two persons living together and sharing household expenditures can live more cheaply and therefore have a greater taxable capacity than two single persons living separately.
7. The choice of tax unit should not be excessively costly in loss of tax revenue.
8. The arrangements involved should be reasonably simple for the taxpayer to understand and for the tax authorities to administer (Meade 1978, p. 377)

As Meade notes: 'the treatment of the tax unit must inevitably be a matter of compromise between a number of conflicting considerations' and 'the choice of tax unit treatment thus depends to an exceptionally high degree on the relative weights which are set on the conflicting objectives' (Meade 1978, pp. 377 and 395). What Meade perhaps underestimated was the degree to which the choice is bound up with ideological and personal considerations so that the opposition to any change among some men, who feel threatened by the idea of women being treated as independent individuals, is likely to be considerable. The relative weights given to the conflicting objectives may also differ with regard to earned and unearned income.

The Meade Committee itself came down clearly in favour of individual taxation of earned income. The response to the EOC discussion paper revealed 'a marked preference for a revised system which would have the individual as the basic tax unit' (EOC 1979, p. 34) for earned income purposes. Similarly, a report by a Conservative Party committee on Women and Tax argued that 'it is essential to make women a "separate entity" for tax purposes' (WNACCP 1979, p. 7). The case was well put by Lord Houghton who, in relation to the principle of the aggregation of income, argued

> This is really what we want to destroy. It will have to be done in taxation. It will have to be done in social security, if women are to have their separate personalities, their separate dignity and their separate economic resources. (Hansard, 1978a)

A change to individual taxation of earned income would be in line with the general trend in OECD countries. By 1977, individual taxation was allowable in seventeen member countries and compulsory, at least for some income groups, in thirteen. Before the late 1960s, only three member countries had compulsory individual taxation.

There is rather less consensus on the question of unearned income. On the one hand, the desire to treat married women as independent requires the disaggregation of all income; on the other, it would encourage wealthier couples to divide up their unearned income so as to reduce their tax bill, and could mean a considerable loss of revenue. The Meade Committee did not appear to know its own mind on the issue. At one point it appears to favour individual taxation of unearned income with the proviso that personal tax allowances should be set against earned income only. In order to protect the less well off who depend on unearned income, it suggests that those aged over forty or so could continue to set personal allowances against unearned income. (A more discriminating way of protecting the more vulnerable would be to combine a higher age limit with special provision for groups such as widows and lone parents.) At another point, Meade seems to suggest that unearned income should continue to be aggregated and that it should be treated as the income of the principal earner (or alternatively be divided up according to the principles of separate assessment). But if unearned income continued to be aggregated it would not meet one of the main objections to the current system, which is that it does not permit women to keep their financial affairs private from their husbands. Some of the letters received by the EOC revealed the misery that this can cause. One woman, for example, wrote:

> I have had a Post Office Investment Account since 1971 and have saved my own money, and never told my husband, because I wanted to feel I could help my family, i.e. my daughter setting up home, and feel independent.
> When I withdrew the whole amount, the interest was calculated and (the information) sent to the tax office.
> They immediately wrote to my husband, and told him he had omitted something from his return and he was very cross – told them he had declared everything. Eventually they wrote and told him about my interest. *I was not consulted* by the tax office.
> This has absolutely upset my marriage of many years. Cannot a woman have a little cash to call her own, without upsetting a marriage and causing a lot of misery?

Another possibility that has been canvassed is that unearned income should be disaggregated but that capital transfer and gains taxes should be applied to inter-spouse transfers so as to mitigate the effects on revenue of income-splitting. There is clearly no easy solution to the question of how unearned income should be treated. Nevertheless, the issue cannot be ignored and the Green Paper should consider all the possible options.

The other main question to be resolved is the future of the MMA.

Although the MMA fell in value relative to the SPA from the mid 1950s until the early 1970s, in recent years the difference between the two has widened from 23 per cent in 1972–4 to 36 per cent in 1978–81. Criticism of the MMA is centring both on the fact that it is the married *man's* allowance and on the tax advantage it gives to married couples. As long ago as 1955, the Royal Commission of Taxation of Incomes and Profits argued that 'the position under which the husband retains the full married allowance although the single allowance is given to the wife in addition, is difficult to defend either on grounds of logic or of taxation principle' (Land 1976). And, of course, this is the position for far more couples today than it was in 1955. In 1959–60, there were 4 450 000 couples in which the wife received EIR; by 1976–77, the number had increased to 7 040 000 (Hansard 1979b). However, the questioning goes deeper than that today. Why, it is asked, should other taxpayers subsidise those who choose to marry? And, it is a very expensive subsidy which in 1979–80 cost the community about £2500 million in lost revenue (Hansard 1979a).

The EOC reported that the reponse to its document 'indicated very decisively that there was little or no support for retaining the MMA on the present basis. The demands were mainly directed at adequate support for those who were dependent due to home responsibilities and those who were being cared for.' It argued that 'reforms should therefore be based on a completely different concept of need which is related to family responsibilities and not simply to marriage' (EOC 1979, p. 21). But, although there has emerged a remarkable degree of consensus in favour of the abolition of the MMA, opinion is divided as to what should take its place beyond the broad agreement that each individual should have a 'unisex' personal tax allowance.

The EOCs original document outlined three broad options, and a number of variations of each. These were: (i) separate taxation using the savings from the abolition of the MMA to improve personal tax allowances and tax allowances for the care of dependants; (ii) joint taxation but with one SPA available to each partner to be claimed against either income; and (iii) separate taxation using the savings from the abolition of the MMA to improve cash benefits for dependants, possibly combined with tax allowances for care of dependants. Two main points of conflict have emerged: the question of whether the savings from the abolition of the MMA should be channelled into tax allowances or cash benefits and the treatment of one-earner couples.

It is the latter issue which has caused the most deep-rooted divisions, although, oddly enough, it is not highlighted in the EOC's report on the response to its discussion paper. The conflict has centred on whether the SPA should be transferable between partners where only one of them has a taxable income. The main proponents of transferability are members of the Conservative Party. In their report the Women and Tax Committee stated that, while they wanted women to be treated as independent, they wished 'at the same time, to encourage and support the family. In particular we wish to end the discrimination which at present exists against the married woman who stays at home, either because she is engaged in caring for a family, or dependent relatives, or simply because she prefers to do so' (WNACCP, 1979, p. 6). Similarly, Sir Geoffrey Howe has argued that transferable tax allowances would mean that 'the role of the spouse who stayed at home would be given equal value with the role of the spouse who went to work, so that the tax system would be neutral' (Hansard 1979c).

But is that really neutrality? As the Women and Tax Committee recognised, it would create a very real disincentive for the partner who stays at home to take up paid employment. However, the Committee dismisses this problem with the extraordinary statement that 'this situation could be an incentive to married women to obtain realistic wages' (WNACCP, 1979, p. 9). An argument that is often put forward to justify a transferable tax allowance where there are no children or other dependants in need of care but where the woman stays at home 'simply because she prefers to do so', is that married women who stay at home do important voluntary work in the community. It must be questionable, though, whether extra tax relief for their husbands is the most appropriate means of rewarding such voluntary work. In fact, Conservative thinking on this question reflects a degree of double standards applied to women and men. For a married woman to stay at home with no incentive to work, partly at the taxpayer's expense, is all right; whereas it is regarded as intolerable that an unemployed man might, even potentially, be in this position.

The Women and Tax Committee's proposals, which would mean a transferable allowance set half-way between the current MMA and SPA, would also be extremely expensive. Paul Lewis (1979) of the National Council for One Parent Families had estimated that they would cost over £3 billion. Even if the tax allowances were set at a lower rate, it would be a very wasteful use of resources, which would, as now, be related to marriage rather than to need arising from family responsibilities. (It would also be expensive in administrative terms for it could mean frequent changes to one partner's tax code if the other partner were in and out of paid employment. However, the Treasury is considering ways of avoiding this problem through the adoption of a partially transferable tax allowance.) And, leaving aside the questionable case for subsidising one-earner couples without home responsibilities, there is the question of whether tax allowances are the most appropriate means of helping families where one partner stays at home because there are children or other dependants in need of care. This brings us to the other source of controversy: the relative merits of tax allowances and cash benefits. Response to the EOC document was divided on this issue, with a narrow majority in favour of cash benefits. The case for tax allowances does not appear to have been spelt out anywhere by its proponents. The case for cash benefits has been argued on two main grounds: they help the very poorest below the tax threshold whereas tax allowances are of most help to those paying higher tax rates; and they give the help direct to the person with the care of the dependants and thus can help to redistribute resources more fairly within the family.

The main alternative strategy to the transferable SPA proposed by the Conservatives is based on shifting resources into cash benefits. It has been favoured by, among others, the Meade Committee (1978), the Child Poverty Action Group (Tunnard 1978) and the National Council for Civil Liberties (EOC 1979). The key principles of such a strategy are that the individual SPAs should not be transferable between partners and that some of the resources saved by abolishing the MMA should be used to improve child benefits and possibly, also, to introduce what Meade has called a 'home responsibility benefit'. This Meade suggests, should be paid to all 'those who have children or other dependants needing home care' (Meade 1978, p. 294) whether or not one partner was at home full-time. The benefit would be taxable so that couples where both parents were in employment would receive less than where one stayed at home. The alternative of paying it only where one partner stayed at home would create yet another 'poverty trap', would be vulnerable to abuse, would ignore the expenses involved when two partners with dependants go out to work and could have the effect of locking married women back into the home (an issue to which we return later). The home responsibility benefit could be paid as an addition to the child benefit paid for the oldest child and as an improved invalid-care allowance. There could also be higher rates for lone parents and those with pre-school children.

If the money saved by abolishing the MMA were used to increase child benefits, the latter could be doubled at a stroke. However, although we shall argue below that such a shift of resources would be totally justified, the loss to the 6-million-odd married taxpayers without children would probably not be politically acceptable. Thus it would probably be necessary to phase out the MMA gradually, and the easiest time to do this would be when taxes were being cut anyway. Similarly, there might have to be special transitional provisions to protect those older couples where the wife has been out of the labour market for most of her married life. However, as the economic activity rate for older women is increasing, this is likely to be only a fairly short-term problem.

The abolition of the MMA would also have implications for one-parent families, 425 000 of whom receive an additional personal allowance which provides them with the equivalent of the MMA. This additional allowance could be retained or, preferably, the money saved by abolishing it could be used to improve the child benefit addition paid for the first children of lone parents. (It is worth noting also that individual taxation would mean that separated wives would be in a much better position to deal with their tax affairs on the break-up of their marriage than they tend to be at present(Tunnard 1978).)

We have focused here on the future of the MMA. It should be noted, however, that the Treasury has been reported to be considering tackling the issue of the tax advantage enjoyed by married couples from the opposite direction. It has been suggested that its target will be the wife's earned income relief. If the government *did* cut the EIR it would be adding insult to injury by widening still further the gap between the take-home pay of married men and married women on the same wage or salary. (*Observer* 1979)

The Case for Redistributing Resources to those with Children
It is crucial that the opportunity provided by the abolition of the MMA to redistribute resources to those with children is not lost. (Although we concentrate here on those with children, there is also a strong case for a more generous invalid-care allowance, and for extending the allowance to married women.) There are three very powerful arguments for such a redistribution of resources. The first is

based on the concept of 'horizontal equity', which recognises that families with children need more money than the childless to achieve the same standard of living and that the community as a whole has a responsibility to the next generation to help families achieve a similar standard of living to those without children. In fact, during the post-war period we have moved further away from achieving horizontal equity rather than towards it. The table shows how child tax allowances had plummeted in value relative to the SPA by the time they began to be phased out under the child benefit scheme. As a result those with children have borne an increasingly large share of the total tax burden. Family allowances suffered even greater neglect during the same period and were worth less when abolished in 1977 than when they were introduced in 1946, at what was then accepted to be an inadequate level.

Child tax allowances as a percentage of the single personal allowance

	Under 11 (%)	11–16 (%)	16 and over (%)
1957/58	71.4	89.3	107.1
1976/77	41.0	46.0	50.0
(after clawback)	(34.0)	(38.5)	(42.5)

Child benefit has not yet made a significant impact on the horizontal distribution of income as between couples with and without children because it was largely financed by the withdrawal of CTAs. Child benefits are still worth less relative to average earnings than the combined level of family allowances and CTAs during most of the post-war period. The failure to increase child benefits in the 1979 Budget and to restore their real value in 1980 represented a further deterioration in the relative position of those with children.

The second argument for redistributing resources towards those with children is the growing incidence of child poverty. Increasingly poverty is to be found among families with children. Unfortunately, comparable figures are available only for the years 1974–7. These show that in 1974, 33 per cent of those living below supplementary benefit level were living in families with children; three years later the figure was 38 per cent. Nearly half a million children were living below SB level in 1977; three and a half million were living in families with incomes less than 40 per cent above SB level. The supplementary benefit level is by no means generous. In 1979/80 for a couple with two pre-school children it amounts to £40.10 a week after housing costs; 74p a day to meet all the needs of each child. Finally, more help for those with children not only means a shift of resources from one section of the population to another, it also represents a redistribution of resources over the lifetime of individuals from a time when their needs are lowest to the child-rearing years when they are greatest.

The move from tax allowances to cash benefits through the introduction of child benefits was widely welcomed. Now that the process has been completed, it is perhaps time to take stock. The treatment of child benefit in the 1979 and 1980 Budgets has given rise to the fear that families with children could lose out under the child benefit scheme because it is no longer open to a Chancellor of the Exchequer to help them through the system of personal tax allowances. If the government continues to treat child benefit as public expenditure and not as part of the tax system, these fears could well prove to be justified. Yet, when in Opposition the present Chancellor and Secretary of State for Social Services both promised they would 'treat increases in child benefit in the same way as reductions in taxation' (see Lister 1979). It is only through an increase in child benefits that the Chancellor can now protect or increase the amount of tax-free income available specifically to families with children. So long as the DHSS has to bid for increases in child benefit as part of the annual public expenditure exercise, the future of the child benefit scheme is likely to be in jeopardy. If the relative standard of living of those with children is to be maintained, let alone improved, it is crucial that child benefit is treated as part of the tax system (as members of the present government had promised). It is also crucial that the benefit should be index-linked in line with other benefits and with the main personal tax allowances. Otherwise it will simply repeat the dismal history of the family allowance scheme. First, though, there appears to be broad agreement among politicians of all parties, the DHSS, the TUC and groups such as CPAG that the immediate goal must be to raise child benefit to the level of child support provided for claimants of unemployment and sickness benefit. This would mean that the child additions to unemployment and sickness benefit could be subsumed by child benefit and it would increase the incomes of low-paid working families relative to those of families out of work.

Although attention is bound to focus on how to achieve this short-term goal, there are a number of other issues which need to be considered in the longer term. The two most important are the contradictory questions of whether more help should be channelled to those with pre-school children and whether the benefit should increase with age. The case for more help for those with pre-school children rests on the fact that this is the group most vulnerable to family poverty. As the Royal Commission on the Distribution of Income and Wealth's Report on Lower Incomes made clear, many families escape poverty only because of the presence of two wages. Although the proportion of mothers of pre-school children who go out to work is growing, it is still only a minority and they work for fewer hours on average than other women. Extra help could be given to families with pre-school children through the child benefit scheme or through some kind of home responsibility benefit as proposed by Meade (see p. 145). There has also been a growing demand recently for tax relief for childcare expenses. Although this would certainly help working parents who incur childcare costs, it is debatable whether it would be the best way of helping parents. As we have already noted, tax allowances do not help the small minority of the very lowest paid below the tax threshold and are of greatest benefit to the wealthiest. There is also the danger that if tax relief were given for childcare expenses, it could undermine the campaign for adequate local authority childcare facilities.

Although parents of school-age children are more vulnerable because of their lower earning capacity, as every parent knows, a teenager costs much more to keep than a toddler. This fact was reflected to a certain extent in the CTAs and is reflected, though inadequately, in the supplementary benefits scheme. Should the child benefit not also be age-related? Age-related child benefits could, for instance, be combined with a home responsibility benefit which favoured those with pre-school children.

One question which is sometimes raised is whether the child benefit should be taxed. It is pointed out that child benefit is expensive and provides a tax-free supplement to the incomes of the rich as well as of the poor. Moreover, as noted in Chapter 4, a tax system is most equitable if *all* income is taxable. Although, in theory, the idea may sound sensible, in practice, there are many drawbacks. In the absence of a significant increase in the level of the tax threshold, the benefit would be taxed back from those on low incomes as well as those on high. Thus, unless the taxation of child benefit was part of a package which included a fairly substantial increase in the level of benefit, it would merely mean a further slide backwards in the relative position of families with children. Another problem would be that, under the present taxation system, taxing child benefits would mean that, by and large, husbands would be paying tax on a benefit received by their wives. In view of some politicians' fears in 1976 of possible male reaction to the switch from CTAs to child benefit, no government is likely to embark on such a course lightly. However, this problem would not arise under a system of individual taxation. On the other hand, the burden of the tax would be borne by working mothers many of whom could ill afford it. There is also the general presentational point made by David Piachaud (1979) that: 'most people would probably regard such a give-and-take operation as an absurd waste of time and money'. Certainly one of the most unpopular aspects of the family allowance was the tax and 'clawback'.

In the present context, the balance of argument would favour tackling the question of the vertical distribution of resources between rich and poor separately from that of the horizontal distribution between those with and without children. As Meade comments:

> there is an argument on grounds of horizontal equity for continuing their [child benefits] exemption from tax, in so far as such benefits are regarded not only as one means of setting a floor for the avoidance of poverty but also as a means of discriminating at all levels of income between the capacity to pay tax of families with and of families without children to support. In the context of a more progressive tax system, the case for taxing child benefits would, however, be much stronger than now. *Meade, 1978, p. 288.*

Conclusion: Taxation and Family Policy

'Taxation', argued the EOC, 'is an instrument of social policy ... the structure of personal taxation can, either deliberately or, more often, unwittingly, contribute to, or hinder progress towards equal opportunities for men and women' (EOC, 1978 p. 3). At present, the tax system clearly hinders progress towards equal opportunities for women. But as we have argued in this chapter, there is no guarantee that reform of the tax system will necessarily contribute to progress towards equal opportunities. The critical question that must be faced in the context of the development of both taxation policy and of a wider family policy is the relationship between family responsibilities and the economy which centres, in particular, on the role of women as mothers and carers. It is a question which has been tackled in Sweden where family policy has developed on the assumption that equal opportunities for women and men depend on providing the facilities to enable both mothers and fathers to combine family responsibilities with participation in the labour market. This stems from the recognition that there is no going back on the trend of increasing economic activity among married women.

So far, British policymakers do not appear to have accepted this fact. And it is no coincidence that at a time of high unemployment there is growing talk of encouraging mothers to stay at home. Underlying the proposals for transferable tax allowances is the Canute-like desire to reassert the position of women in the home in order 'to encourage and support the family'. Thus what may appear to some as rather abstruse arguments about the niceties of taxation policy are in fact reflections of very different ideological beliefs about the position of women in the family and society at large. It is important that, in the ensuing debate about taxation and the family, these fundamental questions of ideology are made explicit. From the point of view of those committed to equal opportunities for women, the danger is that those who see women's place in the home will win by default and that, under the guise of giving women equal rights in the tax system, an attempt will be made to shore up women's unequal position in society through a system of transferable tax allowances. The tragedy would be that resources, which could have effected a significant redistribution to those with the care of children and other dependants, will instead be channelled back into husbands' pay-packets.

References

Department of Employment 1975, *Women and Work: a review*, London, HMSO.
EOC (Equal Opportunities Commission) 1977, *Income Tax and Sex Discrimination*, London, EOC.
EOC 1979, *With All my Worldly Goods I Thee Endow . . . Except my Tax Allowances*, London, EOC.
Hansard 1978a, House of Lords Debates, 24 January, col. 317.
Hansard 1978b, House of Commons Debates, 12 July, col. 1265.
Hansard 1978c, House of Commons Debates, 12 July, col. 1267.
Hansard 1979a, House of Commons Debates, 5 July.
Hansard 1979b, House of Commons, 20 July, col. 871.
Hansard 1980, House of Commons Debates, 26 March, col. 1477.
Hurstfield, J. 1978, *The Part-time Trap*, Low Pay Unit.
Inland Revenue 1978, *Income Tax Separate Assessment*, Leaflet.

IR32, Board of Inland Revenue.

Land, H. Undated, *Family Policies in Britain*, mimeo.

Land, H. 1976, '*Social Security and Income Tax Systems: How the State Determines Who Does the Work*' in Chetwynd and Hartnett (eds), *Sex Role Stereotyping*, London, Routledge & Keegan Paul.

Lewis, P. 1979. Unpublished mimeo.

Lister, R. 1979, *A Budget for the Year of the Child*, London, Child Poverty Action Group.

Observer 1979, 5 August.

Meade, J. E. 1978, *The Structure and Reform of Direct Taxation*, London, George Allen & Unwin/Institute of Fiscal Studies.

OECD (Organisation for Economic Co-operation and Development) 1977, *The Treatment of Family Units in OECD Member Countries under Tax and Transfer Systems*, Committee on Fiscal Affairs, OECD.

Piachaud, D. 1979, 'Who are the poor and what is the best way to help them', *New Society*, 15 March.

Sunday Times 1978, 7 May.

Tunnard, J. 1978, *The Trouble with Tax*, London, Child Poverty Action Group.

WNACCP (Womens National Advisory Committee of the Conservative Party) 1979, *Women and Tax*, WNACCP.

Part III
Proposals for Reform

Previous chapters have illustrated the results of the development of taxation and social policy as two separate and largely uncoordinated systems. In this final section of the book, we turn to consider the possibilities for reform.

The main proposals currently being discussed offer us a choice of two paths to reform. One will lead us to try and resolve the contradictions and inconsistencies of separate systems by integrating the two. The proposals on offer are a Social Dividend or Negative Income Tax Scheme discussed in Chapter 11 or the Tax-Credit approach described in Chapter 12. Our second alternative is to attempt to reform each of the systems according to a consistent set of objectives and criteria, but to retain their separate identity. This is the approach favoured by the proponents of a 'New Beveridge' scheme, as discussed by Ken Judge in Chapter 12. If this second alternative is chosen, there remains a need to consider the shortcomings of the direct tax system itself, and this Geoffrey Whittington does in Chapter 9.

The operation of the tax system should be very much a matter of concern to social policy analysts. As Chapter 4 made clear, it represents a system of welfare and expenditure analagous to that of the social welfare system. Moreover, the extent to which the tax system tackles economic inequality determines the size of the 'job-to-be-done' in the various areas of social policy dealing with the results of that inequality. Finally the ability of taxes to raise revenue with as little loss of economic efficiency, and with as little taxpayer resentment, as possible determines the resources available for social expenditure.

Chapter 9 makes it clear that the British tax system performs poorly on all these counts. Marginal rates of tax tend to be high because of the relatively large proportion of income that is exempted from tax by allowances and reliefs. The result is a system which has high disincentive effects while doing little to modify the distribution of incomes (a result anticipated in Chapters 2 and 4). Both the efficiency and the equity of the tax system could be improved if either a Comprehensive

Income Tax or a Direct Expenditure Tax, both discussed by the Meade Committee, were to be adopted. To refer to a tax 'system' at all is indeed something of a misnomer. As Chapter 9 illustrates, the different elements of taxation are poorly coordinated and the end result is once again a frustration of basic objectives.

Most proponents of the 'Back to Beveridge' approach (who include the Meade Committee and Child Poverty Action Group) agree that a more progressive direct tax system is an important complement to reform of income maintenance. A more progressive system (in which the rich paid higher average or effective rates of tax) would not be incompatible with lower marginal rates to achieve greater economic efficiency, especially if some curtailment of tax expenditures took place (as would be the case under either a comprehensive income tax or expenditure tax). The proponents of New Beveridge, as its name rather explicitly suggests, are in favour of a return to the principles espoused in the Beveridge Report (although, as Ken Judge argues, they may have taken some liberties in interpretation of those principles). An attempt to move people off dependence on means-tested benefits, such as Family Income Supplement or Supplementary Benefit, together with an increase in the tax threshold and an adequate system of child endowment are the essential ingredients of such an approach.

By contrast, those in favour of a negative income tax, social dividend or tax credit schemes prefer to merge, as far as possible, the tax and income maintenance systems. As with plans for separate but co-ordinated reform, such a merging offers the opportunity to overcome many of the difficulties resulting from the present overlap between the two. But the essence of such schemes is their simplicity, and that simplicity has been gained at the expense of a comparatively unprogressive structure of income tax.

An important difference between the two approaches stems from underlying views about the nature of the problem to be tackled. The proponents of the 'integration approach' are concerned with raising the poor above a specified poverty line. The proponents of the New Beveridge approach, on the other hand, tend to believe that poverty is inextricably linked with inequality and that poverty can only be satisfactorily dealt with through a wider distribution of income and wealth.

The choice between schemes therefore is not determined only by technical considerations. A substantial element of political preference enters into the equation. It is for this reason that we turn, in Chapter 13, to the policy debate surrounding the proposals for reform. The seminar from which this book originated called together three people who had been involved in the policy process either at a practical or a political level to explain why they had advocated each of the options considered. The review of their arguments, brought together by Robert Walker, gives a flavour of the debate as it now stands.

9　The Direct Tax System
Geoffrey Whittington

Some Basic Considerations

There are three basic criteria by which tax systems are conventionally judged: equity, efficiency and administrative effectiveness.

Equity has two aspects: vertical and horizontal. Vertical equity implies considerations of distribution between the better-off taxpayer and the worse-off: usually, the capacity of a tax to fall more heavily on the better-off is considered to be important. Horizontal equity implies equal treatment of equals, i.e. that people in similar situations receive similar treatment. This is often a difficult criterion to apply in practice because of the problem of defining precisely who are equals. For example, two taxpayers with equal incomes may have different family responsibilities and we might wish to regard the one with greater responsibilities as being eligible for tax reliefs (as under the present system), but the precise extent of this is difficult to determine, as is the borderline limiting the characteristics which we take account of: should we, for example, allow for the fact that one person has more expensive tastes than another? (The problem of who should be treated as equals figured prominently in Chapter 8, 'Women and the Family'.)

Efficiency deals with the effect of taxes on the allocation of resources. In so far as taxes affect prices, which are the basis of economic decisions, they will affect those decisions, unless demand or supply are completely inelastic to price. Such effects of taxation can be beneficial, e.g. if the tax compensates for costs to society which would not be reflected in prices determined by free market forces, but they are often undesirable, e.g. in the case of high marginal rates of income tax, which provide a disincentive to effort by encouraging earners to substitute untaxed leisure for taxed earnings.

Administrative effectiveness has two aspects. Clearly, we wish the tax assessment and collection system to be as cheap as possible (including costs to the taxpayer as well as to the tax authorities), but we should also like the system to minimise the scope for avoidance and evasion by the taxpayer.

In appraising individual taxes, it will be convenient to distinguish between three different characteristics of a tax, the definition of the tax base, the rate structure of the tax, and the extent to which the tax integrates with other taxes to form a coherent system.

The Direct Tax System

In considering the direct tax system, we should be aware that we are confining our attention to a somewhat arbitrary subdivision of the tax system as a whole. A direct tax is conventionally defined as a tax which is levied on the person who bears the burden. The theory of tax incidence suggests that it is likely to be a relatively rare occurrence for the taxpayer to bear the full burden, but the conventional classification of direct taxation uses only the superficial incidence of a tax. Thus, income tax is classified as a direct tax because it is levied on the person who receives the income, although in fact he may pass at least part of the burden to others.

A wage earner may for instance, pass the tax on to his employer (who in turn may pass it on to the customer) if he successfully bargains for a certain level of 'take-home pay'.

However, confining our attention to direct taxes as normally defined, there are four important direct taxes at present in the United Kingdom which we need to consider: income tax, corporation tax, capital gains tax and capital transfer tax. Of these, income tax is by far the most important (yielding an estimated £19 665 million in 1979/80). Corporation tax is the next most important (£4850 million in 1979/80), but this includes a high proportion of advance corporation tax, which can be regarded as income tax on dividends. (There is also an additional petroleum revenue tax, which will not be discussed here.) Capital gains tax (£410 million including the supplementary development land tax) and capital transfer tax (£385 million) are much less important in terms of yield.

Proposals for a wealth tax reached Select Committee stage in the House of Commons in 1975 and are still part of Labour Party policy, so that it seems likely that wealth tax will be an important issue in future debates on tax reform, but the present discussion will be confined to taxes which are currently in operation.

One important aspect of income taxation which cannot be ignored is the social security system, which amounts to a negative income tax, albeit a very complicated one. Low incomes are supported by the state, the amount received from the state often exceeding the amount paid to it (although, because the levels of income qualifying support can exceed the income tax threshold, it is not unusual for the state to be giving income support to a person through one agency and charging him to income tax through another): hence the net effect is a gain to the individual which could be described as a negative income tax payment. The fact that many social security benefits are means-tested implies a high rate of loss of benefit as the income of the beneficiary rises, i.e. a high marginal tax rate under the negative income tax system. For example, family income supplement, which is available to persons in employment, is withdrawn at a marginal rate of 50 per cent: a married man receiving FIS and earning more than £1815 is currently (January 1980) subject to a marginal income tax rate of 25 per cent, so that his effective marginal tax rate is 75 per cent, assuming that he receives no other means-tested benefits whose withdrawal would increase this rate. By coincidence, the highest marginal rate of income tax payable on high incomes is also 75 per cent (60 per cent is the marginal rate of tax on taxable incomes in excess of £25 000 per year, and there is an investment income surcharge of 15 per cent on investment incomes in excess of £5000 per year). The phenomenon of very high implicit marginal rates of income tax, due to the withdrawal of means-tested benefits at low incomes, is known as the poverty trap. (See Chapters 1 and 5.)

The social security structure also affects the income tax structure in another way: it is partly contributory and the national insurance contributions payable are related to income. It is difficult to regard these contributions as anything other than another direct tax on income, as they appear to be determined more in relation to the government's overall revenue needs than to the cost of the benefits provided, and they certainly do not cover these costs. The current rates of contribution (for 1979/80) for an employed person are 6.5 per cent of income between £19.50 per week and £135 per week (assuming that the employee is not 'contracted-out' of the state superannuation scheme) and the employer has to contribute another 13.5 per cent. If it is borne in mind that the economic incidence of the employer's contribution is unlikely to fall entirely on the employer, some being borne by the employee in the form of lower wages, this means that the effective tax burden on earnings in this range is much higher than the current 30 per cent basic rate of income tax. This additional burden on employed persons is one possible justification for the investment income surcharge, which is levied on high unearned incomes, and which might be regarded as a very crude method of introducing a degree of horizontal equity between earned and unearned income. (Two other possible justifications for the surcharge would imply that unearned income be taxed more heavily than earned income, which is not generally the case at the present time. These are, firstly, that unearned income does not involve the loss of leisure associated with earning and, secondly, that earned income is derived from human capital, which receives no depreciation allowances for tax purposes, whereas physical capital, which gives rise to unearned income, does receive such allowances.)

What's Wrong?

Having defined the main components of the present UK tax system, each main component, in turn, will be examined critically. Petroleum revenue tax and development land tax are both specialised taxes which will not be discussed here.

Income tax

The income tax is central to the entire tax system and should therefore be considered first. In discussing rate structure, it will be necessary to consider the combined effects of income tax and the social security system, but in discussing the base only income tax will be discussed: reform of the social security system is the subject of the following chapters.

Rate Structure. In theory our income tax has always been progressive, i.e. it is designed on the assumption that equity requires its burden to fall relatively heavily on those with higher incomes; because of this, the rate structure of income tax presents a difficult trade-off between considerations of efficiency and vertical equity. High marginal rates of tax are inefficient, implying a disincentive to work effect, but given that we have a common tax schedule for all taxpayers, high marginal rates of tax at some point on the schedule are necessary if those with the highest incomes are to have a high average rate; this is necessary if our view of vertical equity is that the tax burden should be proportionately greater on those with high incomes than on those with low incomes. The trade-off between the disincentive effect and the redistributive effect of an income tax has recently been the subject of a great deal of theoretical investigation in the optimal income tax literature, following a seminal paper on the subject published by Professor Mirrlees in 1971. This is a rapidly developing area of economic theory, but the results obtained to date suggest that for a wide range of social welfare functions (incorporating social preferences for various forms of vertical equity), distributions of earning capacity in the population and disincentive effects, it is optimal to have a low marginal rate of tax on extremely low and extremely high incomes, with higher rates on the middle ranges of income. This 'low-high-low' pattern is the exact reverse of the 'high-low-high' pattern at present prevailing in the United Kingdom, the high tax rates being due to the poverty trap at low-income levels and to the progressivity of the marginal rate of tax at high-income levels. Of course, the optimal tax literature uses assumptions which might not be accepted (e.g. the social welfare functions usually preclude envy of the well off, which would imply that society as a whole was made worse off by the well off becoming even better off), and the subject is still being explored, but at least it puts some burden of proof on those who advocate the complete reverse pattern which is at present being applied.

The June 1979 Budget did, in fact, alleviate the problem of high marginal tax rates on high incomes, by reducing the highest rate on earned incomes from 83 per cent to 60 per cent, and on unearned incomes from 98 per cent to 75 per cent, with corresponding reductions in the other high-rate bands. It does not require the sophisticated analysis of optimal tax theory to demonstrate that a marginal tax rate of 98 per cent provides a strong disincentive for the taxpayer to make much effort to increase his income. It also provides him with a very strong incentive to avoid income tax by converting his income into a form which attracts lower tax rates, such as capital gains. The recent changes in rates, by increasing the post-tax marginal income of such a person from 2p in the pound to 25p in the pound must have alleviated these inefficient aspects of the rate structure.

At the lower end of the income scale, the poverty trap remains. It was somewhat alleviated (between 1978/9 and 1979/80) by the 25 per cent rate of tax for the first £750 of taxable income, and in 1979/80 increases in the tax threshold (£1815 for a married person). The 'Rooker and Wise' amendment to the 1978 Finance Act, which tied the tax threshold to annual changes in the cost of living (in the absence of specific legislation to the contrary), may also have a beneficial effect in preventing further erosion by inflation of the tax threshold, thus preventing an even worse overlap between the income tax system and the scales of income for various means-tested benefits. However, the central problem of the poverty trap still remains: there are far too many unco-ordinated means-tested benefits, with the result that the highest effective marginal rates of income tax are those faced by people on low incomes. This provides a great disincentive to work, either by entering the labour force or by making an effort to earn more when in the labour force, and a large number of people are affected in this way: an official estimate is that 50 000 families could have faced effective marginal tax rates exceeding 100 per cent in December 1977 (Central Statistical Office 1979, p. 145). A final inconsistency in the social security system is that short-term sickness and unemployment benefits are, for administrative reasons, (see Chapter 5, p. 76) not subject to income tax although longer-term benefits (such as state pensions) are taxable. This is horizontally inequitable as between the two types of benefit, leads to considerable loss of tax revenue, and prevents the application of the most consistent method of means-testing, i.e. subjecting benefits to the tax rates appropriate to other forms of income.

The income tax base. Income is a very difficult tax base to implement consistently. This is demonstrated clearly by the voluminous proposals for a comprehensive income tax drawn up by the Carter Commission 1966, in Canada (see Chapter 4, p. 51). The usual definition of income, for practical purposes, is:

$$\text{Income} = \text{Consumption} + \text{Net Savings}$$
$$\text{where Net Savings} = \text{Savings less Dis-savings.}$$

Looked at from the other side of the individual's balance-sheet, savings imply an addition to net assets (and dis-savings, which involve consumption in excess of income, imply a decrease in net assets). Of the two major components of income, consumption is relatively easy to measure objectively for tax purposes because it is mainly reflected in current transactions, although there is the problem that some important components of consumption are not traded (the most notable being the enjoyment of leisure) and are therefore not taxed, and there are also problems in measuring the consumption derived from the purchase of durable goods (notably housing). However, it is the net savings, or increase in net assets, component of income which gives rise to the main measurement problems in using income as a tax base. There are two aspects to this set of problems. Firstly, how do we value assets which are held rather than being bought or sold, so that they give rise to accrued gains or losses? Secondly, how do we measure the opening value of net assets which we use as our benchmark in measuring increases or decreases? The latter problem is made important by inflation: when inflation is at a high rate, comparing the terminal value of net assets for the previous year with that for the current year may lead to the assessment of gains which are monetary rather than real, so that the tax is falling on capital rather than real income.

Another problem of using income as a tax base lies in the choice of theoretical definitions of income. The definition used above is based on capital maintenance, i.e. a gain in value of net assets is regarded as a taxable gain. An alternative definition is based on consumption maintenance, i.e. the taxable income is that level of consumption which the taxpayer could potentially have sustained in the current period and hoped to have maintained indefinitely over future periods. This definition is, in some ways, more satisfactory and leads to a different treatment of capital gains arising from interest rate changes (which do not increase sustainable consumption and are therefore untaxed) and windfall gains (which are of a once-for-all nature and therefore make a proportionately small contribution to sustainable consumption). However, it is an impractical definition from an operational point of view because it depends crucially upon expectations about the future, which are subjective and therefore likely to lead to dispute between the taxpayer and the tax assessors. This definition will not, therefore, be discussed further: the main purpose in mentioning it is that it may have been implicit in some aspects of our present United Kingdom system, for example, the traditional exclusion of capital gains from the income tax might be regarded as being justified by this definition in the case of windfalls.

The present United Kingdom income tax base has developed in a pragmatic manner and does not conform systematically to any particular definition of income. Indeed, as the Meade Committee Report has demonstrated, it is in some respects more like an expenditure tax, basing the taxation of certain transactions on consumption, rather than income, giving tax relief for savings and taxing dis-savings. A good example of this pure expenditure tax treatment occurring within our present so-called income tax is the treatment of occupational pension schemes: contributions are tax deductible, the fund's income is free of tax, but pensions paid out are fully taxed in the hands of the recipient. (See Chapter 7.) Apart from savings reliefs, such as the deductibility of pension fund contributions (and, to a lesser extent, life-assurance premiums), there are two other types of relief which have a similar economic impact. Firstly, there are capital allowances for investment by businesses, which are equivalent to savings relief when the saving is associated with an investment which qualifies for a full initial capital allowance against income tax. Secondly, interest paid is sometimes a deductible expense (when the loan is for business purposes or, up to £25 000, for the purchase of an owner-occupied house.): in such cases, exempting the yield from tax (through interest deductibility) makes saving and investment as attractive, in terms of the post-tax rate of return which it offers, as if the initial act of saving and investment were given tax relief. Of course, there are cases where more than one type of relief is given to a particular activity, e.g. owner-occupied housing receives interest deductibility and the income, in the form of rent avoided, is untaxed (if we ignore local rates). (See Chapter 6.) In such cases, this particular medium of investment is more favourably treated than would be the case under a pure expenditure tax. This situation is exacerbated by the fact that capital gains and company profits are subject to separate taxes which are rather poorly co-ordinated with the income tax. The result is a system in which high rewards accrue to a taxpayer who takes his gains and makes his savings in ways which attract the most favourable tax treatment.

Inflation is not explicitly allowed for at all in the present income tax base. Thus, the purchaser of a fixed-interest government security pays income tax on the interest which he receives, despite the fact that the interest is often inadequate to compensate for the real loss in capital value, so that the interest is really a somewhat inadequate capital repayment rather than real income (although obviously the true incidence is not necessarily on the taxpayer: he might be willing to accept an even lower interest rate if the interest were tax free).

One important measure which was introduced to deal with the problems caused by inflation is stock appreciation relief. Inflation at the rates prevailing during the mid 1970s meant that businesses were paying tax heavily on the increase in the cash value of their stocks even when the physical level of stocks remained constant. This led to cash flow problems and stock appreciation relief was introduced in 1974 as a temporary measure. Currently, any increase in the book value of stocks in excess of 15 per cent of taxable profits is exempt from income tax or (in the case of incorporated businesses) corporation tax. This is a characteristically crude method of dealing with the problem: it is not based upon a systematic calculation of the extent to which stock values might have been expected to rise due to inflation. Instead, it gives full relief to increases above the threshold level in the value of stocks held and therefore provides a strong marginal incentive to businesses to hoard stocks in order to defer taxation.

The main criticisms which can be made of the present United Kingdom income tax, in the light of the criteria stated earlier, are as follows.

Firstly, the tax is inefficient, in the sense that it distorts behaviour without any obvious rationale. For example, the savings reliefs for pension funds and life assurance encourage the institutionalisation of savings, as is reflected in the decline of personal shareholding and the rise of institutional shareholding in recent years. (see Chapter 7.) Equally, the differential rates of capital allowances encourage investment in some forms (e.g. plant and machinery) rather than others (e.g. office building), and the reliefs given to owner-occupied housing may encourage over-investment or under-occupation of this type of housing (see Chapter 6).

Secondly, the tax is horizontally inequitable as between taxpayers who save and invest in different forms. These differences may be due to ignorance of the tax advantages of alternatives, unwillingness to exploit these advantages or lack of opportunity, e.g. the pension scheme will be determined by the employer rather than the employee.

Thirdly, the income tax is vertically inequitable in so far as the factors listed in the previous paragraph are related to income. For example, home ownership is closed to those on low incomes who cannot offer security for a mortgage and the more favourable occupational pension schemes are usually associated with highly paid forms of employment.

Fourthly, the rate structure of the present income tax seems to be a very poor compromise between equity and efficiency, achieving possibly the worst of both. It is not necessary to accept the low-high-low pattern of marginal rates which emerges from the optimal tax literature, or even the compromise linear (constant marginal rate) schedule suggested by Meade (1978, Chapter 14) to recognise that a combination of very high marginal rates for very high incomes with a very wide standard-rate band for middle incomes is likely to combine the maximum disincentive effect for high-income earners with a largely cosmetic appearance of progressivity (since, although marginal rates are high, the average rate of income tax paid by those with high incomes will be much lower than the marginal rate, due to the effect of the broad standard-rate band). The poverty trap induced by high implicit marginal rates of tax on very low incomes is probably an even more serious source of inefficiency, since it affects more people.

Finally, the system is administratively complicated and it offers considerable scope for avoidance. It also offers considerable scope for evasion, because the majority of taxpayers are not required to make an annual income tax return.

Capital gains tax

In theory, it is difficult to justify the separation of capital gains from income, for tax purposes. The advocates of a comprehensive income tax (such as Henry Simons and the Carter Commission) have advocated taxing capital gains within the income tax system. In the United Kingdom, capital gains have traditionally been excluded from the income tax system, and indeed they were exempt entirely from taxation until 1965, when capital gains tax was introduced.

In its present form, capital gains tax has a realisation basis, i.e. only those gains realised by disposal during the year are taxed, unrealised accrued gains being ignored. The realisation basis has the advantage of avoiding the necessity for annual valuations, and it also avoids the problem of liquidity (forced sales of assets resulting from the taxpayer having to raise the cash to pay tax on accrued gains), but it does mean that the taxpayer can defer the tax indefinitely by not disposing of assets which appreciate in value. There are other important restrictions on the base of capital gains tax: exemptions include the first £1000 of annual realised gains, owner-occupied houses used as the main United Kingdom residence of the taxpayer, British government stocks held for more than one year, various forms of National Savings investment and assets realised on death. There are also important 'rollover' provisions for agricultural land owned by working farmers and for family-owned businesses. Despite all these exemptions, which suggest that the tax can easily be avoided by those who are determined to do so, the capital gains tax base is harsh in one respect: it makes no allowance for inflation. Thus, the taxpayer who realises an asset bought ten years ago will be taxed on the monetary difference between the sale value and the cost, despite the fact that the cost was incurred when the real value of the pound sterling was more than twice its present level.

The latter problem is alleviated to some extent (although arbitrarily) by the fact that the maximum rate of capital gains tax is currently only 30 per cent, on annual gains greater than £9500 per annum. The 30 per cent maximum rate has applied ever since the inception of the tax, and the rate structure of capital gains tax has never been integrated into that of income tax (although one of the reliefs for small gains is related to the taxpayer's marginal rate of income tax). Thus, for the taxpayer who is liable to the higher rates of income tax, it has always been attractive to convert as much income as possible into capital gains, e.g. by buying relatively short-dated, low-coupon government securities, which will give a guaranteed gain on redemption.

The capital gains tax can be criticised on all of the basic criteria stated earlier. It is vertically inequitable, allowing those with large capital to avoid income tax, by converting income into capital gains, and by arranging their capital gains in such a way that they attract relatively little tax. It is horizontally inequitable as between those who pay the tax and those who, by accident or design, escape through one of the many loopholes. The failure to deal with inflation is a particularly important source of horizontal inequity in a tax which is based upon changes in the value of assets. There have recently been discussions of possible reforms in this respect, but a currently popular suggestion seems to be total abolition of the tax, which would eliminate (rather than solving) the inflation problem at the price of increasing the attraction of capital gains as an income tax avoidance device. The tax in its present form is also inefficient, since its many loopholes discourage taxpayers from disposing of their assets in the manner which they consider to be most efficient, e.g. the realisation basis produces the 'locking-in effect', discouraging the disposal of assets. Finally, the tax is administratively inefficient in that it produces a relatively small yield but requires detailed returns from a large number of taxpayers.

Corporation tax

The profits of companies are not subject to income tax but are instead subject to corporation tax at a current rate of 52 per cent (42 per cent for small companies). The corporation tax base is profit after deducting capital allowances (the company's own estimates of depreciation not being an allowable expense), interest payments, and stock appreciation relief. These deductions are the same as those given to unincorporated businesses. There are special provisions for bringing capital gains realised by companies into the corporation tax base, at a reduced rate, and dividends are subject to imputation relief through the advance corporation tax system. The effect of this is that dividends are treated like a deductible expense but only at the basic rate of income tax, which is less than the corporation tax rate. The basic rate of income tax on dividends, paid by the company on behalf of shareholders, is regarded additionally as an advance payment of corporation tax.

The result of this system is that corporation tax distorts two types of decision. Firstly, various forms of investment are favoured relative to others: plant and machinery being generously treated under the capital allowance system, and increases in stocks in excess of 15 per cent of taxable profits being generously treated under stock appreciation relief. Secondly, various forms of finance are favoured over others: loan stocks are favoured relative to equity because interest is a fully deductible expense, whereas dividends receive only imputation relief. Retained profits receive no special relief but can be attractive when shareholders are liable to high rates of income tax: in such a case, the shareholder may prefer that the profits be subject to corporation tax (at a maximum rate of 52 per cent) and the benefit to him be the capital gain in the value of his shares resulting from retaining the post-tax profit.

As a result of the generosity of capital allowances and stock appreciation relief, manufacturing companies have paid little 'mainstream' corporation tax (i.e. corporation tax additional to the advance corporation tax on dividends) in recent years (this is demonstrated in the recent book by John Kay and Mervyn King 1978; of twenty leading industrial companies which they studied in 1977, only eight were currently paying mainstream corporation tax on their profits). However, every company has to make complex returns to claim the reliefs, so that the administrative cost to the company, as well as to the Inland Revenue, must be high even when no tax is payable. Service industries, particularly those in the financial sector, which have few assets qualifying for capital allowances or stock appreciation relief, do typically pay mainstream corporation tax, and it might reasonably be asked whether it is horizontally equitable and economically efficient that reliefs (particularly stock appreciation relief, which is a recent relief designed to deal with one of the effects of inflation, a problem faced by all sectors) should discriminate in this way between sectors.

Capital transfer tax

Capital transfer tax replaced the old estate duty in 1974. The latter tax was levied only on transfer at death (or, at reduced rates, in the years immediately preceding death) and was therefore easily avoided by the taxpayer making gifts during his lifetime (known as gifts *inter vivos*). The capital transfer tax base is lifetime gifts by a donor, the total being accumulated from year to year without any form of adjustment for inflation. The rates are progressive with respect to the amount given over the donor's life.

This base was designed to stop the obvious gap in estate duty, but there are important restrictions on the capital transfer tax base. The first £25 000 of lifetime gifts is exempt entirely from the tax, as are gifts between husband and wife up to £2000 given in any one year, and gifts made out of current income. There are also lower rates on lifetime gifts than on gifts on death (although transfers on death do have the advantage of exemption from capital gains tax), and concessions (in the form of a 50 per cent reduction in the valuation of assets) for the transfer of agricultural land and family business assets.

These concessions amount to a very serious limitation on the effectiveness of the tax, apart perhaps for the case of extremely large estates, in the context of which the exemptions (such as the ability of a married couple to transfer £4000 per annum tax-free) are quantitatively small. Even in such cases, there is the possibility of minimising transfers by 'generation skipping' (giving to grandchildren rather than children) and the use of family trusts. Thus, the effect of capital transfer tax on vertical equity is less than might have been hoped, and the system favours those who obtain good tax advice and are willing and able to act upon it. The low yield of the tax, and the failure of the yield to grow as transfers accumulate, testify to its relative ineffectiveness.

For example, the yield of estate duty in 1974/5, the fiscal year preceding the introduction of capital transfer tax, was £337.8 million, which was below its yield of earlier years, but by 1977/8 capital transfer tax, in its third year of operation, was able to yield only £311.2 million: even if we add the £86.7 million yielded by residual estate duty payments in 1977/8, the yield of all capital transfer taxes in that year was, in real terms, much below that of three years earlier, representing 0.28 per cent of Gross National Product, as compared with 0.40 per cent in 1974/5.

One possible basis for the reform of capital taxation is accessions taxation, i.e. assessing the tax on the receiver of gifts rather than on the donor. This would not necessarily remove all the problems of the existing tax, which largely arise from the details of implementation (particularly the loopholes referred to earlier), but it would have the great virtue of basing the progressivity of the tax on individual accumulations of wealth from gifts or inheritance. The fundamental equity objective of transfer taxation is presumably to penalise such accumulations, on the ground that large individual concentrations of inherited wealth are undesirable, and capital transfer tax, in its present donor-based form, does not do this directly. In theory, it is possible to inherit a large fortune without incurring capital transfer tax, provided that the transfer is affected through a large number of routes which qualify for exemption, e.g. ten individuals each with £25 000 available to transfer can, by transferring it to the same person, endow that individual with a total of £$\frac{1}{4}$ million without incurring any tax (assuming that they have made no other gifts). Various forms of accessions tax are discussed in Chapter 15 of Meade (1978).

The System as a Whole

It is clear from the above discussion that we do not have a direct tax 'system', in the sense of a set of taxes with an underlying philosophy. For example, it is clear that capital gains tax and income tax do not match well either in terms of their base or their rate structure, and corporation tax is also rather poorly integrated with the income tax, in so far as there are cases where a business may gain or lose for tax purposes merely by being incorporated rather than unincorporated. Capital transfer tax seems to exist, somewhat ineffectively, in complete isolation from the other taxes, although it would be quite possible to include gifts in the income tax base. This lack of systematic co-ordination creates anomalies and loopholes, and the attempt to prevent these adds much unnecessary uncertainty and complication to the tax legislation.

The pragmatism of our direct tax 'system' is therefore its basic problem. It has grown as an historical process rather than an act of conscious design and it would therefore be unreasonable to expect it to have a coherent, systematic base. Various alternative proposals for reform on a systematic basis will be found in Chapter 23 of the Meade Report. Some of these systems use an income tax and some use an expenditure tax as the main direct tax, but all have a consistency between taxes which is notably lacking in the existing arrangements. Expenditure has some notable advantages over income as a basis of tax reform. The expenditure base is less ambiguous than income for measurement purposes, as it is more closely related to current transactions. Also, perhaps surprisingly, it is in many ways closely related to our present so called 'income' tax, and could be regarded as a rationalisation of the present inconsistent method of giving savings relief, giving a single relief to all forms of saving, and taxing all forms of dis-saving.

However, it is not necessary to believe in an expenditure tax to accept the case for *some* form of systematic reform to introduce greater consistency into our tax system. It would, of course, be naive to expect any tax system to be exempt from expedient adjustments in response to events and the political pressures exerted by interest groups, such as farmers, home owners, and small businesses, all of whom enjoy privileges at present. However, if we were to adopt a system which had a systematic base, such as those suggested by the Meade Report, the following benefits might be hoped for:

1.   The system would be less naturally prone to avoidance loopholes and anomalies. If the direct taxes are properly designed to fit together there should be much less opportunity to gain by converting transactions from one form to another.

2.   Pragmatic concessions to pressure groups would at least be seen to be concessions and would be judged by a common standard. Our present so called 'income' tax, for example, offers such variety of treatment of different transactions that it is difficult to define what is normal treatment.

3.   There might be less distortion of economic activity due to negligence rather than conscious policy. For example, the present corporation tax system, as was described earlier, discriminates in favour of some forms of investment rather than others. This might be justified if it were felt that the favoured forms on investment were particularly conducive to the national interest, but it is desirable that the arguments for this view should be properly aired. Furthermore, there are some other discriminatory features of the tax which seem to be entirely accidental, such as the effective elimination of preference shares, formerly a useful and sensible method of finance but now made uneconomic because interest on loan stocks is a deductible expense, whereas preference dividends receive only imputation relief.

Of course, there will be those who do not believe that reform on a systematic basis is feasible. The argument is that the present system 'works', and that reform is 'all right in theory but not in practice'. It is undoubtedly true that the process of transition from the present system to a better one is likely to be difficult and that it is unlikely that any system will be perfect. However, it is also true that changes are regularly made to the tax system: two of the four direct taxes discussed earlier have dated from 1965 (capital gains tax and corporation tax) and one (capital transfer tax) from 1974. If we are to have changes, then we should make them changes for the better. Furthermore, there is no reason why a system which is 'all right in theory' should not work in practice. Perhaps the fact that our present system is not 'all right in theory' and yet still manages to work in practice should be a source of encouragement rather than discouragement to those who advocate reform.

References

Carter Commission 1966, *Report of the Royal Commission on Taxation*, Ottawa, Queens Printer.
Central Statistical Office 1979, *Social Trends*, no. 10, 1980 edn, London, HMSO.
Kay, J. A. and King, M. A. 1978, *The British Tax System*, Oxford, OUP.
Meade, J. E. (Chairman) 1978, *The Structure and Reform of Direct Taxation*, London, George Allen & Unwin Institute for Fiscal Studies.
Mirrlees, J. A. 1971, 'An exploration in the theory of optimum income taxation', *Review of Economic Studies*, vol. 38, pp. 175–208.

10 Beveridge: Past, Present and Future*
Ken Judge

Social Insurance and Allied Services (Beveridge 1942), or the Beveridge Plan as it was more popularly known, was first published at the end of 1942 and was an instant bestseller on both sides of the Atlantic. In particular, it caught the public imagination in war-weary Britain and put the reform of social welfare firmly on the post-war reconstruction policy agenda. In many ways, Sir William Beveridge's report can be seen as the inspirational source or foundation of many of the social policy initiatives taken by the Attlee government immediately after the cessation of hostilities. Now, almost forty years later, it is rather ironical that Beveridge's name should be used as a clarion-call by those who want to introduce radical and expensive reforms of the social security system Beveridge helped to create.

The purpose of this chapter is to briefly examine some of Beveridge's original proposals for social security and the way in which they were implemented; consider some of the reasons why poverty has persisted since the reform of social security in 1948; examine current proposals for a New Beveridge programme and their associated costs; and, finally, discuss some of the problems connected with these proposals.

The Beveridge Plan
In examining Beveridge's proposals I shall concentrate primarily upon his plan for social security, but it is essential to understand that the scheme was designed on the basis of three critical assumptions. These were that family allowances would be introduced; a National Health Service would be created; and that full employment would be maintained.

* I am very grateful to Peggy Foster and the editors for their helpful comments and suggestions on an earlier draft of this chapter.

Beveridge took a broad view of social security and defined its scope as follows.

> The term 'social security' is used here to denote the securing of an income to take the place of earnings when they are interrupted by unemployment, sickness or accident, to provide for retirement through age, to provide against loss of support by the death of another person, and to meet exceptional expenditures, such as those connected with birth, death and marriage. Primarily social security means security of income up to a minimum, but the provision of an income should be associated with treatment designed to bring the interruption of earnings to an end as soon as possible. (Beveridge 1942, p. 120)

The actual plan for social security consisted of three distinct elements: social insurance for basic needs; national assistance for the few groups not covered by insurance; and voluntary insurance for additions to the basic provision. The most detailed part of the Beveridge Report is concerned with social insurance, but such an emphasis gives a misleading impression of Beveridge's own priorities. In developing his proposals, he had in mind one singularly important guiding principle which was:

> that social security must be achieved by cooperation between the State and the individual. The State should offer security for service and contribution. The State in organising security should not stifle incentive, opportunity, responsibility; in establishing a national minimum, it should leave room and encouragement for voluntary action by each individual to provide more than that minimum for himself and his family. (Beveridge 1942, pp. 6–7)

The purpose of the remainder of this section is twofold. First, to set out some of the most distinctive features of the different elements of the social security plan. Second, to consider three particular aspects of Beveridge's proposals which are central to contemporary debates about the reform of social security: the calculation of benefit rates; the problem of rents; and family allowances.

Social insurance

Beveridge proposed a comprehensive insurance scheme to provide financial cover against a range of predictable risks, such as old age, sickness and unemployment, in which the participants would pay flat-rate contributions so as to ensure equality of treatment for all workers. In return, those eligible would receive flat-rate benefits only which would encourage personal responsibility. In addition, there were another four distinguishing characteristics of the scheme: unification of administrative responsibility; adequacy of benefit; comprehensiveness; and classification. The most important aspects of these features were that the:

> flat rate of benefit proposed is intended in itself to be sufficient without further resources to provide the minimum income needed for subsistence in all cases ... [and that] social insurance should be comprehensive in respect of both of the persons covered and their needs. (Beveridge 1942, p. 122)

National assistance

The safety net for those not fully covered by social insurance was to be a scheme of national assistance which would meet financial needs up to subsistence level. In order to maintain the attractiveness of the contributory principle, however, it was thought that national assistance should be seen as considerably less desirable than insurance benefits. Beveridge decided, therefore, that entitlement to national assistance needed to be subject to rigorous tests of means and needs, and that 'it will be subject also to any conditions as to behaviour which may seem likely to hasten restoration of earning capacity' (Beveridge 1942, p. 141).

Voluntary insurance

The final part of the social security plan, voluntary insurance, is one to which we have already suggested Beveridge attached considerable importance. He recognised that the standards of living of different sections of the population differed enormously and was convinced that making provision for the maintenance of standards higher than the minimum he envisaged was a matter of free choice for the individual. Beveridge was anxious, however, that the assumption of greater personal responsibilities by individuals should be strongly encouraged by the state.

> In so far as voluntary insurance meets real needs, it is an essential part of security; scope and encouragement for it must be provided. The State can ensure this negatively, by avoiding so far as possible any test of means for its compulsory insurance benefits, and by limiting such benefits to subsistence and primary needs. The State can ensure this positively by regulation, by financial assistance or by itself undertaking the organisation of voluntary insurance. (p. 143)

Benefit rates

Beveridge went to a great deal of trouble to try and identify, on as scientific a basis as possible, what level of subsistence benefits should be provided to people in different circumstances. He concluded that a family of two adults and three children should receive, at 1938 prices, an allowance of £2.16½p plus a standard addition for rent of 50p. Beveridge also explained in considerable detail the calculation of benefit rates because he thought it essential to illustrate the relationship between benefits and contributions, and the relative cost of the scheme to be borne by employees, employers and the state. It is crucially important to understand, however, that his calculations were very much illustrative ones. He was not firmly committed to a particular set of benefit rates.

> The Plan for Social Security proposed in this Report is first and foremost a plan of how social insurance should be organised, with national assistance and voluntary insurance as subsidiary methods, for maintenance of income. The method of organisation is independent of the precise amounts to be given each week as benefit or pension. It might be difficult today to take definite decisions on questions of amount, because the future level of prices is uncertain; the final figures must be written into the plan when the time and conditions of its coming into operation are known. (Beveridge 1942, p. 103)

In other words, Beveridge was firmly committed to the concept of subsistence levels of benefit, or a minimum acceptable standard of living, rather than any particular set of benefit rates included in his report.

The problem of rent

The major problem for Beveridge in trying to establish subsistence levels of benefit was that rents payable for similar accommodation varied enormously.

> The attempt to fix rates of insurance benefit and pension on a scientific basis with regard to subsistence needs has brought to notice a serious difficulty in doing so in the conditions of modern Britain. This is the problem of rent ... In this ... the framing of a satisfactory scheme of social security depends on the solution of other problems of economic and social organisation. (Beveridge 1942, p. 15)

The most obvious solution to this would have been to allow *actual* rents, but Beveridge raised a number of objections of administration and principle against this and concluded that a flat-rate allowance for rent should be included in the scale rates for insurance benefits. In contrast, actual rents were to be taken into consideration when assessing national assistance entitlement.

It should be recognised, however, that Beveridge's design was sufficiently flexible to accommodate conclusions different to his own and he stated that if adjustments for individual rents were thought to be desirable, within the social insurance scheme, 'this change ... could be made without affecting the main structure' of his overall plan (Beveridge 1942, p. 84). The primary reason why Beveridge himself did not support individual adjustment was his belief or hope that:

> The launching of the Plan for Social Security will coincide with a determined and successful effort to deal with urban congestion and shortage of housing. If and so far as this hope is realised, inequalities of rent bearing no relation to the accommodation obtained will disappear; a high rent will then represent a free choice by the householder and it will become indefensible to favour that form of expenditure over other forms of expenditure in fixing scales of benefit. (Beveridge 1942, p. 83)

Family allowances

Strictly speaking, the proposals for family allowances contained in the Beveridge Report were not part of the social security plan, but they were an essential complement to it. Beveridge supported the principle of family allowances for three reasons. First, because he recognised that they were efficient instruments for tackling that aspect of poverty caused by the existence of a large number of dependent children within a household. The second reason was that, in the absence of allowances, large families would receive financial assistance for their children only when they were in receipt of insurance benefit or national assistance and Beveridge thought it was 'dangerous to allow benefit ... to equal or exceed earnings during work' (Beveridge 1942, p. 154).

The final reason was Beveridge's belief that family allowances would encourage the maintenance of a satisfactory birth-rate. In practice, Beveridge believed that the subsistence costs of children should be shared between their parents and the community. This division of responsibility could be achieved either by paying subsistence-level allowances to all except the first dependent child in a family, or smaller benefits for all children. Finally, Beveridge supported the proposition that family allowances should be age-related 'since the needs of children increase rapidly with age' (Beveridge 1942, p. 157).

Summary

Beveridge's plan was intended to provide a comprehensive system of social insurance so as to ensure a minimum level of benefits for individuals whose earnings were interrupted by predictable risks. Such a system was to be reinforced in two ways. First, by providing family allowances for the children of parents both in and out of work. Second, by personal saving through voluntary insurance. Finally, if all else failed, national assistance would be available as a safety net for those with no other means of financial support. But a major objective of the Beveridge Plan was to minimise the numbers of people dependent upon means-tested national assistance.

The Persistence of Poverty

Much of what Beveridge proposed in 1942 was implemented by the Labour government after 1945; but despite his intentions, the number of people dependent upon national assistance, and its successor supplementary benefit, has increased rather than diminished since the scheme was introduced in 1948. For example, the total number of claimants and their dependents increased from 1.5 million, or 3 per cent of the population, in 1948 to almost 5 million, or 9 per cent of the population, in 1977, and the numbers continue to grow. Among the many reasons which account for this increase we should consider three in particular: improvements in the relative poverty standard; inadequate levels of insurance benefits; and limitations in the coverage of insurance benefits.

Relative or absolute poverty?

If we are to make statements about the numbers of people in poverty we need some definition of the term. For example, one persuasive commentator has argued that:

> Poverty can be defined objectively and applied consistently only in terms of the concept of relative deprivation ... Individuals, families and groups in the population can be said to be in poverty when ... their resources are so seriously below those commanded by the average individual or family that they are, in effect, excluded from ordinary living patterns, customs and activities. (Townsend 1974, p. 15)

This kind of approach has been very influential but the most common poverty standards in Britain are the official supplementary benefit scales which are less generous than Townsend (1979) and others believe to be essential even though they have improved considerably in real terms in the post-war era. It has been suggested from time to time, however, that the use of even these crude approximations to relative poverty standards gives a false picture of the numbers in poverty and that the adoption of a relatively fixed or absolute poverty standard is more illuminating. In particular, it has been suggested that Beveridge had in mind absolute rather than relative scales of poverty in designing his benefit rates. The difference in approach certainly affects the numbers classified as being in poverty, as Table 10.1 illustrates.

Table 10.1   Numbers in poverty (receiving Supplementary Benefit) in Britain, 1953 and 1973

Year	£ per week	Individuals (millions)	% of population
1953/4 standard			
1953	3.84	2.4	4.8
1973	8.78	0.1	0.2
1971 standard			
1953	5.83	10.6	21.0
1973	13.83	1.3	2.3

Note: Basic-scale rates, excluding any long-term addition after 1976, for a married couple, plus 30 per cent for rent and other discretionary additions.
Source: G. C. Fiegehen, P. S. Lansley and A. D. Smith, 1977, *Poverty and Progress in Britain 1953–73*, Cambridge, CUP, Table 3.4.

However, it seems that Beveridge was not averse to the concept of relative poverty. His biographer has written that Beveridge 'was sympathetic to the view that an administrative definition of "subsistence" should take account of changing social perceptions of human needs' (Harris 1977, p. 397), and Beveridge himself wrote that:

Social insurance should aim at guaranteeing the minimum income needed for subsistence. What the actual rates of benefit and contributions should be in terms of money cannot be settled now ... determination of what is required for reasonable human subsistence is to some extent a matter of judgement; estimates on this point change with time, and generally, in a progressive community, change upwards ... But the provisional rates themselves are not essential ... If social policy should demand benefits on a higher scale than subsistence, the whole level of benefit and contribution rates could be raised without affecting the structure of the scheme. (Beveridge 1942, p. 14)

Inadequacy of benefit levels

If the national assistance or supplementary benefit level is accepted as the poverty standard, then it is quite clear that the benefit scales for insurance benefits have always been below that level which is contrary to what Beveridge suggested. It is also the case that family allowances were introduced, and maintained, at lower levels than that envisaged by Beveridge. Table 10.2 compares levels of national insurance and assistance benefits for old-age pensions in 1948 and 1979. The 1979 pension was below the scale rate available to those pensioners

Table 10.2   Comparison of national insurance and social assistance benefit levels, 1948–79 (£ per week)

Year	Retirement pension[a]	National assistance supplementary benefit[b]
1948	2.10	2.00 + rent, etc.
1979	37.30 + rent rebate	37.65 + rent, etc.

Notes: [a] Married couple under 80
    [b] Long-term scale rate in 1979.

dependent on supplementary benefit even when rents are excluded from consideration. The 1948 pension was slightly above the introductory national assistance rate, but the difference of 10p was hardly sufficient compensation for the rent adjustment applicable to national assistance. It will be remembered that Beveridge had suggested a flat-rate rent of 50p per week at 1938 price levels. The 1980 social security legislation will reduce some of these anomalies by bringing supplementary benefit and some national insurance benefit rates into line but the major problem of differential rents will remain.

Limitations of coverage

Despite Beveridge's clear intention that his social security plan should be as comprehensive as possible it has become increasingly apparent since the 1940s that large groups of potential beneficiaries have inadequate contribution records and are ineligible, therefore, for insurance benefits. These groups include the long-term unemployed and single-parent families – Beveridge had hoped to include the latter but the practical problems proved insurmountable – who are among the faster growing set of dependents on supplementary benefit, as well as the disabled and the self-employed.

Defects in social security

Whatever the causal factors are, it is indisputable that very large numbers of people are dependent on supplementary benefit, at least in part, for their weekly income. It has been estimated that the number of claimants and their dependents at the end of 1977 totalled about 5 million (DHSS 1978, p. 3). Advocates of reforming the social security system are critical of this level of dependence on means-tested benefits for four main reasons. First, that levels of take-up are inadequate. The Supplementary Benefits Commission estimated that as many as one million people were eligible for, but not claiming, benefit (SBC 1977, p. 136). Second, that many of those in receipt of supplementary benefit are stigmatised and humiliated by the experience. Third, that means-tests are associated with high marginal rates of taxation and poverty traps and so create severe disincentives to seek employment. Finally, it is thought that selective income maintenance programmes are more costly to administer than universal ones. For example, the administrative costs of the supplementary benefits system as a proportion of benefits paid were 13.4 per cent in 1975 whereas they were only 3.8 per cent for national insurance benefits in 1973–4 (Meade 1978, Appendix 13.3).

Moreover, in addition to the particular defects of supplementary benefit, there are many other criticisms of the income maintenance system as a whole. Two examples will have to suffice. First, there is a lack of co-ordination between the tax and social security systems. Field, Meacher and Pond have highlighted the seemingly absurd situation where:

> a married couple with two small children earning £35 a week were eligible (at July 1976 rates) to receive a poverty wage supplement of £3.50 from the Department of Health and Social Security on the grounds that their income from employment was inadequate. At the same time, they would be required to pay £3.80 to the Inland Revenue in the form of income tax and national insurance contributions (1977).

Second, there is a plethora of overlapping means-tested benefits scattered across various agencies and tiers of government which are difficult to describe let alone understand (NCC 1976). In fact, after reviewing all aspects of the present tax and social security system, the influential Meade Committee established by *The Institute for Fiscal Studies* concluded that there 'is a widespread feeling ... that some rationalisation and simplification of this whole apparatus is to be desired' (Meade 1978, p. 270).

Back to Beveridge?

In the past, various proposals for a radical restructuring of income maintenance programmes have been put forward which include different kinds of social dividend, tax credit and negative income tax schemes. Some of these are discussed in other chapters, but the purpose of this section is to examine what has been described as a 'Back to Beveridge Strategy' or a 'New Beveridge Plan'. Such an approach was first suggested by Professor Atkinson in his book *Poverty in Britain and the Reform of Social Security* (1970). Since that time, Atkinson has been closely associated with two publications, both influential in their different ways, which have urged that Beveridge's ideas should be exhumed. First, he has been an adviser to the Child Poverty Action Group (CPAG) which set out its proposals for a Back-to-Beveridge strategy in Ruth Lister's pamphlet *Social Security: the Case for Reform* (Lister 1975). Second, he was one of the original members of the Meade Committee which included in its final recommendations the proposal for a New Beveridge Plan (Meade 1978, Chapter 13).

My intention is to set out what a New Beveridge Plan entails using the CPAG pamphlet and the Meade Report as guides, although other groups have made similar suggestions (cf. NCC 1976, Chapter 8). One small introductory point to make, however, is that although the general tenor of the two publications is clear they both fudge their approach to some of the more important details as well as differing to some degree in their attitude to certain questions. Their fundamental proposals, though, can easily be presented in bald outline. First, they define the long-term supplementary benefit scale rate as the 'minimum acceptable standard of living' for everyone. Second, they wish to see all insurance benefits and tax thresholds raised to at least the supplementary benefit level. Third, they advocate a substantial improvement in child benefits and the introduction of a new cash benefit – a home responsibility allowance. Finally, they suggest that the contribution requirements for insurance benefits should be substantially relaxed. Before examining these proposals in a little more detail, though, it might be helpful to indicate the rates of personal tax allowances and main social security benefits for a married couple effective in November 1979, and these are set out in Table 10.3.

Table 10.3   Tax allowance and benefit rates for married couples (November 1979)

Allowances and benefits	Rate per week (£)	Rate for year (£)
Married men's tax allowance	34.90	1815
Unemployment and sickness benefit[a]	29.95	1557
Retirement pension	37.30	1940
Long-term supplementary benefit[b]	37.65	1958

Notes: [a] Excluding earnings-related benefits
 [b] Excluding rent.

The poverty line

The problem with using supplementary benefit rates as a poverty standard is that they vary according to claimant's circumstances which, of course, may change over time. Most people dependent upon supplementary benefit have their income in any period brought up to a level which is determined by a number of factors. The supplementary benefit entitlement of an elderly married couple with no other financial resources of their own will be calculated by adding their housing costs to the long-term scale rate together with any discretionary payments. The DHSS review of the supplementary benefit scheme reported that the average addition for rent and rates, etc., was about £5 per week. In addition, almost two-thirds of elderly claimants in 1976 were in receipt of weekly additions to their benefit (ECAs) for items such as heating, laundry and special diets, and also had the possibility of occasional lump-sum payments for exceptional needs (ENPs). We can illustrate the scale of these discretionary additions by reference to the fact that in 1976 more than 900 000 claimants received ECAs for extra heating costs worth between 95p and £2.85 per week (at November 1979 rates) and in 1977 more than 1.1 million ENPs worth an average of about £25 each were awarded. Table 10.4

Table 10.4   Illustrative calculation of supplementary benefit for an elderly married couple (November 1979)

Item	£ per week
Long-term scale rate	37–65
Rent and rates	5–45
Extra heating	1–90
Total	45–00

provides a hypothetical example of by how much some of these various additions could influence the weekly benefit of an elderly married couple.

The point about discretionary additions is that they enable people in different circumstances to achieve similar standards of living, but they also create major problems for any proposal to achieve greater harmonisation of fiscal and social programmes. In order to achieve a degree of consistency between tax, insurance and assistance benefits, one needs to establish a relatively fixed monetary entitlement. A choice has to be made, therefore, between two different approaches. Option A would specify the poverty standard as the basic scale rate only and suggest other ways of dealing with the discretionary extras such as rent. Option B would seek to consolidate the average discretionary payments into the scale rates. The second option would involve a degree of rough justice for those with particularly expensive special needs or circumstances but would still produce a substantially higher poverty line than option A. If we take the figures in Table 10.4 as an illustration then option A would specify a poverty line for an elderly married couple at £37.65 per week and option B the greater sum of £45 per week. It is difficult to say which option should be selected for a New Beveridge Plan because neither of the chief advocates make their position absolutely clear, but, broadly speaking, Meade appears to favour option A and Lister, option B.

Improvements in tax and insurance benefits

Both Meade and Lister fudge the issue of how best to make arrangements for household costs and discretionary additions, but in different ways. Meade harks back to the original Beveridge report in declaring that the problem of rent depends on 'measures taken to reform the housing market ... which we regard as being beyond the scope of the Committee' (Meade 1978, p. 293), and quietly omits to discuss such issues as extra heating additions. The Meade proposals, therefore, are quite straightforward and would involve the harmonisation of personal tax allowances and national insurance benefits with the appropriate long-term supplementary benefit scale rate. Lister would also prefer to deal with housing costs separately through 'the introduction of some form of universal non-means-tested housing allowance' (Lister 1978, p. 42), but unlike Meade she also has some more practical suggestions to make. In order to compensate for factors such as rent she advocates that national insurance benefits, and by implication tax allowances, should be set at levels substantially higher than the long-term SB scale rates. 'As a first step, we suggest that the adult rates be set at £3 above the long-term supplementary benefit scale rates, which would allow for an average rent of £3' (Lister 1975, p. 41). In fact, by 1978 the average rent payment for supplementary benefit recipients was estimated to be £6.50 (Hansard 1979d, col. 221). It is important to emphasise, however, that Lister was adamant that the £3 extra was only a first step and even that was at 1975 prices. Nevertheless, we can use that figure to illustrate the different proposals of Meade and Lister in Table 10.5.

Despite the differences both Meade and Lister propose substantial increases in the level of allowances and benefits for most groups. The only exception being the very small increase in retirement pensions proposed by Meade, but even this needs to be seen in the context of Meade's assumption that additional assistance with rents, etc., would be forthcoming from somewhere.

Family benefits

Meade and Lister differ in their detailed discussion of family benefits but their broad conclusions point in the same direction. First, they are in agreement that child benefits should be substantially increased. Meade proposes that for each child they should be worth 25 per cent of the adult personal tax allowance, 'although there would be nothing to prevent the adoption of the arrangement whereby the amount of the benefit depended upon the age of the child, on the grounds that the support of an older child involves more expense than that of a younger child' (Meade 1978, p. 286). Lister, on the other hand, proposes a more complicated set of arrangements which would link the level of child benefits to average male manual earnings. It is not easy to specify exactly what level of child benefits Meade and Lister favour because their proposals are contingent upon other factors which are continually changing. Nevertheless, leaving aside the complication of age-related benefits, it is clear that the minimum increase necessary to satisfy Meade would be 50 per cent whereas Lister would probably have something approaching a 150 per cent increase in mind. Average child benefits, therefore, would need to be raised to between £6 and £10 per week at November 1979 rates compared with the actual level of £4.

In principle, both Meade and Lister are agreed that new benefits should be paid to an 'adult who needs to make arrangements to look after children or other dependents needing home care' (Meade 1978, p. 286), although once again they differ over the details of their proposals. In this instance, however, it is the principle of introducing something such as a *home responsibility payment* which is the most important consideration and we need not concern ourselves with the practicalities other than to say that the absolute minimum level for such a benefit would not be below that proposed for child benefits.

Relaxation of contribution conditions
The final positive element of a New Beveridge Plan is not one that we need examine in detail. It was suggested above that many people had to claim supplementary benefit because either they had a zero or reduced entitlement to benefits. In order to alleviate this situation, therefore, and reduce what is seen as an unnecessary reliance on means-tested benefits, it is proposed that contribution conditions should be considerably relaxed by increasing both the scope and the value of *credited* contributions. It is the principle rather than the details which matter and the important point is that a revised scheme would 'aim to extend coverage to groups not at present receiving national insurance' (Meade 1978, p. 285).

Financing the proposals
Whatever the precise details, the gross cost of introducing a New Beveridge Plan would be very considerable. Some savings would be obtained from a reduction in expenditure on SB and other means-tested benefits, but others are simply illusory. For example, Lister claimed that 'as much as £327 million should already be available in the form of unclaimed supplementary benefits' (Lister 1975, p. 67), but as such expenditure is not actually incurred it can hardly be saved.

In fact, there can be little doubt that even the net cost of a New Beveridge Plan would require a huge increase in public expenditure and taxation. It is difficult to say how much the proposals would cost, but they would almost certainly require a substantial increase in tax rates even if certain changes in the tax base which have been proposed were adopted. The proposals put forward by the Meade Committee would involve an increase in the standard rate of income tax of between 4p and 7p *and* changes in the tax base. The Lister proposals would be even more expensive. For example, simply raising the tax thresholds alone to levels consistent with the benefit rates set out in Table 10.5 would in themselves probably require an increase in the basic rate of income tax of at least 4p in the pound. In addition to increases in the rate of tax, though, both Lister and Meade favour raising extra revenue through extending the tax base.

Table 10.5   Proposed benefit rates (£) for a married couple[a]
(at November 1979 rates)

Benefit or allowance	Annual rate	Meade proposal	Increase	Lister proposal	Increase
Tax allowance	1815	1958	143	2114	299
Unemployment and Sickness benefit[b]	1557	1958	401	2114	557
Retirement pension	1940	1958	14	2114	174

Notes: [a] Under 80 and wife not working
[b] Excluding earnings-related benefits

One suggested extension of the tax base is 'the removal of the anomaly whereby a married couple, both members of which are earning, can receive a tax allowance which is approximately two and a half times the tax allowance of a single person' (Meade 1978, p. 498). In other words, the married man's tax allowance should be abolished. This would cost the standard-rate taxpayer an extra £3.75 in income tax each week (Hansard 1979a, col. 284). Another proposed change is the taxation of all benefits so as to 'concentrate maximum benefit on those in greatest need without recourse to a means test' (Lister 1975, p. 43). Table 10.6 illustrates how much more progressive a policy of taxing benefits is than having either untaxed benefits or tax allowances. Lister has also suggested two other ways of extending the tax

Table 10.6   The tax treatment of social benefits

Social benefit	Value (£) to taxpayer with marginal rate of tax of:		
	0%	40%	60%
Tax allowance of £500	0	200	300
Untaxed benefit of £200	200	200	200
Taxable benefit of £333⅓	333⅓	200	133⅓

Source: Derived from Meade 1978, Table 13.5.

base. The first would be to abolish the ceiling on national insurance contributions so that higher-income groups paid more. It is estimated that such a step would have raised approximately £730 million in 1979 (Hansard 1979b, cols. 501–2). The second and more controversial proposal challenges Beveridge's belief in the importance of voluntary provision by individuals on the grounds that 'it reflects a strategy aimed at abolishing subsistence poverty without tackling the issue of inequality' (Lister 1975, p. 49), and advocates the withdrawal of tax reliefs from occupational and private pension schemes. It is difficult to calculate exactly the value of these tax expenditures but the Treasury estimate for 1979–80 is that they represented a revenue loss of £500 million on employees' contributions and £1150 million on employers' contributions (Hansard 1979c, cols. 693–4). One thing only is absolutely clear. Whichever way one shuffles the various fiscal instruments proposed there would be inevitable increase in the total tax burden, although the distributional consequences would differ from one package to another.

Conclusion
The New Beveridge proposals represent an extensive and expensive package which, whatever its attractions, has a number of problems associated with it. First, one must question whether the level of increased taxation envisaged is politically feasible especially after the Conservative victory on a tax-cutting platform in the 1979 general election. Moreover, are some of the proposed shifts in the tax burden such as higher tax rates in exchange for increased thresholds really necessary? Even some members of the Meade Committee have expressed reservations about the harmonisation of tax thresholds with

supplementary benefits. For example, Kay and King have argued that:

> A situation in which resources for those with low incomes have been deployed in raising the supplementary benefit level rather than the tax threshold is not necessarily irrational, but a possibly appropriate response to the difficult trade-offs between equity, efficiency, and incentives. (1978, p. 113)

Second, one must ask whether the New Beveridge proposals are sufficiently close to the original spirit of Beveridge to warrant the association with his name. For example, both Lister and Meade mount a sustained attack on the contributory insurance principle. But it is in Lister's opposition to tax reliefs for occupational pensions that she departs most clearly from the original Beveridge Plan for, as we have seen, support for voluntary insurance was a central tenet of Beveridge's approach. Furthermore, this particular reform can be criticised on economic grounds. The abolition of tax reliefs on occupational pensions to help pay for improved social security benefits might reduce the flow of new investment to productive industry. Such a policy might well have damaging consequences for future economic growth. Feldstein (1974), for example, has argued that the development of public social security programmes in the USA between 1929 and 1971 had a detrimental affect upon personal saving and economic growth in the same period. Munnell (1974) has challenged the details of Feldstein's results for the past, but she is more inclined to accept that in the future 'the influence of social security on private saving must be taken into account' (Munnell 1977, p. 121). Finally, there is the danger that excessive advocacy of a radical Back-to-Beveridge strategy will divert attention away from reforms of the supplementary benefits system which are more attainable in the foreseeable future (cf. SBC 1979, para. 3.20). Nevertheless, despite the validity of these criticisms there is much in the Lister and Meade proposals which is worthy of support. The great advantage of the New Beveridge Plan is that the reforms do not have to be introduced in one giant step. Instead, they could 'be carried out in a piecemeal fashion, stage by stage, at whatever speed political and economic conditions permitted' (Meade 1978, p. 294).

References

Atkinson, A. B. 1970, *Poverty in Britain and the Reform of Social Security*, Cambridge, CUP.
Beveridge, W. 1942, *Social Insurance and Allied Services*, Cmd 6404, London, HMSO.

DHSS 1978, *Social Assistance: A review of the supplementary benefits scheme in Great Britain*, DHSS.

Feldstein, M. 1974, 'Social security, induced retirement, and aggregate capital accumulation', *Journal of Political Economy*, vol. 82, September-October.

Fiegehen, G. C., Lansley, P. S. and Smith, A. D. 1977, *Poverty and Progress in Britain 1953–73*, Cambridge, CUP.

Field, F., Meacher, M. and Pond, C. 1977, *To Him Who Hath: a study of poverty and taxation*, Harmondsworth, Penguin Books.

Hansard 1979a, House of Commons Debates, *Written Answers*, 12 July.

Hansard 1979b, House of Commons Debates, *Written Answers*, 30 October.

Hansard 1979c, House of Commons Debates, *Written Answers*, 2 November.

Hansard 1979d, House of Commons Debates, *Written Answers*, 7 November.

Harris J. 1977, *William Beveridge: A biography*, Oxford, Clarendon Press.

Kay, J. A. and King, M.A. 1978, *The British Tax System*, Oxford, OUP.

Lister, R. 1975, *Social Security: the case for reform*, Poverty Pamphlet no. 22, CPAG.

Meade, J. E. (Chairman) 1978, *The Structure and Reform of Direct Taxation*, London, George Allen & Unwin/Institute for Fiscal Studies.

Munnell, A. H. 1974, *The Effect of Social Security on Personal Saving*, Cambridge, Massachusetts, Ballinger.

Munnell, A. H. 1977, *The Future of Social Security*, Washington D.C., Brookings Institution.

NCC (National Consumer Council) 1976, *Means Tested Benefits: A Discussion Paper*, NCC.

SBC 1977, *Supplementary Benefits Commission Annual Report 1976*, Cmnd 6910, London, HMSO.

SBC 1979, *Response of the Supplementary Benefits Commission to 'Social Assistance: A Review of the Supplementary Benefits Scheme in Great Britain'*, SBA Paper no. 9, London, HMSO.

Townsend, P. 1974, 'Poverty as relative deprivation: resources and style of living' in Dorothy Wedderburn (ed), *Poverty, Inequality and Class Structure*, Cambridge, CUP.

Townsend, P. 1979, *Poverty in the United Kingdom*, Harmondsworth, Penguin Books.

HM Treasury 1979, *The Government's Expenditure Plans 1979–80 to 1982–83*, Cmnd 7439, HMSO.

11 Social Dividend and Negative Income Tax
David Collard

There is something fresh and appealing about the family of schemes considered in this chapter: they are simple, comprehensive and thorough, unlike the truncated and half-hearted tax-credit proposal of 1972 or tinkerings with the 1942 Beveridge Scheme. At one sweep they deal with the problem of poverty *and* offer a great simplification of the tax system. Yet they have not been adopted. Why? In this chapter the various important versions of social dividend (SD) and negative income tax (NIT) are outlined, the basic question of 'cost' is examined and the future of the scheme is considered.

Basic Schemes

The basic idea may be seen from Figures 11.1(a) and 11.1(b)

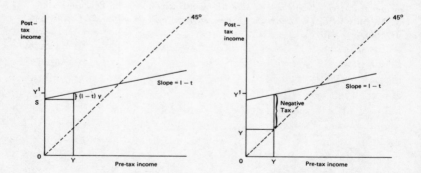

Figure 11.1 (a) *Social dividend,* (b) *negative income tax*

In financial terms there is nothing to choose between the social dividend and the negative income tax: the intercept and slope of the two solid lines are exactly the same. But the *mechanisms* are quite different. Under the social dividend everyone is entitled to a universal payment S: all income is then taxed at a rate t. Final income is therefore made up of two parts, the social dividend and post-tax other income. Under the negative income tax scheme, on the other hand, the poor are entitled to their pre-tax income Y together with a supplement or negative income tax to bring it up to target income.

(a) Final income = social dividend + post-tax other income
$$= S + (1 - t) Y$$
(b) Final income = pre-tax income + negative income tax
$$= Y + [S + (1 - t) Y - Y]$$

Either way the individual or family with income Y ends up with Y^1 but the need for regular weekly payments suggests that the SD might be best administered as a universal weekly cash benefit (payable perhaps through post offices) whereas the NIT might be administered as a weekly subvention to earnings by the employer. Thus the Conservative tax-credit proposal was much more like a negative income tax than a social dividend.

Advantages of the basic schemes
Both NIT and SD sweep away a whole lot of social security and national insurance payments; in the SD case, by a weekly 'social dividend' based on household characteristics (family composition, age) and possibly, though not necessarily, on employment and health status. There would be no means-tested element in the social dividend, hence it would be *universal* not selective. The paradigmatic schemes also simplify the tax structure itself by having just one marginal rate across all incomes (though see the various modified schemes discussed below). This would also enable the cumulative basis of PAYE to be abandoned and the constant marginal tax to be collected weekly or monthly without annual adjustment; it would also automatically remove the 'poverty trap', provided the social dividend was itself totally comprehensive.

Two further major advantages over the present system are that poverty relief would be *absolutely certain* and that workers would have no incentive to stay out of the labour force; they could always obtain more net income by working than by not working (This point does not wholly dispose of the efficiency problem – see below.)

Clearly there is room for argument about the level at which S, the social dividend, would be set. From the political 'right', notably Friedman (1962) the wholesale replacement of benefits in kind (e.g. social work) by cash payments has been advocated; from the 'left' have come suggestions for housing and family responsibility allowances; everyone agrees that special dividends would be necessary for the disabled and other groups with special needs. These latter would have to be additional as they could not reasonably be included in the general dividend.

Criticism of the basic schemes
So much for the bare bones which have been fleshed out in the literature from time to time. The original proposal by Lady Juliet Rhys Williams (1943) was overshadowed in that creative era of social reform by the Beveridge Report. The main features of her scheme were: a weekly social dividend for all at adequate rates of support; abolition of national insurance contributions, income tax and surtax; a proportional tax on all income except the social dividend. Milton Friedman (1962) in *Capitalism and Freedom* proposed the replacement of a whole range of social expenditures by a social dividend. The practicability of SD and NIT reforms was widely discussed in the USA in the late 1960s (see, for example, J. Tobin *et al.* 1967) and in the early 1970s Senator George McGovern advocated a 'demo-grant' (i.e. a demographically-based grant financed by a 33.5 per cent tax rate). By this time, however, much more attention was beginning to be paid to the Achilles' heel of all such schemes, their cost.

The central difficulty about cost is this. To be sure of raising everyone above supplementary benefit levels (and thus eliminating poverty) the social dividend would have to be set at something like 40 per cent of average earnings (Meade 1978). But the tax rate would have to provide not merely the social dividend but revenue for expenditure on goods and services (say, 15 per cent of average earnings). Hence the marginal tax rate would need to be of the order of 55 per cent. In June 1979 the top UK income tax rate was fixed at 60 per cent: a rate of 55 per cent was paid only on taxable income of over £20 000 per annum. It is plausibly argued that the electorate would jib at marginal tax rates of 55 per cent on all income. Hence social dividend reformers have been forced to abandon their simpler schemes and look for less elegant but cheaper alternatives.

An excellent presentation of both sides of the social dividend case, on traditional lines, is to be found in C. V. Brown and D. A. Dawson (1969) and in A. B. Atkinson (1969). Atkinson has constantly argued for a strengthening of Beveridge (see Chapter 10) rather than a major reform of the SD type. His reservations about SD in 1969 were along the following lines:

(i)   the need to tailor social benefits to special cases would mean retaining at least part of the supplementary benefits structure; hence the saving in administrative costs would be less than suggested by SD advocates;

(ii)   some national insurance beneficiaries (e.g. those with industrial injuries) would be worse off under any plausible flat-rate system;

(iii)   while it would always be better to work than not to work (the incentive effect noted earlier), the high marginal tax rates required by the schemes would be disincentive to extra work at the margin for those in employment; it is at the margin that disincentive effects really matter;

(iv)   the flat-rate tax schedule imposes a less progressive tax structure than could be achieved by one with increasing marginal rates.

Atkinson's objections, it should be noted, did not emphasise the most common criticism, that of cost. On this question there is a common misapprehension, for the 'cost' is the amount of money (command over goods and services) transferred to the poor, not the marginal tax rate. The average household is affected in three ways:

(i)   it is a little worse off because the problem of poverty is being tackled.

(ii)   the composition of its income has changed; earnings are taxed at a higher rate than before but the fixed element in income has increased. The great bulk of middle-of-the-road taxpayers will essentially be paying extra taxes to finance (a little more than) their own social dividends. There are some scenarios, for example that of long-run technological unemployment, in which a major 'social dividend' element in income would make a great deal of sense. Behind this lie deep political questions concerning how far one wishes to go in the direction of a society based on 'to each according to his need'.

(iii)   the intra-family composition of income will have changed if the social dividend is received by the wife rather than the husband. In another context, that of the tax credit proposals, this has become

known as the wallet-to-handbag issue and many (particularly tradi-
tionalist male workers) find the transfer distasteful.

Modified Schemes

Multiple rate

Tax reformers have accepted that the public would, in fact, be
reluctant to pay marginal rates of the order of 55 per cent and because
of this they have produced various modifications of the basic proposal.
Some of these are now briefly discussed. One set of contributions has
come from the Institute of Economic Affairs under the heading of
reverse income tax (RIT), in principle equivalent to NIT but usually
embodying a higher marginal rate of taxation at the lower end (a
higher rate of 'clawback' of the reverse tax payment). In its most
extreme form this simply becomes a minimum-income guarantee with
an implicit marginal tax rate of 100 per cent (IEA 1970). The high rate
of clawback enables the 'standard rate' of tax to be as low as 35 per
cent. Somewhat less severe is a scheme due to Clark (1977) whereby
RIT would be clawed back at 70 per cent giving a standard rate of 40
per cent. Rather similarly, Meade (1975) had proposed a social
dividend with a 40 per cent standard rate but higher rates of 75 per
cent at the top and bottom to replace the present system. Of special
interest, in view of the later Meade Report, was his discussion of the
mechanisms whereby his social dividend might be operated. VAT
could easily be converted into a general sales tax of 40 per cent and at
the bottom and top ends of the distribution respectively there could be
a 35 per cent national insurance contribution and a 'surtax' of 35 per
cent. All of these modified schemes have in common a reduction in the
required standard rate: in this respect they are therefore more
acceptable to the bulk of taxpayers. On the face of it they appear to be
inequitable (one would not, in an ideal scheme, expect to see high tax
rates at low incomes) but if they enable otherwise impossible schemes
to be implemented they deserve serious consideration.

The Meade Report (1978) referred to this broad type of scheme as
modified SD or minimum-income guarantee. It is useful to think of the
full social dividend and the minimum-income guarantee as standing at
the two extremes with Meade, Clark and others in between. The
relationship between the standard rate and the rate on the first slice of
income is a simple linear one as in Figure 11.2.

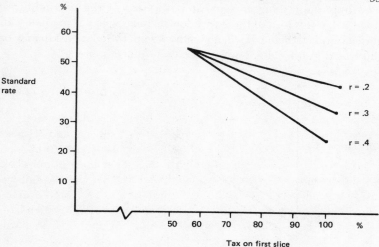

Figure 11.2   Some two-rate schemes

The graph shows that the higher the rate on the first slice, the lower the standard rate has to be. The relationship differs according to where we decide to 'split' total income. Thus in Meade (1978) the illustrations are based on r = .3., but the greater the proportion of total income (r) below the split, the easier the trade-off between the two rates becomes. Figure 2 provides a do-it-yourself tool kit for constructing a two-rate modified social dividend, e.g. a first-slice rate of 78 per cent requires a 45 per cent standard rate if r = .3. It is relatively straightforward to extend modified schemes to deal with multiple splits.

Two tier
Other variations are possible. In 1967 Lees suggested a NIT for families only. The NIT would have enabled family allowances and child tax allowances to be abolished and would have carried a 40 per cent marginal tax rate. However it was specifically aimed at relieving poverty due to family size and made no attempt to sweep away social security and national insurance benefits. In the same tradition schemes have been devised for 'two-tier' social dividends (Meade Committee 1978). There would be a high conditional benefit (going to the old, the sick, etc.) and an unconditional lower benefit going to everyone else.

The important thing to look at is the size of the unconditional dividend; if it is low all those with low incomes who fail to qualify for the conditional dividend will do badly. Again, the relationship may be illustrated graphically, Figure 11.3.

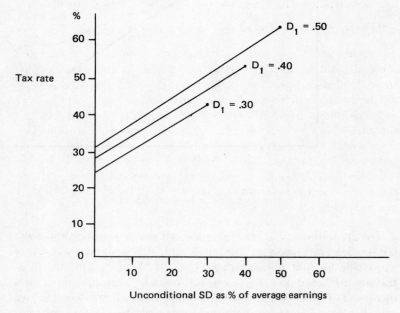

Figure 11.3   Some two-tier schemes

It is assumed that one-third of the population would be entitled to the conditional dividend (D_1). The three lines on the diagram show the levels at which the tax rate would need to be set to finance various combinations of the conditional (D_1) and unconditional (D_2) social dividends. The central assumption of $D_1 = .40$ was the one made by the Meade Committee on the grounds that $D_1 = .30$ would not adequately deal with poverty and that $D_1 = .50$ would require unacceptably high tax rates. From the diagram it may, for example, be seen that a conditional dividend of .40 of average earnings together with an unconditional benefit of only half that (.20), could be financed by a tax rate of 42 per cent, whereas to pay the same universal benefit of .40 to everyone would have required a tax rate of 55 per cent.

Thus the two-tier scheme, like the modified one-tier schemes, appears to do the job of poverty relief more economically than the pure social dividend. But, as in the modified scheme, the poor pay a price for economy and simplification. Consider, in the above example, the case of someone entitled only to the unconditional dividend (.2). To reach the poverty line (.4) he or she would need to earn just under a third of average earnings. This is because net earnings would be $.20 + (1 - .42)$ gross earnings: for this to *equal* .40 we have gross earnings $= \dfrac{.40 - .20}{.58}$ or roughly one-third. Many individuals would be unable to earn this much depending on how harshly the distinction is drawn between those entitled and those not entitled to the conditional dividend (the old distinction between the deserving and undeserving poor in another guise). If the unemployed were entitled to an unconditional dividend these individuals would be better off working than not working, i.e. there would be serious disincentive effects. If not entitled they could suffer considerable hardship. Therefore the two-tier scheme cannot be relied upon to eliminate poverty because it may not be assumed that those receiving the unconditional dividend will be able to make their incomes up to the conditional level.

The two-tier scheme is, next to a Beveridge-type reform, the preferred solution in the Meade Report where the detailed implementation of the two schemes is discussed together. It would be intended to pay unemployment benefit to the long-term unemployed unless the principal erstwhile earner ceased to be so; to allow the dividend to vary with severity of disablement for the disabled; to pay home-responsibility payments and to include the self-employed. Meade also discusses how the taxation of benefits (which it broadly favours) could be administered.

Once one has abandoned the grand simplicity of the pure social dividend, the various schemes run into the sands of reality and when they have run their course there is very little to choose between them. If the social dividend is not to be set at above the poverty level for everyone there might as well be a hierarchy of social dividends, each devised for its own particular client groups. Provided that the 'causes' of poverty (old age, family size, illness, unemployment, etc.) have benefits especially tailored to them there is no longer a need for a universal dividend, even an inadequate unconditional one of .20. However, we know from Professor Townsend's *Poverty Survey* (1979) that incomes differ enormously *within* the classical poverty groups. Under a Beveridge-type reform one would try to deal with the awkward cases under the supplementary benefits heading; but it is most unlikely that the awkward cases could be covered by the unconditional benefit in a two-tier system.

The Basic Schemes Reconsidered

In this section we consider again some of the more positive aspects of the basic or pure social dividend scheme as we tend to lose sight of these once the cost argument has caused us to modify it almost out of recognition.

Hard cases

It has to be agreed that the social dividends could not hope to cope with all the difficult cases at present dealt with as discretionary 'special needs' under supplementary benefit or as cases requiring mobility allowances, constant-attendance allowances, etc. To the extent that social dividend advocates have suggested that it could do so, they have oversold their case. However, the hard cases have to be dealt with separately under almost every conceivable reform and in comparing them should be left to one side.

Elimination of poverty

The really major advantage of an adequate social dividend which cannot be too strongly emphasised is that it does, at a sweep (except for the hard cases), get rid of poverty. And it does so without using means tests of any kind: the dividend is solely determined by readily attainable demographic information; it depends in no way on earnings, contribution records, employment status or whatever. This is a very positive contribution which should not lightly be abandoned. In this respect it is superior both to the two-tier SD and to Beveridge reforms but not to the 'two-rate' schemes.

Elimination of the poverty trap

The social dividend is universal, not selective; the authorities do not 'claw' it back when other income increases. There is no family income supplement (FIS) representing a 'tax' rate at 50 per cent, no national insurance contribution: in principle, just a single marginal rate (of say 55 per cent). Under the two-rate system the poverty trap would, of course, remain, as the first-slice rate could be anywhere between 55 per cent and 100 per cent. But even under the social dividend scheme proper a great deal would hang on the fate of other means-tested benefits. It is well known that there are dozens of means-tested benefits not all of which could easily be absorbed into a universal social dividend. Some means-tests could be abandoned and absorbed into a higher child benefit element of the social dividend, for example, free school meals, uniform allowances, etc. Others would require substantial increases in the social dividend and therefore in tax rates: for example, rent rebates, rate rebates and mortgage interest relief (see below) could be replaced by a housing component of social dividend (see also the housing credit referred to in Chapter 13, p. 225). Where it would be ludicrous to provide a benefit for all (e.g. meals on wheels, school transport from remote areas, home helps, physical aids) it would be in the spirit of social dividend reform to allocate it on the basis of 'need': further hurdles based on income would reduce take-up *and* contribute to the poverty trap (Collard 1971). But, as was argued above, the treatment of hard cases may be discussed separately from the basic choice of scheme.

Economic efficiency
Both the two-tier and two-rate schemes have undesirable effects on economic efficiency. Two-tier schemes (as has already been shown) could enable low-paid workers to earn more when unemployed than when in work. Two-rate schemes carry a heavy tax rate on the first slice of income which could have adverse effects on the number of hours worked or on the pace of piece-work. On the basis of experiments in New Jersey, Clark (1977) argued that the lower paid would not react much to high first-slice rates: but in the British context a panoply of means-tests could make the effective marginal tax rate very high indeed, with much greater effects than those reported. Unlike both schemes the pure SD does not encourage non-work at the expense of work: the marginal tax rate is high (55 per cent) but much less likely to generate a serious poverty trap problem than in a two-rate system.

Figure 11.4 compares the pure social dividend with Meade's (1978) central two-rate system. The effects of taxation on hours worked may conveniently be split into a substitution effect which causes a movement opposite in direction to the tax and an income effect which (generally) causes a movement in the same direction as price. The substitution effect depends on the marginal rate of tax and the income effect on the average rate. Thus it is convenient to consider the three ranges marked. In range I the substitution effect would cause more hours to be worked (a positive hours effect) under the pure SD scheme

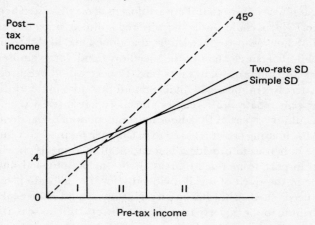

Figure 11.4   Incentive comparison between a pure SD and a two-rate SD

and the income effect fewer hours to be worked (a negative hours effect), so the overall effect on hours is ambiguous. In range II (which contains most earners) both the substitution and the income hours effects are negative. In range III the substitution hours effect is positive and the income hours effect negative. Altogether then the hours effects are ambiguous in ranges I or III but unambiguously adverse in range II. The general weight of the evidence is, however, that these effects are unlikely to be large. (Brown and Jackson 1978, Chapter 13).

The linear schedule
The pure social dividend has just one marginal rate of taxation, a major administrative simplification emphasised by its early advocates. But there is no essential reason why a social dividend should be associated with a linear schedule. From the progressivity standpoint the 'ideal' social dividend/tax schedule would look like SD[1] figure 11.5: as income rises the marginal tax rate rises as well as the average tax rate.

Relative to the linear SD the bulk of taxpayers would be slightly better off and the 'rich' considerably worse off. Note that after point 'a' taxpayers would be paying a higher marginal rate of tax than under a pure social dividend. Again, the great mass of taxpayers would experience negative income and substitution hours effects. The extent

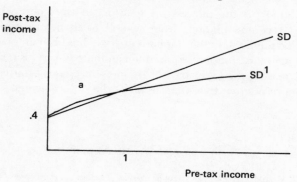

Figure 11.5   Two progressive schedules

to which one is willing to put up with this depends partly on how serious these effects are likely to be and partly on the other issues, (i) the relative importance of poverty and inequality and (ii) the feasibility of administering a non-linear system. Taking issue (i), the more progressive schedule would not be adopted if one was concerned only with poverty (*that* is taken care of by the dividend itself) but it might be if one wanted to reduce inequality, not merely poverty. In technical language, the choice depends on the social welfare function: if this embodies a strong aversion to inequality the linear SD will be preferred to both the two-tier and the two-rate systems but the non-linear, increasingly progressive SD will be preferred to any of them. Taking issue (ii), a linear schedule is much easier to operate on a weekly system (without end-of-year adjustments) than a non-linear one. Therefore the SD can accommodate a non-linear scheme much more readily than can a NIT. The dividend payments could be made weekly and all other income could be taxed under a PAYE system, possibly introducing a larger element of self-assessment. Unfortunately some of the major administrative advantages claimed for the SD would then disappear.

Conclusion
There is no painless way of redistributing income in favour of the poor. Given the need to keep the typical taxpayer's average and marginal rates as low as possible, the original schemes for a social dividend have

been diluted (in the interests of realism) to the point where the practical recommendations from several of them are remarkably similar. To some extent the emphasis on 'cost' has been unfortunate in that the net redistribution required to eliminate poverty is rather low. For this reason, the latter part of the present essay has attempted a rather more positive view than usual of the pure schemes.

References

Atkinson, A. B. 1969, *Poverty in Great Britain and the Reform of Social Security*, Cambridge, CUP.

Brown, C. V. and Dawson, D. A. 1969, *Personal Taxation, Incentives and Tax Reforms*, London, PEP.

Brown, C. V. and Jackson, P. M. 1978, *Public Sector Economics*, Oxford, Martin Robertson.

Clark, C. 1977, *Poverty Before Politics*, London, Institute of Economic Affairs.

Collard, D. 1971, 'The Case for Universal Benefits' in D. Bull (ed.), *Family Poverty*, London, Duckworth.

Friedman, M. 1962, *Capitalism and Freedom*, Chicago, University of Chicago Press.

Institute of Economic Affairs 1970, *Policy for Poverty*.

Lees, D. 1967, 'Poor families and fiscal reform', *Lloyd's Bank Review*, no. 86, October 1967.

Meade, J. E. 1975, *The Intelligent Radical's Guide to Economic Policy*, London, George Allen & Unwin, Chapter 6.

Meade, J. E. 1978, *The Structure and Reform of Direct Taxation*, London, George Allen & Unwin/Institute for Fiscal Studies.

Tobin, J. Pechman, J. A. and Mieszkowski, P. 1967, 'Is a negative income tax practical?', *Yale Law Journal*.

Townsend, P. 1979, *Poverty in the United Kingdom: A Survey of Household Resources and Standards of Living*, Harmondsworth, Pelican.

Rhys Williams, J. 1943, Something to Look Forward To, McDonald.

Origins and Description

In the later 1960s both the Labour Party and the Conservative Party were showing interest in the possibility of integrating the income tax and social security systems, an interest in part resulting from work in the United States where Milton Friedman (1962) had popularised the idea of a negative income tax (see Chapters 5 and 11). Perhaps because of the nature of its American parentage, the Conservatives explored the possibilities more enthusiastically than Labour and particular interest was shown in the idea by Brendon Sewill, Director of the Conservative Research Department from 1965 to 1970. His encouragement led to two publications by the Conservative Political Centre; *AUNTIE* (Automatic Unit of National Taxation and Insurance), a computerised model for linking tax and social security benefits (Sewell 1966) and *Must the Children Suffer?* (Hayhoe 1968).

In their Election Manifesto of 1970 the Conservatives declared:

A scheme based upon negative income tax would allow benefits to be related to family need; other families would benefit by reduced taxation. The government has exaggerated the administrative problems involved and we will make a real effort to find a practical solution.

As this statement implies, the Conservatives had no clear-cut scheme when they took office in 1970 and in fact what emerged was very different from the kind of scheme on which the Research Department had been working whilst the party was in Opposition. The tax credit proposals were very much the brainchild of Arthur (now Lord) Cockfield, the Chancellor's special adviser on taxation and a former Commissioner of Inland Revenue. As Lord Barber himself tells us (Barber 1974), a scheme was worked out in detail before being submitted either to the Inland Revenue or the Department of Health and Social Security. When the Heads of these two departments confirmed that it would work, the Chancellor and the Secretary of State for the Social Services set up a working group of officials, known as the Tax-Credit Study Group, to take the planning further. The Study Group contained representatives of the Department of Health and Social Security, Treasury, Inland Revenue, Department of Employment and Civil Service Department.

The Chancellor made an announcement about the scheme in his Budget speech on 21 March 1972 and published a Green Paper in October 1972 (Cmnd 5116). In accordance with the suggestion of the Green Paper, a Select Committee of the House of Commons was set up, examined the scheme and reported in June 1973 (HC 341). The majority of the Select Committee recommended the scheme but there were two dissenting reports from Labour members. In the Green Paper the government had simply 'commended' the proposals but subsequently they accepted the scheme as a policy commitment and proposed to implement it in 1977, which was the earliest date at which it was considered possible to do so.

The failure of the Conservatives at the 1974 election ended this possibility. In his first Budget speech in 1974 Mr Healey stressed the 'serious drawbacks' of the scheme and shelved it; but the Labour government introduced child benefits. The approach adopted by the Conservatives in their 1979 Election Manifesto was cautious. They welcomed the new child benefit 'as the first stage of our tax-credit scheme', but stated:

> Further progress will be very difficult in the next few years, both for reasons of cost and because of technical problems involved in the switch to computers. We shall wish to move towards the fulfilment of our original tax-credit objectives as and when resources become available.

Thus the tax credit scheme remains on the agenda – but not for early implementation.

The Green Paper proposals

The objectives set out in the 1972 Green Paper were to 'improve the system of income support for poor people', 'to simplify and reform the whole system of personal tax collection', and in so doing, to reduce the overlap between the tax and social security provision and offer a new system which people could more easily understand.

The essence of the scheme was the introduction of a new system of tax credits which would replace (1) the main personal allowances, i.e. granted for purposes of income tax: the single, married person's and child allowances; (2) the family allowance (FAM), paid through the

Post Office to the mother in respect of second and subsequent children; and (3) the Family Income Supplement (FIS), a means-tested benefit for low-paid married wage earners with at least one child.

Everyone covered by the scheme (the exceptions are discussed below) would receive the appropriate tax credits, and the whole of their income (excluding the credits) would be taxed at the basic rate of tax, then 30 per cent. If the tax bill exceeded the value of the credits they would pay (net) tax, as before; but if the value of the credits exceeded their tax bill they would receive a net addition to income. For illustrative purposes the tax credits were set at £4 per week for a single person, £6 for a married couple (whether or not the wife was working), £6 for a single parent and £2 per child. Table 12.1 illustrates the working of the scheme for families of different sizes and on different levels of income; the examples are simplified by omitting national insurance contributions.

The Green Paper envisaged that married and single persons' credits would be paid through the employer to those in work and on

Table 12.1   Illustrations of the operation of the tax credit system

Family size	Weekly pay £	Less tax at 30% £	Plus credit £	Pay after tax and credit[a] £
Single persons	10	3	4	11
	25	7.50	4	21.50
	50	15	4	39
	100	30	4	74
Married persons	10	3	6	13
	25	7.50	6	23.50
	50	15	6	41
	100	30	6	76
Married persons with two children	10	3	10	17
	25	7.50	10	27.50
	50	15	10	45
	100	30	10	80

[a]National insurance contributions ignored.

Tax credit rates: single £4; married £6; child £2.

occupational pension schemes; through the Department of Health and Social Security to people drawing national insurance benefits like sickness or retirement benefits; and through the Department of Employment to those temporarily unemployed. Each individual in the scheme would receive a notification of credit entitlement which he would give to the paying authority. The authority would then deduct tax at the basic rate and pay over the net sum after allowing the credits.

The method of payment of the child credit (which replaced the child tax allowance and the family allowance) was left open in the Green Paper. To pay the child credit along with the married allowance would offer significant administrative savings, but it was recognised that there was a strongly held view that some, at least, should be paid to the mother through the Post Office as a separate source of family income. To pay all the benefit to the father involved a 'handbag to wallet' transfer of that part of the credit which replaced FAM, whilst to pay it all to the mother involved a transfer to the wife of the equivalent of the tax allowances which had previously benefited the father. The Green Paper suggested the possibility of a compromise by which the credit for the first child went to the father whilst that for subsequent children was paid to the mother – a solution nearer to the existing situation but still effecting some transfer to the wife where there were two or more children. The government indicated that it would decide the issue in the light of public discussion and the views of the Select Committee; but before the Select Committee reported, the Chancellor gave the assurance that the government would 'not adopt any arrangement which leaves mothers being paid less than they are at present' (*Hansard* 6 March 1973, col. 242).

The tax credit scheme was intended to cover most employed persons, the main national insurance beneficiaries, both short- and long-term (including all on state retirement pensions) and most occupational pensioners. The principal groups excluded were the self-employed and those with earnings (in 1972) of less than £8 per week (about one-quarter of the average male industrial earnings). Those with less than the qualifying level of earnings were excluded because they needed a level of support well above the credit levels which it was necessary to relate to each family according to individual circumstances. The Green Paper stressed that the tax credits had not been designed with the intention of guaranteeing each family enough to live on without further help from the state – to have done so would have made the cost prohibitive. The self-employed were omitted for a different reason; they pay tax not on a weekly basis but in half-yearly instalments some time after their profits have arisen. Hence there was no weekly income against which the credits could be set and to have paid in full would have increased subsequent tax bills (not all of which might have been easily recoverable). The self-employed would therefore continue to receive tax allowances, corresponding to the value of the tax credits, and for those with dependant children and incomes below the tax threshold the Green Paper suggested a support scheme on FIS lines would be introduced, offering benefits on a comparable scale to those of the tax credit scheme. On the basis of the Green Paper proposals it was claimed that nine out of every ten people in the country would be covered by the scheme. The hope was also expressed that, once the scheme was running, it would prove possible to extend its coverage.

If all basic-rate taxpayers were to be taxed at 30 per cent on the whole of their income and at the same time end-year tax adjustments were to be avoided for the majority of taxpayers, it was necessary, besides replacing the main personal allowances, to abolish or alter the form of the most common tax allowances. Thus the dependant relative relief was to go; many such relatives would be helped directly by the tax credits, giving them a measure of financial independence, or, where they were outside the scheme, by supplementary benefit. Life-assurance relief was to take the form of a reduction on premium payments with the balance made up by the Exchequer. The payment of mortgage interest would be net of basic rate (which would enable the option mortgage scheme to be discontinued). There would be a standard deduction for expenses of an employee incurred in the performance of his duties to cover allowances currently given for items such as tools, clothing, professional expenses and subscriptions. This standard deduction, set at £30 in 1972 values, would be taken into account in fixing the initial level of tax credits; employees with heavier expenses could claim extra (possibly subject to a *de minimis* rule) and claims agreed would be met by a repayment at the end of the tax year. Age allowances would also disappear.

For higher-rate taxpayers the main personal allowances would continue to be given against higher-rate tax; regular tax deductions would continue, but on a non-cumulative PAYE basis with end-year adjustments.

The Green Paper, after reviewing possible alternatives, proposed that the tax allowance for working wives, the wife's earned income relief, should be held at the current level and paid as a tax allowance against the wife's earnings. To have converted it into a credit equivalent to a single-person credit would have given an additional benefit to couples with working wives. Thus, in the normal case, the married woman at work would not be within the scheme in her own right; but where the husband was not within the scheme and not self-employed, the wife as the family breadwinner could, if otherwise qualified, receive the credit appropriate to the family.

The total net cost (in current prices) of implementing the scheme was estimated at £1300 million.

The Select Committee

On three main issues the Select Committee made specific recommendations of considerable importance for the operation and development of the tax credit scheme.

First, they recommended that the child credits should be paid in full to the mother (or whoever had the day-to-day care of the child) and that they should take the form of a cash payment on a universal basis through the Post Office. They would thus be paid in respect of the children of the self-employed who to that extent would be brought into the scheme. Secondly, they supported a scheme, suggested by the Tax-Credit Study Group, by which married women earning should receive a single person's credit if they qualified for entry into the scheme. If by reason of low or nil earnings they did not qualify for the scheme in their own right, they could transfer, say, half their credit to their husbands. On this basis, the married man with a wife who was not working would receive the same credit (£6) as that proposed in the Green Paper; if the wife had small casual earnings the remaining £2 could be set against them; the need for retaining PAYE allowances to provide for the married women's earned income relief would be obviated with administrative savings to Inland Revenue and firms; and the working wife was given a similar standing in the scheme to that of the working husband. The proposal also put a working husband and wife in exactly the same tax credit position as two single persons (instead of being in a superior position) with a considerable saving to the Revenue. Thirdly, the Committee recommended that the secondary personal allowances for blind persons and for men with children whose wives are incapacitated should be replaced by a tax credit rather than the retention of a tax allowance, as the Green Paper had proposed. Further, the tax credit scheme should be planned with sufficient flexibility to make it possible to pay further credits to defined groups at selected levels.

In general, the Select Committee took the view that in deciding whether or not to recommend the scheme as a whole, the criterion should be whether the scheme had sufficient flexibility to meet any required policy objectives concerned with the relativities of particular groups, irrespective of whether particular groups would have been made relatively better or worse off on the basis of the illustrative figures and the estimated cost or an alternative distribution of the cost. The majority conclusion was that the scheme did offer the necessary flexibility and should be adopted.

Merits of Tax Credits

The tax credit scheme offered a number of advantages compared with the system it was designed to supersede.

The easement of poverty

Necessarily, tax allowances can only benefit in full those who have sufficient income to bring them up to the tax threshold. The replacement of the personal tax allowances by tax credits thus of itself offered significant gains to those with sufficient income to bring them into the scheme but not enough to be taxpayers. Further, such people benefited from the compensating changes resulting from the proposed abolition of other allowances. Thus, the incorporation of a standard expenses allowance within the credits benefited employees with expenses whose income fell short of the tax threshold; and similarly they gained from the proposed reduction of insurance premiums, to replace the 15 per cent tax relief.

It had always been an attraction of negative income tax schemes that this use of the income tax mechanism made for impersonal and automatic poverty relief with a high take-up. The tax credit scheme carried this advantage. At the same time the weekly basis of the tax credit (associated with a non-cumulative tax deduction on all income) met one of the practical objections to most schemes of negative income tax; namely, that because tax is assessed on an annual basis the tax mechanism is unsuitable for meeting welfare needs which are generally of a week-to-week nature. Moreover, there is no stigma attaching to benefits administered as part of the tax system; tax credits are benefits left in the wage packet and, as Professor Abel Smith (1973) has put it,

'Less stigma attaches to retaining what one has earned than to receiving what one has not.'

The tax credit scheme would have reduced dependence on means-tested benefits. FIS was to disappear, completely or almost completely, while the higher income levels for the poor would have taken some of them above the level of eligibility for other means-tested benefits like rent and rate rebates, school meals and milk. Many thousands of pensioners would also have been floated off supplementary benefit.

The poverty trap would have been eased. The Department of Health and Social Security estimated for the Select Committee (1973, p. 17) that there were currently 36 000 people who might conceivably be worse off by receiving an additional £1 of gross income; 29 000 who would be less than 25p better off; and 172 000 who would only be better off by an amount between 25p and 50p. The corresponding figures with the tax credit scheme in operation at the illustrative levels (but without any other adjustments of the means-tested benefits) would have been 15 000, 5000 and 40 000 respectively. The biggest change was the abolition of FIS which, apart from tax, involves a withdrawal rate of 50 per cent. The withdrawal rate with tax credits, if one moved from net credit to net taxpaying, was only 30 per cent. The marginal 'tax' rates would therefore fall, reducing disincentive effects (Piachaud 1973). The reservation must be added, however, that these figures make no allowance for the method of financing the increased cost of the tax credit scheme which might, for example, have raised the basic rate of income tax by several per cent.

Taxation of short-term benefits

The problem of taxing short-term national insurance benefits has been outlined in Chapter 5. The administrative problems are almost insuperable with a cumulative PAYE system, but under the tax credit proposals the basic rate could be deducted and weekly credit allowed for without difficulty. That sickness benefit and unemployment pay should be liable to tax is widely regarded as fair (see Chapter 13). For anyone dependent on these benefits the credit would be likely to exceed the tax. No tax rebates would have been available (unlike the current situation) but the benefit of the weekly tax credit would have been felt immediately when it was most needed, whereas the repayment of tax is more haphazard. The anomalies which can arise at present, by which tax-free unemployment pay together with tax rebate may approach or even exceed the income available in work, would be unlikely to arise because the tax credit would be received in both situations, thus eliminating any financial disincentive to return to work.

Whether or not tax credits would be paid to workers on strike is an open question. Paragraph 42 of the Green Paper refers to credits being allowed to continue for periods of 'short duration in which the qualifying conditions for credit were not met'. This seems to carry with it the implication that tax credits to strikers would not be allowed for a long strike (Prest 1973). But a change which some would welcome and others deplore, necessarily resulting from the introduction of the tax credit scheme, would be that strikers would not receive tax rebates to help them support themselves during a strike.

Simplification

One aspect of the proposals which figured less prominently in discussion than its importance warrants is the simplification which the proposals would make to income tax.

Much of the complication of the existing income tax system, both for the Revenue authorities and for employers, arises from the coding to take account of allowances and from the cumulative basis which requires the tax office to maintain contact with all employees through their employer, no matter how frequently they change jobs. The introduction of a non-cumulative system would much reduce the tax problems associated with the ten million job changes a year.

The simplification was expected to result in considerable savings in administrative and compliance costs. The Green Paper expected an eventual saving of some 10 000 – 15 000 Civil Servants if the proposals were implemented. Savings for employers could also be expected and there would also be an easement in compliance costs for the personal taxpayer from the radical simplification of the system of allowances (Sandford 1973). The changes on both the tax and social security side would make for a more understandable structure, for simplification goes hand in hand with comprehension. Also the changes would have made desirable inroads into the number of tax expenditures (Chapter 4).

Flexibility

Simplification in some ways makes for flexibility; in particular to move to a non-cumulative PAYE would make it much easier, administratively, to implement a change in the basic rate of income tax. The

Select Committee (1973) was struck by the potential flexibility of the tax credit scheme, in particular the range of effects which could be secured by variations in credit rates, basic- and higher-rate tax and their interaction with social security benefit rates, as well as the possibility of introducing special credits for identifiable groups. On the other hand, as we shall see below, critics were concerned at the inflexibility which the tax credit scheme would give to the rate structure of income tax.

Let us conclude this section by quoting from the Green Paper (Paragraph 115), on the merits of the proposals.

> The tax credit scheme cannot of itself offer a complete solution to all the problems of poverty. But to those within it, and this includes the great majority of people at work and everyone in receipt of the main national insurance benefits, it offers the prospect of a system of family support which would be easier to understand than the present one, which would provide its benefit largely automatically and which, being integrated with the tax system, would extend the benefit of tax allowances to people who have insufficient income to pay tax. By doing so it would relieve hundreds of thousands of pensioners from the need to claim supplementary benefit. It would also bring significant increases in income to a further three or four million pensioners who already have some margin, but not a great one, above the supplementary benefit level, and would similarly prove of great help to hard-pressed families of working age – especially those with children – many of whom cannot be helped effectively through FIS and other means-tested schemes. Some means-testing – and the flexibility which only means-testing can secure – would remain, but its role in the social services as a whole would be reduced.

Limitations and Criticisms

To many it seemed, however, that the Green Paper overstated the case and claimed too much. The main criticisms of the scheme are summarised in two draft reports, one in the names of Mr Joel Barnett and Mr Robert Sheldon and the other in the name of Mrs Barbara Castle, which were published with the Select Committee Report (1973). The criticisms are interconnected but can conveniently be considered under several subheadings.

Limited coverage and impact on poverty

Even considered on its own terms the tax credit scheme did not go far in its attack on poverty. Some groups – the self-employed and those with an income of less than £8 per week – were outside the scheme altogether. But, even for those within it, the impact was limited. The majority of those on supplementary benefit would stay on supplementary benefit and of the forty-four means-tested benefits identified for the Select Committee by the Tax Credit Study Group, forty-three would remain; more significantly, of the six means-tested benefits which provided continuous support for comparatively large numbers of people – FIS, rent rebates, rent allowances, rate rebates, free school meals and welfare milk – only FIS was to be abolished by the tax credit proposals. Because the tax credit scheme consisted of uniform flat-rate benefits, it was difficult to use the scheme to make payments related to expenditure, hence it would not be easy to replace benefits such as those related to housing costs by means of a tax credit.

Financing the scheme

Critics argued that the terms on which the tax credit scheme was presented were misleading. The illustrative figures in which all comparisons were made required a net increase in expenditure of £1300 million. The Green Paper did not discuss in any detail how this cost would be met, except to say that 'with the growth of national income, more resources will become available' (paragraph 118). The tax credit levels of the Green Paper seem to have been fixed so that no one was made worse off – but any scheme could be made to look attractive on such terms. A valid comparison with the existing situation required either an indication of the method of finance, e.g. increased VAT or income tax and its effect on the distribution of income, or a revenue-neutral basis, which implied a reduction of some 17–18 per cent in the value of the credits. On a revenue-neutral basis the whole scheme looked very much less attractive, and considerable sections of the lower-income groups would finish up worse rather than better off.

Superior alternatives

If, in fact, an additional £1300 million was going to become available, it could be used much more effectively to combat poverty than by means of the tax credit scheme. It was estimated that, of the £1300 million, at 1973 income levels only £150 million went to those with incomes below £1000, with a further £400 million going to those with incomes between £1000 and £1600. Thus some £750 million went to those with incomes above £1600 per annum. The application of a smaller sum than this to raising national insurance benefits, especially pensions, and introducing a child endowment scheme would have had a much more powerful impact on poverty.

Inflexible tax structure

A particular objection to the tax credit scheme was its dependence on a simple rate structure for income tax, with a very wide basic-rate band applying to all but a few per cent of taxpayers who paid higher rates. That a wide band of income should be taxed at a flat rate was not new to the scheme – it was already operative at that time and had applied since the abolition of the reduced rate in 1969. But it was considered that the tax credit scheme would fasten this undesirable feature on to the tax system, with the result that it would continue to lack a consistent element of progression. Whilst it was possible to introduce a reduced rate or lower the threshold for higher-rate tax under the tax credit scheme, to do so would lose the administrative economies and the simplicity of the scheme. In general, the cumulative PAYE scheme was more flexible and allowed considerably more scope for equitable distinctions like the variation in tax allowance for children of different ages, which was to be replaced by a uniform child credit under the scheme.

Let us conclude by quoting one of the strongest and best informed critics of the scheme, Professor A. B. Atkinson, whose evidence much influenced the dissenting members of the Select Committee. His astringent verdict (1973) was as follows:

> Despite the claims made for it, the Green Paper is a half-hearted document. It recognises the need for a substantial transfer of resources to those with low incomes, but does not have the courage to say how this should be financed. It is described as a radical reform, but it nowhere examines the structure of benefits to be provided to different groups and the redistribution which would ensue is based on no coherent principles. It aims both to simplify the tax system and to improve income support, but fails to recognise that these objectives may well be in conflict. It acknowledges that means-tested benefits are ineffective, yet it offers no hope of going further than the abolition of FIS. It stresses the importance of the poverty trap, but leaves many families facing marginal tax rates of nearly 50 per cent. Such a document does not appear the best foundation for social policy in the next quarter of a century.

Conclusions

There is no doubt that, as Professor Pinker (1947) has aptly expressed it, 'By comparison with the Beveridge Report the Green Paper on proposals for a tax credit scheme is a welfare technician's paper.' Nowhere is there in it any reference to the moral principles on which the relief of poverty should be based or even to the psychological consequences of financing it by one means rather than another. Again, to quote Pinker (1974), 'Tax credits are the pragmatist's solution to poverty.'

The tax credit scheme is not necessarily the worse for that, especially as the insurance principle which dominated Beveridge's thinking has been discarded, at least in part, whilst no wholly acceptable alternative has taken its place in the public mind.

Some of the criticism of the tax credit scheme, that only a relatively small proportion of the extra expenditure involved would go to aid the poorest, is not necessarily to the point. The ultimate question is how much redistribution the large majority of taxpayers are prepared to accept. *If* they are only prepared to accept the redistribution of a sum equivalent to 10 per cent of the extra cost of the scheme it matters little, perhaps not at all, that nine-tenths of the cost goes in benefit to those who finance the scheme.

In principle a tax credit must be a more effective way of helping the poor than a tax allowance, as those with insufficient income to bring them up to the tax threshold cannot take full advantage of the allowance. Moreover the attractions of an automatic, stigma-free, high take-up form of benefit are not to be lightly discarded, quite apart from the widening of the tax base involved in the scheme. With the hindsight of 1980 one cannot help but feel that, for all the limitations of the tax credit scheme, had it been adopted the chaos in the tax/social security field would have been less than it now is. Since 1973, the only reform, apart from the reintroduction of the reduced rate of income tax (see Chapter 5), has been the introduction of child benefit. While child benefit could be claimed to be an application of a part of the tax credit scheme, it is not indexed, nor is it differentiated to provide different benefits for children of different ages, which critics of the tax credit scheme sought (see Chapter 5). Furthermore it is set in real terms at a level below that of the 'revenue-neutral' child credit of 1972.

The Select Committee, rather more than the Green Paper,

revealed the potential of the tax credit scheme to provide credits for particular identifiable groups in need. Whilst the scheme as a whole may never be revived, it should be possible to draw on its merits by adopting credits instead of personal tax allowances for particular groups (see Chapter 13) and by implementing some of the simplifications or replacement of other tax reliefs which the scheme proposed. Indeed, both these developments, it could be argued, have already begun with the introduction of child benefit and the new form of providing tax relief for insurance premiums.

References

Abel-Smith, B. 1973, 'Social security and taxation' in B. Crick and W. A. Robson (eds), *Taxation Policy*, Harmondsworth, Penguin Books, p. 172.
Atkinson, A. B. 1973, *The Tax Credit Scheme and Redistribution of Income*, London, Institute for Fiscal Studies, p. 85.
Barber, Lord 1975, *Great Britain's Tax Credit Income Supplement*, New York, Institute for Socioeconomic Studies.
Friedman, M. 1962, *Capitalism and Freedom*, Chicago, University of Chicago Press.
Hayhoe, B. 1968, *Must the Children Suffer?*, London, CPC.
Piachaud, D. 1973, 'Tax credits and disincentives' in *Conference on Proposals for a Tax-Credit System*, London, Institute for Fiscal Studies.
Pinker, R. 1974, 'Social Policy and Social Justice', *Journal of Social Policy*, vol. 3, pp. 1–19.
Prest, A. R. 1973, 'Proposals for a tax credit scheme', in *Conference on Proposals for a Tax Credit Scheme*, London, Institute for Fiscal Studies.
Proposals for a Tax-Credit System 1972, Cmnd 5116, London, HMSO.
Sandford, C. T. 1973, *Hidden Costs of Taxation*, London, Institute for Fiscal Studies, pp. 152–3.
Select Committee on Tax Credit 1973, HC 341, London, HMSO.
Sewell, H. 1966, *AUNTIE*, London, CPC.

13 The Policy Debate: Where Do We Go From Here?
Edited by Robert Walker

The Sunningdale Seminar concluded with a discussion led by two politicians and a former senior administrator. Frank Field, Labour MP for Birkenhead and formerly director of the Child Poverty Action Group, was asked to speak in favour of the 'New Beveridge' proposals which have long been associated, rightly or wrongly, with the Child Poverty Action Group. Sir Brandon Rhys-Williams spoke as a leading advocate of social dividend schemes. He is Conservative MP for Kensington and represents the South East London Region at the European Parliament. Finally, Tony Crocker was invited to present the case for tax credits. As the Under Secretary responsible for tax credits at the Department of Health and Social Security from 1972 to 1974 he led the Department's evidence to the Select Committee on Tax Credit and was responsible for the Child Benefit Scheme.

The speakers' opening remarks and the ensuing discussion are summarised below.

Introduction

The speakers agreed that none of the schemes on the agenda provided a complete answer to the problems posed by the mutually confounding effects of the tax and welfare systems. Indeed, Tony Crocker, in his talk on tax credits, carefully spelt out the reasons why such a scheme could not be considered a priority programme. First, it would involve enormous administrative upheaval, especially for employers. Secondly, it would need an extensive operational system which could not be envisaged until the Inland Revenue and Department of Health and Social Security had finished their current Automatic Data Processing development programmes. Thirdly, there remained the unsolved problem of how to treat married women earners within a tax credit scheme when so many worked for only part of the year. Finally the introduction of tax credits would in practice require substantial extra resources.

Similarly Frank Field drew attention to the 'phenomenal' cost of implementing a full Beveridge scheme. Furthermore, in developing his proposals, he not only suggested moving away from the strict insurance principles on which the original Beveridge proposals were founded but also proposed the introduction of a tax credit scheme for pensioners.

There was also a large measure of agreement on what the main policy objectives ought to be, although in each case speakers were able to offer a distinctive set of policy options. At the risk of over-simplifying, it might be said that there was broad agreement on the following propositions:

(a)   reliance on means-tested benefits should be reduced;
(b)   the level of family endowment should be increased;
(c)   any new scheme which is introduced must be inherently flexible; and
(d)   it is desirable to tax short-term benefits and thought should be given to how this might be done.

Policy Objectives

Means-tested benefits

The first objective was to take people off supplementary benefit and to eliminate personal casework as far as possible. Sir Brandon identified three routes by which a citizen might claim entitlement to benefit: via a record of contributions; by reference to citizenship and by showing that he had a genuine need. He argued that it was

> vital not only for the dignity and respect of the citizen – but also because one wants, in a modern effective industrial society, to have an easy, obvious, cheap and automatic administrative system . . . [to bring] . . . large numbers of people off need as the route of entitlement and onto either citizenship or contributions.

Furthermore since many people were forced to rely on supplementary benefits primarily because of the high level of their rent, Sir Brandon believed that it was necessary to reform the housing subsidy system, perhaps by integrating it with a reformed system of personal tax allowances, and by introducing a household dividend. (See below.)

In a not dissimilar fashion Frank Field believed that society should guarantee people the right to benefits which matched their lifetime needs. Therefore he suggested the introduction of a pensioner tax credit scheme for the aged (see below); an extension of the coverage and rate of national insurance benefits for the unemployed (see below); and, ideally, a special allowance for single-parent families or, failing that, additional help for them through a generous system of family support.

Finally, Tony Crocker believed that one of the main reasons why a tax credit scheme, broadly similar to that outlined in the 1972 Green Paper (Cmnd 5116), should not be ruled out was that it would enable substantial numbers of people to be 'floated off' supplementary benefit while at the same time permitting national insurance and supplementary benefit rates to be continually increased so as to ensure that the poor shared in the improved living standards of the population as a whole.

Improving family endowment

The second policy objective identified by the speakers was a need to improve the level of family endowment. It was agreed that the introduction of child benefit was an important step forward but that the level of state support for the family remained inadequate. Frank Field further argued that the level of child benefit should be set to equal the rate paid for the children of higher-rate national insurance beneficiaries.

Once this was done it would be easier to raise the level of benefit paid to the unemployed, since even fewer would then be better off out of work than in work. Higher child benefit might also enable the introduction of a special family allowance for single parents. Currently there is not the political support in the country for reform which advocates large cash payments to single women with children if they are not widows. However, increased child benefit might lessen opposition to such a reform by reducing the amount that would need to be paid to single parents on top of their child benefit.

Flexibility

Thirdly, the speakers were clear that whatever approach was finally adopted it had to be inherently flexible. Tony Crocker saw flexibility as the main advantage of tax credit proposals. It would be possible, by varying the rate of credit (even up to social dividend level), the rate of tax (including the higher rates) and the levels of benefit, to give a very wide range of distributional options. Moreover, such a system would ensure that taxes and benefits would always be considered at the same time. Equally, Frank Field felt that proposals which built on the existing national insurance scheme would permit a programme designed to help different groups in poverty to be implemented by staging the introduction of adequate benefits. This would mean that major administrative upheavals could be avoided and that reforms would be introduced to match the resources that the government made available.

Taxing short-term benefits

Fourthly, whether or not the taxing of shorter-term national insurance benefits was inherent in the schemes proposed, the speakers were convinced of the advantages of doing so. First, it was logical that all income should be taxed, although it was acknowledged that in practice there might always be exceptions, e.g. disablement benefits. Secondly, it was important both in terms of equity with those that work and also in connection with the effects of incentives, whether real or supposed. The intention would not be to cut the actual weekly benefit payments to the unemployed or the sick but to make the benefit part of taxable income for the year, thus obviating the need for tax refunds which are currently paid on top of benefits.

Policy Options

Four of the policy options proposed by the speakers were considered in detail during the plenary discussion: (a) a pensioner tax credit scheme; (b) improved family endowment based on increased horizontal redistribution; (c) reform of the national insurance scheme; (d) a household allowance or dividend. The remainder of this chapter is a summary of points that were made in discussion.

Pensioner tax credits

The objectives of a pensioner tax credit scheme would be to provide a short-term bridging mechanism until the new pension scheme finally breaks the link between poverty and old age in 1998. The tax credit scheme would be built into the insurance system so that the state retirement scheme and supplementary benefits would be retained, but the income tax basic allowance for pensioners would be withdrawn. All their income would then become taxable. Depending on the size of the credit, the effect of the scheme would be to float considerable numbers of pensioners off supplementary benefits and some off rent and rate rebates.

Pensioners floated off supplementary benefits would gain varying amounts from the scheme depending on how far their post-credit income was above supplementary benefit level. However, the people who would gain most from the scheme would be those pensioners who were not previously in receipt of supplementary benefit and who did not pay tax (and so would not have benefited or benefited fully from the age allowance under income tax). Those pensioners whose post-credit income meant that they were still eligible for supplementary benefit would gain nothing from the scheme. The larger the credit, the more people would be floated off supplementary benefit with varying amounts of gain, but the larger would also be the proportion of total benefit going to those in the middle slice of income who were previously neither paying tax nor receiving supplementary benefit.

The costs of the scheme and its redistributive impact would depend on the size of the credit and the numbers to be floated off means-tested benefits. At one extreme, the amount of revenue allotted to the scheme might be limited to the revenue currently lost through allowing tax allowances to pensioners. Theoretically, such a scheme could have zero cost but would then simply represent a positive redistribution of income among the elderly. To introduce a scheme under which no pensioner would be made worse off would mean that the cost would have to be met by other groups. For around £600 million it might be possible to float a million people off supplementary benefits but many, if not most of these, would only be floated off if they were still in receipt of means-tested housing benefits. Nevertheless, it is possible that housing benefits are considered by many to be more acceptable than supplementary benefit.

Despite its attractions, a tax credit scheme confined to pensioners presents real difficulties. The present income tax age allowance does not extend to women between sixty and sixty-five, and decisions would also be needed as to the distribution of the credit to replace it for a pensioner husband and wife. Pensioners alone would be taxed on all their other income, however small, which poses problems of equity. Administratively, pensioner tax credits would necessitate a substantial increase in manpower and would be dependent on the solution of a number of technical problems. One effect of the scheme would be to bring large numbers of pensioners into tax. Related to this, methods have to be found to collect tax on small amounts of income which the Inland Revenue does not have to concern itself with currently and also to ensure that all income was in fact taxed. There would also be problems for employers including those not in PAYE and for pensions funds who would have to operate two schemes side by side.

Increased family endowment

The introduction of child benefit was an essential structural step towards the attainment of a level of child endowment which was sufficient for low earners without resort to means-tested benefits. It was also seen at the time as a symbolic gesture on the part of the state to share more fully in the costs of child-rearing. Nevertheless the contribution of child benefit to the problem of family poverty has been less than satisfactory for a number of reasons. First, child benefit is treated as a component of public expenditure, which inevitably means that governments have been reluctant radically to increase levels of benefits. (It might be noted that Sir Brandon argued in his talk that transfer payments, such as child benefit, should properly be regarded merely as private expenditure in the reorganisation of which the state has played a part.)

Secondly, child benefit is not indexed against inflation and, although rates were substantially increased in April 1979, Sir Geoffrey Howe's Budget did not provide for subsequent increases although the former child tax allowances would normally have been increased along with other forms of tax allowance. This would not have been important in the circumstances under which the cause of child benefit was first taken up by the poverty lobby, at a time when very few families paid tax. However, now that the majority of people with children do pay tax and therefore would have benefited from increased tax allowances, the loss to families could be significant.

Thirdly, it can be argued that even the 1979 level of child benefit has been set too low, which in part explains why the majority of the poor are now below pensionable age. Indeed it is also arguable that the costs of rearing children have been consistently undervalued throughout the tax and social security system (relative to the subsistence costs of other people) because the precise cost of rearing children has never been established empirically.

However, defining the appropriate level of child support has its difficulties. Assuming that the technical problem of budgetary studies could be overcome and the cost of maintaining a child established, to do so might hinder attempts to increase the living standards of recipients in line with the living standards of the community as a whole, and especially efforts to increase their relative position. On the other hand, it might be possible to establish through research the amount of money various groups in the population would require in order to attain particular standards of living. Once this was known, it would be for society to decide what living standards it was prepared to support through the tax and social security systems.

However, improved living standards for families with children can only be achieved through increased horizontal redistribution. At the moment, the living standards of a breadwinner with a wife and family to support are hardly comparable with the standard of living of a married couple with similar income but without children. Increased family support is dependent upon those without children, who currently have financial advantages over those involved in child rearing, relinquishing their advantaged position. If child benefit was raised to the rate paid to the children of higher-rate national insurance beneficiaries it would, as a welcome by-product, help to relieve the presumed disincentive effects of social security payments. Child benefit exists as a vehicle for redistribution of this sort, but at the moment it is nowhere near sufficient.

Reform of national insurance
The national insurance system is under severe pressure and is simultaneously coming in for more outspoken criticism. Demographic changes and rising unemployment have rapidly increased the numbers entitled to benefit. The scheme is very labour-intensive, reflecting the difficulty of calculating how much the claimant is entitled to in any given week. This difficulty arises partly because of the complexity of the earnings-related component of national insurance and partly because the direct contribution principle has been eroded to bring within the scheme groups who have not in practice contributed fully. At the same time, the strict logic of the insurance principle means that divorced and unmarried mothers are still excluded from the scheme, while payments to the unemployed are restricted to a twelve-month period and are even then dependent on an adequate insurance record. One consequence of these restrictions on entitlement to national insurance is to add to the already enormous pressures on the supplementary benefits system.

Nevertheless, there remain real administrative advantages in persevering with the national insurance scheme which become apparent when alternative proposals are considered. For example, the high level of take-up generally associated with national insurance benefits may stem from a belief on the part of the claimants that 'they have paid and are therefore entitled'. Judging by the low take-up of the other benefits, belief in the right of entitlement does not yet extend to citizen rights dependent on the payment of general taxes.

A related argument is that it should theoretically be possible to collect and increase national insurance contributions more readily than other taxes simply because people see direct benefit stemming from their payments. However, while this may be true, the low level of benefits payable under the national insurance scheme suggests that claimants gain little from this flexibility.

Again, the TUC has always been heavily in favour of the contributory principle, partly because of the fear that once the link with contributions is broken for any part of the national insurance scheme, that part would become a very attractive proposition for a future government to cut when seeking public savings.

Nevertheless, one possible line of development might be to maintain the existing national insurance scheme but to alter radically the eligibility rules. This would enable most of the advantages of the present scheme to be retained while at the same time reducing complexity – and thereby administrative costs – and increasing the numbers of people who benefit from the scheme. One way of achieving this would be to adopt an entry fee principle under which any person fulfilling the 'need' criteria (i.e. sickness, unemployment, etc.) would be entitled to benefit provided they had made one contribution to the scheme, however meagre.

Alternatively, as Frank Field suggested in his talk, it might be possible, whilst still using the language of insurance, to guarantee a right to benefit to *all* people falling into certain categories of need: children, the sick, old and unemployed. It should be possible to sell such a scheme to the electorate by stressing that everybody is especially vulnerable, either to poverty or to relative deprivation, during particular periods of their lives.

Funding for the schemes outlined above could point ultimately to the introduction of a hypothecated social security tax. But other changes could be made more quickly. For instance, the present ceiling on contributions should be abolished and a higher degree of earnings-relation above the basic level introduced with respect both to contributions and benefits. This would make the national insurance scheme less regressive and float large numbers of people off the supplementary benefit.

The householder credit

The rationale behind the positive household allowance or householder credit proposed by Sir Brandon is threefold. First, there is a need to do something about the large numbers of people who are dependent on supplementary benefit solely because they cannot meet their housing costs. Secondly, the existing system of housing subsidies is in need of reform because it has become too complex, too confusing and, in Sir Brandon's view, very luxuriant. Thirdly, the personal allowance, which was introduced in William Pitt's original income tax scheme to take account of the responsibilities of the householder, has now become a lavish gift that the community makes to the individual, because not every earning person who is entitled to a personal allowance is in fact responsible for household outgoings. Transformed to a positive cash benefit, Sir Brandon estimated the current personal allowance to be worth about £7 per week for the single person and £12 for a married couple.

In principle, the householder credit could be financed through the abolition of personal allowances. The householder credit, geared to a person's housing outlay, would then be paid as a positive allowance rather than a negative one. Tax relief on mortgage interest payments might be phased out and the rent rebate and allowances schemes abolished. Some funding would also be drawn from the housing element in supplementary benefit and from the latent, or concealed, householder element which may be identified in the national insurance scheme (currently estimated by Sir Brandon to be about £9.30 per week). The relevant elements in national insurance and supplementary benefit payments would then be included in the householder allowance, resulting in a rationalisation of both the tax and benefit systems.

Such a scheme would not be without its problems. First, relating the benefit to people's housing costs would involve inquiry into their financial circumstances. This would not be possible through the medium of tax return which is completed only once every five years on average. Consequently, a parallel system for assessing housing costs would need to be developed which would be expensive and might be seen by the public as an excessive intrusion into their affairs.

Secondly, relating the householder credit to full housing costs might lead to the over-consumption of housing while partial payment of housing costs would be difficult to implement.

Finally, a householder credit scheme might be very expensive, although it is impossible to establish the true cost without detailed study. For example, a zero-cost scheme which covered the full housing costs of people with incomes at or below supplementary benefit level could only be achieved if the savings resulting from the abolition of personal tax allowances, etc., precisely matched the housing costs of people on low incomes who, for one reason or another, currently do not receive supplementary benefit. Unfortunately any attempt to reduce the cost of the scheme, by lowering the proportion of housing costs covered by the credit, would rapidly reduce the numbers who would be lifted clear of supplementary benefit.

Conclusion

Three approaches which have been suggested to overcome the confounding effects of the tax and social security systems – 'New Beveridge', social dividend and tax credits – were discussed in detail in Chapters 10, 11 and 12.

The opening speakers had been invited to act as advocates of these different approaches. What emerged from the debate, however, was a marked consensus amongst the speakers as to the nature of the problems and the objectives of reform, and also, more surprisingly, a large measure of agreement on the kind of solutions proposed.

The two main objectives, as they saw it, were to reduce reliance on means-tested benefits and to increase the level of child-benefit. The former might, if and when practicable, be achieved by the introduction of tax credits for specific groups, or by modifications to the rules of entitlement for national insurance benefits. The latter objective required the level of child benefits to be raised with the additional costs met by increased horizontal redistribution.

The suggested reforms which were likely to prove practicable sooner rather than later were those which could proceed by stages and would improve existing forms of provision rather than radically restructure the tax and welfare systems. Such reforms, therefore, can only be partial in their impact on the problems identified in earlier chapters of this book. Realistically, such reforms would place a limit on the escalation in costs, be flexible and avoid major administrative upheavals. The emphasis would therefore be on an alternative allocation of existing resources so that people's needs might be met more satisfactorily.

14 Conclusions
Cedric Sandford

It is an editor's dream that in the concluding chapter of a book which, like this one, has revealed a series of complex problems, he can draw all the threads together and offer a comprehensive list of neat and satisfying solutions. Unfortunately the problems of politics and society rarely lend themselves to such treatment; and, indeed, to attempt to offer a comprehensive list of easy solutions would smack loudly of arrogance. The objective of this final chapter is therefore more modest. In it we attempt to draw out some of the broad general conclusions from the interlocking areas of taxation and social policy considered earlier in the book, to illustrate the relevance of these conclusions to particular aspects of social policy and, where possible, to point the direction in which reform may be sought. Although it may help the reader to have the conclusions listed out under separate headings, like taxation and social policy, the conclusions are intimately interconnected.

Inter-relationship and Ad Hocery
The first conclusion to emerge, with almost overwhelming force from the book as a whole, is the extent and complexity of the inter-relationship between taxation and social policy. To start with, there are three major divisions of social policy as identified by Titmuss (1958) and referred to particularly in Chapter 4: social welfare – those provisions, traditionally described as the social services, like the NHS and national insurance benefits, financed by explicit public spending; fiscal welfare – the reliefs and allowances under the tax system; and occupational welfare – such as pensions and private health care provided by employers. If taxation supplies a welfare system of its own, it also permeates the other two. The most obvious and well-known example of overlap is, of course, the poverty trap, but few will have appreciated the subtleties of the relationship between the poverty trap and income tax rate structure before reading Chapter 5. Nor will many people have realised the full complexities of the

relationship between taxation, tax reliefs and explicit subsidisation, as applied to different forms of housing tenure, described in Chapter 6. Chapter 7 reveals similar complexities in relation to occupational welfare from the intricacies of the taxation and non-taxation of the contributions, earnings and benefits of pension schemes.

Nor are things always what they seem. Tax benefits become capitalised, so that, for example, in housing the main consequence of a tax concession to owner-occupiers is to raise housing prices and give a tax-free capital gain to all existing owner-occupiers on their principal private residences with little effect on the supply of houses. With regard to pensions, as Mike Reddin puts it, 'It is not just that taxes bear on pensions: pensions in turn bear on tax systems'.

Moreover, social policy is not separate and distinct from economic policy. Housing is a major source of national investment and, as such, cannot be divorced from demand management policies in the economy as a whole. The rate of interest is vitally relevant to the level of investment in the economy and to the financing of the public sector borrowing requirement, but also has a special social significance because of its effect on housing costs. Pension funds not only provide the wherewithal for retirement incomes but are a major source of investment funds to industry and the government. Social security measures, especially in conjunction with taxation provisions, may influence the supply of labour.

We could go on. Much of the inter-relationship and complexity is a necessary outcome of a sophisticated socio-economic system. But not all the complication can be accounted for or justified in this way. What emerges from the book is muddle, inconsistency and lack of purpose in social policy, a product of *ad hocery*, of actions taken in isolation and with insufficient regard for their effect on the remainder of the system. The growth of means-tested benefits, generating the poverty trap, is a good illustration. As David Piachaud (1973) has put it:

> The road which has led to this situation has been paved with good intentions. Each new means-tested scheme was introduced if not to benefit the poorest households, at least to shelter them from some new charge, or from an increase in an established charge ... Each means-test appears to have been evolved by the particular central or local government department with scant regard to other means tests. In this field co-ordinated action has been sadly lacking.

Housing policy abounds in contradictions. To start with one can query the logic of heavily subsidising housing whilst taxing it by local rates – although it is arguable that this apparent contradiction is justifiable because rates are particularly suitable as a *local* tax. That apart, however, there appears no logic in abolishing income tax on the imputed rent of an owner-occuped house (and thereby ceasing to treat it for tax purposes as an investment) but then retaining the deductibility of mortgage interest payments. Likewise zero-rating new building for VAT whilst standard-rating repairs appears contradictory, especially in the context of a history of rent control which has led to such a decline in the quality of the housing stock that improvement grants have had to be introduced to repair the damage.

The Need for Systematisation

Clearly the corrective to this lack of co-ordination and *ad hocery* is a more systematic approach and broader vision; in particular, viewing tax and social policy measures together. This is easy to say, but, within a large government machine, much less easy to achieve. In the introductory chapter we identified one way in which co-ordination might be furthered – namely wider pre-Budget discussion of possible Budget changes. Another way is suggested by the discussion in Chapter 4, the regular presentation of tax expenditure data along with and as part of the spending on social service programmes to promote both understanding and co-ordination. (Not least of the attractions of the tax credit scheme was the replacement of many tax expenditures either by tax credits or by other forms of explicit government expenditure, as with mortgage interest and insurance premiums.)

Making good the knowledge gaps

To provide a tax-expenditure budget would mean the development of information beyond what is at present available. As Chris Pond outlines in Chapter 4, the Treasury published for the first time in 1979 a list of tax allowances and reliefs, with, where possible, their estimated cost to the taxpayers, but the Treasury has been reluctant to proceed as far as the Americans, and latterly the Canadians, and allocate these tax expenditures to spending programmes. Whilst in some cases the allocation might be somewhat arbitrary, this is not sufficient reason for not making the attempt; explicit expenditures raise similar problems, e.g. is expenditure on a school for the children of soldiers in Germany to be classed as education or defence spending? The harm of not allocating tax expenditures to programmes seems greater than any possible harm from so doing. Ideally, too, the distributional effects of tax expenditures should be analysed – and this ought to be possible if fuller use were made of the family expenditure survey.

This brings us to another area where our knowledge is deficient – the effect of taxes and benefits on the distribution of income. Income distribution lies at the heart of social policy and, as Chapters 2 and 3 reveal, whilst the CSO has been publishing for some time annual estimates (based on FES data) of the distributional effects of taxes and benefits and has been steadily refining these estimates over the years, much remains to be done. Less than 50 per cent of total government expenditure and less than 60 per cent of government receipts is taken into account in the CSO's analysis and, as Michael O'Higgins indicated in Chapter 3, the procedures used in allocating benefits and the assumptions about tax incidence are open to question. It is good news that the CSO has its own programme of research to improve the quality of the FES data and the accuracy of its interpretation, and private researchers are likewise seeking to fill the gaps using FES data made available to them. Particularly useful is sensitivity analysis to indicate whether, first, the results are significantly affected by using different assumptions about the allocation of those benefits and taxes included in the survey and, second, how far the total picture is influenced by alternative assumptions for allocating taxes and benefits not now included.

Adequate and accurate data is a necessary condition for sound social policy, but it is not a sufficient condition. Constraints may be imposed by administrative practicality, political myopia and social attitudes. It is to those we now turn.

Administrative and Political Constraints
One conclusion for which evidence is to be found in many chapters is the practical constraints on action.

Equity between citizens is a complex matter, both to define and to implement, and in making changes account must be taken of reasonable expectations that have become established. Whatever the intrinsic merits of a particular policy it is unfair if the state changes the rules too drastically and too quickly. It is very difficult to justify the extent of the tax concessions to owner-occupiers; there can be little doubt that they have an unfair and undeserved advantage especially as compared with a tenant in private accommodation. Yet apart from the political consequences to any government which attempted it, suddenly to remove the mortgage interest concession and put nothing in its place would be unfair. A large proportion of family income goes on housing. People have bought houses and entered into mortgage commitments in the perfectly reasonable expectation that tax relief would be granted. The rapid withdrawal of the relief would result in a big drop in house prices, and would leave some people with housing debts in excess of the value of their house, and interest payments too heavy to meet. The most that might reasonably be done would be gradually to reduce the concession; or leave the concession intact and reintroduce the taxation of imputed income by stages spread over a long period; or simply (and this is perhaps the most likely 'action') leave the £25 000 limit on the mortgage concession unchanged in the face of rising prices.

Many reformers (as illustrated in Chapters 8, 10 and 13) have stressed the case for a much bigger child benefit. It is argued that the costs of bringing up children have always tended to be underestimated and that, in recent years, the balance has gone still further against families with children. To raise child benefit would be one of the most practical ways of striking at a major cause of poverty. Thus horizontal redistribution of income is required from those without to those with children. The argument is very strong; but the pace of change may have to be slower than many reformers would readily accept. There is, to start with, the 'wallet to handbag' argument that so influenced the Labour government when child benefits were introduced. Perhaps more serious, if child benefit were substantially and rapidly increased, whilst couples who had not yet started a family would have no cause to complain for they would have the opportunity to benefit later, older couples whose children were beyond the eligible age might feel unfairly treated. They had to struggle to bring up children when child support was low and might consider it inequitable that they now had to pay for someone else's children. Again, if the tax benefits accorded to pensioners under private schemes have become excessive, as Mike Reddin suggests, established expectations cannot in fairness be frustrated by any severe curtailment of these advantages.

However, not all constraints need be accepted. One, which has figured prominently in our discussions, has been the cumulative PAYE system. It might be noted that a *cumulative* PAYE is unique to the United Kingdom. Other countries operate PAYE schemes but on an approximate basis requiring end-year adjustments. The tax authorities in the United Kingdom have retained their system because of the advantage that it requires only a minority of taxpayers to complete annual returns, and end-year adjustments are restricted to a very small proportion of taxpayers. These merits may have been too dearly bought. Apart from its inhibiting effects in any attempt to tax short-term benefits, the cumulative PAYE system has been attacked from two directions, as we have seen. First, it prohibits a smoothly progressive income tax structure. Second, it is incompatible with a full tax credit scheme. Despite their common target, both groups of attackers have very different objectives. Those who seek a smoothly progressive income tax envisage a solution to the problem of poverty and the poverty trap by co-ordinating the tax and a social security systems so that they complement each other. In this solution the rate structure of income tax is an essential component of a policy of income redistribution. This is the 'New Beveridge' approach. On the other hand, the tax credit supporters – and advocates of the social dividend would be found in the same camp – seek distributive justice primarily through an integration of tax and social security provisions rather than co-ordination. Over most ranges of income, income tax would be proportional and the desired progressivity in the system would be provided by the tax credits or social dividends. In their full-blown version neither of these approaches is compatible with a cumulative PAYE; nor are they compatible with each other.

It is, indeed, in Chapter 13, the policy debate, which was concerned with the three 'options' of 'New Beveridge', tax credit and social dividend that the practical administrative and political constraints are most fully recognised. The three advocates conceded the impossibility of early implementation of the solution each espoused. All agreed, without argument, that the incremental approach was the only way forward. Although the objectives might be radical, we had to start from where we were and proceed in small stages. The particular proposals emerging from the debate, like that of a pensioner tax credit (to apply at least until the new pension scheme floats pensioners off supplementary benefit) reflect this approach. Despite difficulties the idea of the pensioner credit seems well worth further exploration. Another idea, the householder credit, illustrates the constraints provided by the complicated linkages of one social policy with another and both with tax, for it is difficult to see how a householder credit might be implemented unless some order were first restored to the housing market. Another restraint and inter-relationship was implied if not explicitly stated both in Chapter 13 and in several other chapters – the relationship of social policy to economic growth. The cost of implementing some of the reform proposals was recognised to be a major obstacle. Whilst cost (reflecting the alternative use to which scarce resources can be put) will always constitute a limitation, this restraint is the more severe in the present absence of any economic growth.

Social Purpose and Social Mores

If incrementalism is the order of the day, it may be asked, how does this differ from *ad hocery*. The answer is that small changes must be seen as part of an overall purpose and pattern; incrementalism needs to be the step-by-step application of a coherent philosophy. Politicians must act with much more clearly defined social purposes than has often been the case hitherto. In a political system, like ours, of adversary politics, it may be particularly difficult to obtain sufficient consensus to ensure the consistent application of social policy beyond the five-year term of a government; but at the least we have a right to expect a particular administration to act in accordance with a consistent and well-thought-out philosophy. As we have seen, politicians have not always acted in this way. As we have argued before, providing a more comprehensive and reliable data base will help, but it offers no guarantee of success.

Another lesson of the book is that policy is conditioned by social practice and social ethics. Policy cannot run too far ahead of, nor should it be too far behind, what society practices and believes. An example of lagging policy is the income tax practice which treats a wife as a dependent of the husband. This view has in many cases ceased to correspond either with the facts, because of the large proportion of working wives, or with social attitudes, because of the wider belief in equality between the sexes. Income tax should not be an instrument for constraining social relationships into undesired patterns; the tax therefore needs modification, as argued in Chapter 8, to take account of social change. An example of social beliefs holding back what might in many other respects be desirable change relates to the continuation of the national insurance contributions. It can be argued with some force that the insurance principle is something of a myth, and that it would rationalise the tax system if the national insurance contributions of employees and the self-employed were incorporated into income tax and if the employer's contribution became a straight payroll tax (Meade 1978). On the benefit side, this would involve abandoning contribution conditions as a test for benefit. However, it is doubtful if this would sufficiently accord with social attitudes. The work ethic implied in the Beveridge insurance concept remains strong and the feeling of having earned an entitlement helps to secure a high take-up. The tax credit principle, as we saw in Chapter 12, is not so far removed from this view, but the principle presented especially in Chapter 13, of benefits being by right of citizenship, seems some way from acceptance. People do not have the same attitude to paying tax as to paying NI contributions; nor the same attitude to receiving other benefits as to receiving NI benefits.

There is much of casual empiricism about these judgements for, to the author's knowledge, no empirical work has been undertaken to assess such attitudes. But if the judgements are correct and if we are to move away – in habits of thought and in practice – from the insurance principle to a new principle, a major educational task awaits to be done.

A Royal Commission on Taxation and Social Policy?

The main purpose of this book has been to explore the implications of the unco-ordinated growth of the tax system and the 'welfare state'. It is now a quarter of a century since the last comprehensive examination of the tax system was undertaken by a Royal Commission or Commission of Inquiry; it is even longer since Beveridge considered the basic principles and objectives of social security. No official body has undertaken a review of the two systems together and the way they interact. Such an exercise is long overdue.

We have already referred to the need for consistent and well-prepared philosophy by governments in the area of social policy and taxation. Each administration will have its own view on emphasis and priorities, and governments change. But there is a need for a thorough review of the basic principles and objectives in the light of current social beliefs. A Royal Commission on Taxation and Social

Policy, with the resources and access to information that only an official body can command, could provide such an overview. It would consider both the changes that have taken place and the options for reform. The setting up of a Royal Commission would, of course, be no more than a first step. Governments have a record of ignoring the recommendations of such bodies. But it could play a valuable role in stimulating a public debate about what we as a society expect from our tax and welfare system. Only then can we begin to replace 'ad hocery' with rational and consistent reform.

References

Meade, J. E. (Chairman) 1978, *The Structure and Reform of Direct Taxation*, London, Institute of Fiscal Studies George Allen & Unwin.

Piachaud, D. 1973, 'Poverty and taxation' in B. Crick and W. A. Robson (eds), *Taxation Policy*, Harmondsworth, Penguin Books.

Titmuss, R. M. 1958, 'The social division of welfare: some reflections on the search for equity', reprinted in *Essays on 'The Welfare State'*, London, George Allen & Unwin.

Index